365 DAYS OF

CROCHET

365 Crochet Patterns for 365 Days

White Lemon

BOOK NAME

—————— ⌇ ——————

by White Lemon

Contents

Introduction..1

January 3

January 1 4
January 2 4
January 3 5
January 4 5
January 5 6
January 6 6
January 7 7
January 8 7
January 9 7
January 10...8
January 11...8
January 12...9
January 13...9
January 14...10
January 15...10
January 16...11
January 17...11
January 18...12
January 19...12
January 20...13
January 21...13
January 22...14
January 23...14
January 24...15
January 25...15
January 26...16
January 27...16
January 28...17
January 29...17
January 30...18
January 31...18

February 21

February 1...22
February 2...22
February 3...23
February 4...23

February 5...24
February 6...24
February 7...25
February 8...26
February 9...26
February 10...27
February 11...27
February 12...27
February 13...28
February 14...28
February 15...29
February 16...29
February 17...30
February 18...30
February 19...31
February 20...31
February 21...32
February 22...32
February 23...33
February 24...33
February 25...34
February 26...34
February 27...35
February 28...35
February 29 (Leap Year Bonus Pattern)..36

March 37

March 1...38
March 2...38
March 3...39
March 4...39
March 5...40
March 6...40
March 7...41
March 8...41
March 9...42
March 10...42
March 11...43
March 12...43
March 13...44
March 14...44
March 15...45
March 16...45
March 17...46
March 18...46

March 19 47
March 20 48
March 21 48
March 22 48
March 23 49
March 24 50
March 25 50
March 26 51
March 27 51
March 28 52
March 29 52
March 30 53
March 31 53

April

April 55
April 1 56
April 2 56
April 3 57
April 4 57
April 5 58
April 6 59
April 7 59
April 8 60
April 9 60
April 10 61
April 11 62
April 12 62
April 13 63
April 14 64
April 15 64
April 16 65
April 17 65
April 18 66
April 19 66
April 20 67
April 21 67
April 22 68
April 23 68
April 24 69
April 25 69
April 26 70
April 27 70
April 28 71
April 29 71
April 30 72

May 73

May 1 74
May 2 74
May 3 75
May 4 75
May 5 76
May 6 77
May 7 77
May 8 78
May 9 78
May 10 79
May 11 79
May 12 80
May 13 80
May 14 81
May 15 82
May 16 82
May 17 83
May 18 83
May 19 84
May 20 85
May 21 85
May 22 86
May 22 87
May 23 87
May 24 88
May 25 88
May 26 89
May 27 89
May 28 90
May 29 90
May 30 91
May 31 91

June 93

June 1 94
June 2 94
June 3 95
June 4 95
June 5 96
June 6 96
June 7 97
June 8 97
June 9 98

June 10...98
June 11...99
June 12...99
June 13..100
June 14..101
June 15..101
June 16..101
June 17..102
June 18..102
June 19..103
June 20..103
June 21..104
June 22..105
June 23..105
June 24..106
June 25..106
June 26..107
June 27..107
June 28..108
June 29..109
June 30..109

July 111

July 1...112
July 2...112
July 3...113
July 4...114
July 5...114
July 6...114
July 7...115
July 8...115
July 9...116
July 10...117
July 11...118
July 12...118
July 13...119
July 14...119
July 15...120
July 16...120
July 17...121
July 18...121
July 19...122
July 20...122
July 21...123
July 22...123

July 23 124

July 24 125

July 25 125

July 26 126

July 27 126

July 28 127

July 29 128

July 30 128

July 31 129

August 131

August 1 132

August 2 132

August 3 133

August 4 133

August 5 134

August 6 135

August 7 135

August 8 136

August 9 136

August 10 137

August 11 137

August 12 138

August 13 139

August 14 139

August 15 140

August 16 140

August 17 141

August 18 141

August 19 142

August 20 142

August 21 143

August 22 143

August 23 144

August 24 144

August 25 145

August 26 145

August 27 146

August 28 147

August 29 148

August 30 148

August 31 149

September 151

September 1 152

September 2 152
September 3 153
September 4 153
September 5 154
September 6 154
September 7 155
September 8 155
September 9 156
September 10 157
September 11 157
September 12 158
September 13 158
September 14 159
September 15 159
September 16 160
September 17 160
September 18 161
September 19 161
September 20 162
September 21 163
September 22 163
September 23 164
September 24 164
September 25 164
September 26 165
September 27 165
September 28 166
September 29 167
September 30 167

October 169

October 1 170
October 2 170
October 3 171
October 4 171
October 5 172
October 6 173
October 7 173
October 8 174
October 9 175
October 10 175
October 11 176
October 12 176
October 13 177
October 14 178

October 15 178
October 16 179
October 17 179
October 18 180
October 19 181
October 20 181
October 21 182
October 22 182
October 23 183
October 24 184
October 25 184
October 26 185
October 27 185
October 28 186
October 29 186
October 30 187
October 31 187

November

November 189

November 1 190
November 2 190
November 3 191
November 4 191
November 5 192
November 6 192
November 7 193
November 8 194
November 9 194
November 10 194
November 11 195
November 12 195
November 13 196
November 14 197
November 15 197
November 16 198
November 17 199
November 18 199
November 19 200
November 20 200
November 21 201
November 22 202
November 23 202
November 24 203
November 25 203
November 26 204

November 27 204

November 28 205

November 29 206

November 30 206

December 207

December 1 208

December 2 208

December 3 209

December 4 209

December 5 210

December 6 211

December 7 211

December 8 212

December 9 213

December 10 213

December 11 214

December 12 214

December 13 215

December 14 216

December 15 217

December 16 218

December 16 218

December 17 219

December 18 219

December 19 220

December 20 221

December 21 221

December 22 222

December 23 222

December 24 223

December 25 223

December 26 224

December 27 224

December 28 225

December 29 225

December 30 226

December 31 226

Tips and Tricks 229

Conclusion 231

Pattern Pictures (For Reference Only) 233

Introduction

Do you love to crochet, but you don't have a lot of time to get involved with big projects? This doesn't mean that you can't still enjoy your favorite hobby. All you need to do is find patterns that you can make up in a few hours. There are loads of great patterns out there that you can whip up easily while you're sitting around watching television, riding in a car on a long trip, or in your spare time (if you actually have any). In this e-book, we are giving you a whole year's worth of patterns, and each one can be made in a single day. In fact, you can make many of these patterns in a couple of hours or less, although you may want to set aside 5-6 hours if you plan on trying some of the bigger projects like blankets and ponchos. You will find loads of great ideas for items for your home, wearables, gifts, and a whole lot more. So, grab your crochet hooks and yarn, and start the year off right with a special pattern for every day of the year.

January

Once the holidays are over and everything is settled once again, it is time to dive back into crafting. What better way to do it than by working on these easy crochet projects. This month, you will be making dishcloths, purses, a friendship bracelet, a granny square afghan, and a whole lot more. Grab your yarn and crochet hooks and beat the winter blahs with these fun and easy patterns.

January 1

Fast and Easy Crochet Dish Cloth

Materials

- 1 50-gram ball cotton yarn (you can make 3-4 dish cloths with one skein)
- Crochet hook size H/8 – 5 mm

Directions

- Crochet 35-stitch chain
- Row 1: 1 single crochet in third chain from hook. *Chain 1, skip a stitch, 1 single crochet. Repeat from * to end of row. Chain 1 and turn.
- Row 2: 1 single stitch in first single crochet, chain 1. *Skip a stitch, 1 single crochet in next stitch. Repeat from * to end of row. Chain 1 and turn.
- Repeat rows one and two until you have a square piece of cloth. Bind off and weave ends through work.

At this point, you can leave the cloth as it is, or put a border with the same color or a contrasting color. Simply add new yarn, and do a single crochet in each stitch all the way around. Bind off and weave ends through work.

January 2

Easy Baby Blanket

Materials

- 4-5 5-ounce balls baby yarn for main color
- 1 5-ounce ball baby yarn for edging
- Crochet hook size 5.5 mm

Directions

- Crochet 65-stitch chain.
- Row 1: 1 double crochet in second chain stitch from hook (chain counts as first stitch). *chain one, skip a stitch, 1 double crochet in next chain. Repeat from * until the end of the row. Chain one and turn.
- Row 2: Continue in the same pattern until work is square (you can continue if you want a longer blanket). Tie off ends and weave into work.
- Edging: Once the blanket is the size you want it, finish it off with a pretty edging. With the contrasting yarn, begin at one corner. Attach the yarn with a slip stitch, and chain two. 2 double crochet in the next stitch. *Chain 1, skip a stitch, 3 double crochet in next stitch. Continue from * all the way around the blanket. Bind off and weave yarn end through work.

January 3

Super-Easy Granny Poncho

Materials

- 350-400 grams of double knitting yarn. You can use contrasting colors for stripes, or do the whole poncho in a single color.
- Crochet hook size 4 mm

Directions

- Crochet 4-stitch chain, join with a slip stitch to create a ring. Do not tie the end, as you will be unraveling some of this later.
- Round 1: Chain 3 (counts as one treble stitch). 2 treble stitches in the middle of the ring, chain 2. *3 treble stitches in the middle of the ring, chain 2. Repeat from * until you have four clusters. Connect with a slip stitch.
- Round 2: Chain 3. 2 treble stitches in the first space (2 chain stitches). *Chain 2, 3 treble crochet in next space. Continue all the way around from * until the end, and join with a slip stitch. Continue in this pattern for five more rounds. Now you can stay with the same color, or tie off and begin a new color if you are doing stripes.
- Round 3: Continue in the same pattern, alternating colors for each row if you are doing stripes, until poncho is the length you want.
- Neck Hole: Unravel the first five to seven rounds (from the middle) to make a head hold. Go around this edge with single crochet for a border.

The poncho is ready to wear, or you can add fringes around the outer edges if you like. You can also make a 2-3 foot chain, weave it through the neck hole, and put a pompom on either end to use as a drawstring.

January 4

Winter Hand Warmers

Materials

- 5-oz ball worsted yarn
- Crochet hook size 5.5 mm
- Tapestry needle

Directions

- Crochet a chain that is approximately 3-3.5 inches long
- Row 1: Skip a chain, 1 double crochet in each stitch. Chain 1 and turn.
- Repeat row 1 until you get to the desired length (it should go from the bottom half of your fingers to the wrist, or longer if you like). Tie off, leaving a long tail for stitching.
- Fold the piece in half lengthwise. Using the tapestry needle, stitch along the side, leaving a space for a thumb hole. Tie off and weave yarn through work. You can single crochet around the thumb hole to make it sturdier if you like.
- Turn inside out so seam is on the inside.

January 5

Shoulder Bag

Materials

- 1 364-yard skein Red Heart yarn, any color
- 1 1-inch button, same color as yarn or contrasting
- Crochet hook size 5.5 mm
- Needle and thread to sew on button
- Stitch marker

Directions

- Crochet a 6-inch chain.
- Round 1: 1 single crochet in second stitch from hook. Single crochet to end of row, 1 single crochet along edge, 1 single crochet along bottom side of chain back to first stitch. Place a stitch marker.
- Round 2: Chain 1, single crochet in each stitch all the way around. Continue rounds until piece reaches about 10 inches long.
- Side Round 1: Chain 1, skip a stitch, single crochet in rest of stitches in round. Repeat this round until the bag reaches the desired size.
- Top Round: In last round, chain 1, single crochet to the middle. Chain 10, skip a stitch, single crochet to end of round

Strap and Closure
- Mark 10 stitches on one side of the bag. Single crochet in each stitch. Chain 1, skip a stitch, single crochet to end of row. Repeat row until desired strap length is reached, and stitch to other side of bag.
- Sew a button on the front, and close with chain loop on back side.

January 6

Simple Striped Scarf

Materials

- 2 5-oz balls worsted weight yarn in contrasting colors
- Crochet hook size 5.5 mm or size needed for a gauge of five stitches per inch

Directions

- Crochet 40-stitch chain.
- Row 1: Skip first chain, double crochet in next chain. *Chain 1, skip a chain, one double crochet. Repeat from * to end of row. Chain 1 and turn.
- Row 2: 1 double crochet in chain space. *Chain 1, skip a stitch, one double crochet in next chain space. Repeat from * to end of row. Chain 1 and turn.
- Rows 3 and 4: Repeat row 2. Tie off and add second color with a slip stitch.
- Row 5: Chain 1, 1 double crochet in chain space. *Chain 1, 1 double crochet in chain space. Repeat from * to end of row. Chain 1 and turn.
- Rows 6, 7, & 8: Repeat row 5. Tie off and switch to other color.
- Repeat this pattern until the scarf reaches the desired length. Weave yarn ends through work. Add fringes on either end to finish the project.

January 7

Clutch/Wallet

Materials

- 1 5-oz ball double worsted or cotton yarn
- Crochet hook, size 5.5 mm or size needed for a gauge of five stitches per inch
- Tapestry needle

Directions

- Crochet 40-stitch chain.
- Row 1: Skip the first chain, single crochet in each chain to end of row. Chain 1 and turn.
- Row2: Skip the first stitch, single crochet in each stitch to end of row. Chain 1 and turn. Continue in this manner until piece measures 8.5 inches in length. Tie off and weave ends through work.
- Measure 6 inches from the bottom, and mark this spot. Next, fold the six inch section in half at the bottom. Using the tapestry needle, stitch the sides in place. This leaves a flap at the top. Sew a button, Velcro, or other fastener to the front of the folded section and to the inside of the flap to keep the clutch/wallet closed.

January 8

Set of 6 Cute Coasters

Materials

- 1 5-oz ball of double worsted yarn
- Crochet hook size 5.5
- Stitch markers

Directions

- Crochet a 5-stitch chain, join with a slip stitch to make a loop.
- Round 1: 1 single crochet in each stitch all the way around. Mark the end of the round with a stitch marker.
- Round 2: 1 single crochet in each stitch all the way around. Move marker to this point. Continue to work in rounds until the coasters reach the desired size.
- Final Round: Chain 3, skip a stitch, slip stitch. Continue the round like this for a lacy edge around the coasters.
- Repeat pattern for 5 more coasters, or as many as you like.

January 9

Cozy Shawl

Materials

- 2 364-yard skeins Lion Brand yarn, any color
- Crochet hook size 5.5 mm

Directions

- Crochet a 4-foot chain.

- Row 1: Skip first chain, 1 double crochet in every chain to end of row.
- Row 2: Chain 2, decrease by making 1 double crochet in two stitches together. Double crochet to last two stitches, 1 decrease stitch. Continue the rest of the rows in this manner until the piece is a triangle.

Edging (3 options)
- Option 1: *4 triple crochet in 1 stitch, skip 2 stitches. Repeat from * all the way around to form a shell edge.
- Option 2: Add 6-inch fringes to the 2 shorter sides of shawl.
- Option 3: Pick up stitch at 1 corner of shawl. Along short end, *chain 10, skip 3 stitches, slip stitch, chain 10. Repeat from * all the way around to the other corner, only putting loops on the short sides.

January 10

Fast Friendship Bracelet

Materials

- Scrap yarn, any c olor
- Pony beads, any color
- Crochet hook size 5 mm

Directions

Crochet a chain of 5 stitches.

Main section: Skip first chain, single crochet in next four stitches. Chain 1 and turn. Repeat row 1 until bracelet is long enough to go around your wrist.

Crochet an 8-inch chain. String pony beads onto chain to equal the length of the main section of the bracelet. Secure each end of the chain to each end of the bracelet, letting the chain ends dangle so you can tie the bracelet onto your wrist.

You can make this wider if you want simply by making the first chain longer. Follow the directions in the same manner.

January 11

Giant Granny Square Throw Blanket

Materials

- 4-5 364-yard skeins of double worsted variegated yarn
- Crochet hook size 5.5 mm

Directions

- Crochet a chain of 4 stitches, join with slip stitch to make ring.
- Round 1: Chain 3, two double crochet in center of ring, chain 2. Repeat 3 more times so there are 4 clusters of stitches. Join with slip stitch in the top of the first chain 3.
- Round 2: Chain 1. In first corner chain space, 2 double crochet, chain 2, 2 double crochet. *Chain 2, 2 double crochet in chain space, chain 2. Repeat from * to end of round.
- Work in this pattern until piece measures the desired size.

Finishing Options
- Option 1: Make 6-inch fringes all the way around throw.
- Option 2: Add a 6-8 inch tassel to each corner of throw.
- Option 2: Shell edging all the way around throw. Join yarn, chain 3, 2 triple crochet in same stitch. *Chain 1, skip a stitch, 3 triple crochet in next stitch. Repeat from * all the way around throw.

January 12

Drawstring Pouch Purse

Materials
- 1 364-yard skein double worsted yarn
- Crochet hook size 5 mm
- ½ inch ribbon for drawstring

Directions

Purse Bottom
- Crochet a chain of 5 stitches, join to form a ring.
- Round 1: Chain 1, 8 half double crochet in ring. Place stitch marker to mark end of round.
- Round 2: Chain 1, half double crochet all the way around. Continue working in rounds until piece measures 6 inches across.

Sides
- Round 1: Chain 1, half double crochet to end of round. Repeat round 1 until sides reach 8 inches.
- Top Round: 2 double crochet in every stitch. Weave ends through work.

Strap
- Crochet a chain of 10 stitches.
- Row 1: Skip a stitch, half double crochet in next 9 stitches. Chain 1 and turn. Repeat row 1 until strap is desired length (make it a handbag or a shoulder bag).
- Connect each end of the strap to either side of the bag with slip stitches. Tie off and weave ends through work.

Drawstring
Weave ribbon through shell edge, leaving ends long enough to tie a bow.

January 13

Slouchy Hat

Materials
- 1 364-yard skein worsted yarn
- Crochet hook size 5 mm
- Tapestry needle

Directions

- Crochet a chain of 5 stitches, join to make a loop.
- Round 1: Chain 2, 11 double crochet in ring, join to first chain in the chain 2.
- Round 2: Chain 2, double crochet in first stitch, 2 double crochet in each stitch to the end of round.
- Round 3: Chain 2, double crochet in next stitch, 2 double crochet in next stitch. *Double crochet in 2 stitches, 2 double crochet in next stitch. Repeat from * to end of round.
- Round 4: Chain 2, 2 double crochet in next stitch. *Double crochet in next 3 stitches, 2 double crochet in next stitch. Repeat from * to end of round.
- Rounds 5-8: Follow as previous round, but instead of double crochet in next 3 stitches, increase it by 1 stitch every round. At the end of round 8, you should have a total of 72 stitches.
- Round 9: Chain 2, double crochet rest of round.
- Rounds 10-30: Repeat row 9. You can add or remove rows depending on how slouchy you want the hat.
- Rounds 31-34: Chain 1, single crochet in each stitch around, decreasing every 6 stitches. Fasten off and weave ends through work.

January 14

Sweet-Smelling Sachets

Materials

- 1 small skein worsted yarn
- Crochet hook size 4.5 mm
- 8 inch piece of ¼ inch wide ribbon (a contrasting color looks really pretty)
- Potpourri (in a cheesecloth bag so the scent can be released but the potpourri doesn't crumble and come out of the sachet)

Directions

- Crochet a chain of 25 stitches.
- Row 1: Skip first chain, single crochet to end of row. Chain 1 and turn.
- Row 2: Skip first stitch, double crochet to end of row. Chain 1 and turn.
- Repeat rows 1 and 2 until you have a piece that is 10 inches in length.
- Fold piece in half lengthwise, and sew with crochet hook along the edge using slip stitches. When you finish the second edge, go all around the top edge with 2 double crochet in each stitch to make a little ruffle. Weave ribbon into the work just under the ruffle.

January 15

Lanyard

Materials

- Scraps of medium weight yarn'
- Crochet hook size 4 mm
- Tapestry needle
- Key ring (available at craft stores, or take one from an old keychain)

Directions

- Crochet a chain of 100 stitches. Thread key ring through chain, and join with slip stitch to make a large loop.
- Round 1: Chain 2, half double crochet in each chain, ending with a slip stitch in the top of the first chain 2.
- Round 2: Single crochet in each stitch all the way around. Tie off and weave ends through work.
- Using the tapestry needle, sew the lanyard straight across just above the key ring to keep it from moving around. You can also dress up your lanyard with beads, variegated yarn, etc. to make wearing it more fun.

January 16

Bad Hair Day Bun Holder

Materials

- 1 small skein worsted yarn
- Crochet hook size 4 mm
- Stitch marker
- Hair elastic (optional)

Directions

- Crochet a chain 6 inches long, join to make loop.
- Round 1: Skip first chain, single crochet to end of round, mark with a stitch marker. Continue going in rounds until piece measures 5 inches, moving the stitch marker at the end of each round so you know where you are. Tie off ends, but leave a long end and don't weave it through at this point.
- Now you can decide if you want to add the elastic or not. It does help to make the bun holder tighter so it stays in place.
- Finishing without elastic: Fold work in half lengthwise, and slip stitch all the way around using the tail you left dangling. Tie off and weave ends through work. You now have a donut-shaped bun holder.
- Finishing with elastic: Before sewing bun holder, slide hair elastic and wrap ends around it.

January 17

Snow Day Fairy Princess Tiara

Materials

- 1 skein bright yellow yarn
- Crochet hook size 5 mm
- Pony beads (different color than yarn for contrast)
- Velcro

Directions

- Crochet a chain of 72 stitches.
- Row 1 (with wrong side facing): Skip a chain, single crochet in each stitch to end of row and turn.
- Rows 2-3: Chain 1, single crochet in every stitch to end of row and turn.
- Row 4: Slip stitch in first 26 stitches, chain 1, decrease (single crochet over 2 stitches), single crochet in 18 stitches, decrease again, and turn (don't work the rest of this round).
- Row 5-12: Chain 1, decrease 2 times, single crochet to last 2 stitches, decrease, and turn.
- Row 13: Chain 1, decrease 2 times, decrease 2 more times and turn.
- Row 14: Chain 1, decrease, fasten off and weave ends through work.

- Decorate with pony beads around edges and any place else you want to add some bling. Get creative and add all kinds of fun decorations.

January 18

Snow Day Fairy Wand

Materials

- Bright yellow yarn (use yarn left over from Snow Day Fairy Princess Tiara)
- Crochet hook size 5 mm
- Tapestry needle
- ½ inch dowel rod, 1 foot long
- Paint to decorate dowel rod

Directions

- Crochet a chain of 5 stitches, join with slip stitch to make a ring.
- Round 1: 15 double crochet in ring, join with slip stitch.
- Round 2: *Chain 6, single crochet in third stitch from hook. Half double crochet in first chain stitch, double crochet in next 2 chains, skip 2 stitches, slip stitch in next stitch. Repeat from * 4 times so you have 5 star points.

Make 2 stars. Sew together with slip stitches, leaving bottom center part open about a half an inch. Once the dowel rod has been decorated and left to dry, use the hot glue gun to put some glue on one end, and slid it in the opening between the star halves. Voila, one magic fairy wand, ready to use.

January 19

Fun and Funky Shoelaces

Materials

- Scraps of variegated yarn (or any color that you want…something bright is great for those dark winter days)
- Crochet hook size 5.5 mm
- Colorful duct tape, cut into ½" wide strips

Directions

- It doesn't get much easier than this, and you can make these in a few minutes. First, using 2 strands of yarn, crochet a chain of 151 stitches.
- Row 1: Turn, and slip stitch in every stitch to the end of the row. Tie off and weave ends through laces.
- Finish the Ends: using the duct tape, wrap each end tightly 3 or 4 times so you have shoelace ends. You may have to play with this a bit to make sure that the ends are going to be small enough to fit through the lace holes in your shoes.

January 20

Photo Mat/Frame

Materials

- 1 skein cotton yarn, any color
- Crochet hook size 4 mm
- Cardboard, 7" X 9"

Directions

Top and bottom pieces
- Crochet a 10" chain, turn.
- Row 1: Skip first chain, single crochet across row. Chain 1 and turn.
- Row 2: Skip first stitch, single crochet across row. Chain 1 and turn.
- Repeat row 2 until piece is 1.5 inches wide. Make a second piece the same as the first.

Side pieces
- Crochet 5" chain, turn.
- Row 1: Skip first chain, single crochet across row. Chain 1 and turn.
- Row2: Repeat row one until piece is 1.5" wide. Make a second piece the same as the first.
- Assembly: Lay out all four pieces so they look like a photo frame. Join each piece with slip stitches. Put some glue on 3 sides of the cardboard, and place crochet frame on top, pressing hard to make sure it sticks to the cardboard. The open end is where you will slide your photos in and out. You can use this as a mat, or add some starch to it to make it stiffer and use as an actual frame.

January 21

Leg Warmers

Materials

- 8 ounces 4-ply yarn
- Crochet hooks sizes 5.5 mm and 6 mm

Directions

- Crochet a chain of 35. Join with a slip stitch, chain 2, don't turn.
- Row 1: Single crochet in each chain. Join with a slip stitch in the top of the first chain 2. Chain 2, don't turn.
- Row 2-8: Single crochet in each chain. Join with a slip stitch in the top of the first chain 2. Chain 2, don't turn.
- Row 9: Switch to larger hook. Chain 2, half double crochet in each stitch. Join with a slip stitch in top of first chain 2. Chain 2, turn.
- Row 10-desired length: Repeat row 9.
- Last 8 rows: Switch back to smaller hook, and repeat first 8 rows of pattern to create another cuff. Tie off and weave ends through work.

You can also do this pattern in a striped version. Simply do the cuffs in one color, then switch the colors every 3-4 rows to add stripes.

January 22

Easy Apron with Pocket

Materials

- 8 ounces 4-ply yarn
- Crochet hook size 5 mm

Directions

- Crochet a chain that is 18" in length.
- Row 1: Skip first chain, single crochet rest of row. Chain 1 and turn.
- Row 2: Skip first stitch, half double crochet rest of row. Chain 1 and turn.
- Repeat rows 1 and 2 until piece reaches desired length.
- Pick up a stitch in one corner, and add 2 single crochet in each stitch all the way around 3 sides of the apron. The open side will be the top portion of the apron.

Pocket
- Crochet a chain that is 8" in length.
- Skip first chain, single crochet rest of row. Repeat this row until piece is 6" tall.
- Stitch pocket to front of apron with slip stitches.

Strap
- Crochet a chain that is 30-36" in length.
- Row 1: Skip first chain, single crochet rest of row. Repeat row 3 times. Tie off and weave ends through work.

Attach Strap

Center apron piece on strap so even lengths of strap are hanging from each side. Sew together with a slip stitch. You can sew it straight, or use a bit of yarn to gather the top of the apron and sew it with the gathers to form pleats.

January 23

Mug Cozy

Materials

- Scrap worsted weight yarn
- Crochet hook size 5 mm
- Tapestry needle

Directions

- Crochet a chain of 5 stitches, join with slip stitch to create a ring.
- Round 1: 6 single crochet in ring.
- Round 2: 2 single crochet in each stitch around.
- Round 3: *Single crochet in next stitch, 2 single crochet in next stitch. Repeat from * to end of round.
- Round 4: Repeat round 3, but add a single crochet at the beginning of each round.
- Round 7: Slip stitch in next stitch, chain 1, single crochet in same stitch. *Skip next stitch, 2 single crochet in next stitch. Repeat from * 16 times, chain 1.

- Rounds 8-16: Single crochet in first stitch. * Skip next stitch, 2 single crochet in next stitch. Repeat from * to end of round.
- Round 17: Single crochet, chain 1, single crochet in first stitch. Single crochet to last stitch, chain 1, and join to the other side (top of mug handle part).
- Finishing: Slip stitch all the way around handle opening. Tie off and weave ends through work.

January 24

Key Ring Change Purse

Materials

- Scraps of 4-ply yarn
- Crochet hook size 5 mm
- Key ring
- Velcro

Directions

- Crochet a chain that is 4 inches in length, with a 24 inch tail for stitching later.
- Row 1: Skip a stitch, single crochet to end of row. Chain 1 and turn.
- Row 2: Skip a stitch, single crochet to end of row. Chain 1 and turn.
- Rows 3-12: Repeat row 2.
- Row 13: Decrease by single crochet in 2 stitches together. Single crochet to last 2 stitches in row, then decrease again.
- Row 14 to end: Repeat row 13 until piece comes to a point. Tie off and weave end through work, leaving original tail.

Finishing
- Fold piece so one end touches the beginning of the triangle end.
- Sew up each side.
- At end of one side, chain 10, slip a key ring onto the chain, and secure with a slip stitch.
- Glue or stitch a square of Velcro to the front of the change purse to keep it closed.

January 25

Kids' Crayon Bag

Materials

- 50 ounce skein of 4-ply yarn
- Crochet hook size 5 mm
- Button
- Needle and thread to sew button on

Directions

- Crochet a chain of 5 stitches, join with a slip stitch and chain 1.
- Round 1: Single crochet 5 stitches in ring, join with a slip stitch. Chain 1, don't turn.
- Round 2: Single crochet in each stitch around.
- Rounds 3-desired size: Continue working in single crochet rounds until piece measures 6" across. This is the bottom of the crayon bag.

- Side round 1: Chain 1, single crochet to end of round. Continue working this round until piece measures 6-8" tall.
- Strap row 1: Chain 1, single crochet 5 stitches. Chain 1 and turn.

Finishing
- Pick up a stitch on the top row of bag, centered between the straps. Chain 10, and slip stitch in next stitch to secure. This creates a button loop on the back of the bag.
- Near the top of the bag at the front, attach the button.

January 26

Retro Lampshade Fringe

Materials

- 1 5-oz skein crochet thread
- Beads (with holes big enough for a needle to go through)
- Crochet hook size 4 mm
- Large-eye sewing needle
- Glue gun and hot glue

Directions

- Crochet a chain long enough to fit around the lampshade you want to add fringes to, making sure that the amount of stitches is a multiple of 10, with an extra 2 inches to spare.
- Row 1: Skip first chain, single crochet rest of row. Chain 2 and turn.
- Row 2: Skip first stitch, 3 triple crochet in next stitch. * Chain 2, skip next stitch, 3 triple crochet in next stitch. Repeat from * to end of row.
- You can stop here, or add as many rows of shells that you like depending on how long you want this part to be.
- String fringes of beads, and stitch them to each shell.
- Glue fringe to outside edge of lampshade with hot glue gun.

January 27

Fast and Easy Baby Bib

Materials

- 50 yards medium-weight yarn
- Crochet hook size 5.5 mm

Directions

- Round 1: Chain 3, 8 half double crochet in third chain from hook. Slip stitch at start of chain 3.
- Round 2: Chain 2 and turn. * 2 half double crochet in next stitch, half double crochet in each stitch around. Slip stitch at the top of first chain 2.
- Work in rounds until piece is about 8".
- Next round: Chain 4, turn, two triple crochet in next stitch, double crochet in next 2 stitches, half double crochet in next 4 stitches. *2 half double crochet in next stitch, half double crochet in next 6 stitches. Repeat from * 5 times, followed by 2 half double crochet in next stitch, half double crochet in next 2 stitches, double crochet in next 2 stitches, triple crochet in next 2 stitches.

- Add chain stitching to make straps. Tie off.

January 28

Adorable Hair Bows

Materials

- Scraps of 4-ply yarn
- Crochet hook size 5.5 mm
- Hair clip (use an old clip or get new clips at your local craft store)
- Hot glue gun and glue stick

Directions

- Crochet a chain of 11 stitches for small bows, 16 stitches for larger bows.
- Row 1: Skip first stitch, single crochet in next stitch. Single crochet to end of row. Turn.
- Row 2: Chain 1, single crochet to end of row. Turn.
- Row 3: Repeat row 2 four times, or more for larger bows. Tie off and weave end to the middle part of the bow, leaving a long tail.
- Pinch crochet rectangle in center, and wrap tail yarn around this spot several times. Tie off and weave end through work.
- Using the glue gun, attach the bow to the hair clip.

January 29

Door Draught Stopper

Materials

- 1 large skein Red Heart yarn, any color (you may want more than one color if you want to do stripes)
- Crochet hook size 5.5 mm
- Polyfill stuffing

Directions

- Crochet a chain of 5 stitches, join to create a ring. Chain 1.
- Round 1: 5 double crochet in middle of ring.
- Round 2: Continue working in rounds with double crochet until piece measures about 5" across.
- Tube Round 1: Chain 1, skip first stitch, double crochet all the way around. Continue in this manner until piece reaches desired length (usually about 3'). Do not tie off
- Stuff draught stopper with polyfill stuffing.
- Double crochet in every other stitch around. Do this for 2-3 rounds, then pull yarn end tight to close hole at end.

January 30

Checker Board and Checkers for Cold Day Indoor Play

Materials

- 2 skeins Red Heart yarn (1 black, one red)
- Crochet hook size 5

Directions

Checker Board
- Crochet a chain of 64 stitches with black yarn. Chain 1 and turn.
- Row 1: Skip first stitch, single crochet in next 7 stitches. Switch to red, and single crochet 8 stitches. Switch back and forth between red and black to end of row, ending with red.
- Rows 2-8 (or enough rows to make each section a square): Beginning with black, chain 1 and skip the first stitch. Single crochet in the next 7 stitches. Switch to red and continue in same manner until you have the second row of squares. Repeat pattern until you have a total of 64 squares.
- Finishing row: Single crochet all the way around checker board with black yarn. Tie off and weave ends through work.

Checkers (make 12 of each color)
- Crochet a chain of 3 stitches.
- Round 1: 11 half double crochet in third chain from hook.
- Round 2: Single crochet all the way around, tie off and weave ends through work.

January 31

Remote Control Caddy

Materials

- 1 skein 4-ply yarn
- Crochet hook size 5.5 mm

Directions

- Crochet a chain of about 50 stitches (or 10 inches).
- Row 1: Skip first stitch, single crochet to end of row. Chain 1 and turn. Repeat this row until piece measures 18" in length. Tie off and weave in loose ends.

Pockets
- Crochet a chain of 50 stitches, or 10 inches.
- Row 1: Skip first stitch, single crochet to end of row. Chain 1 and turn. Repeat until piece measures 6" in length. Tie off and weave in loose ends.

Finishing
- Place shorter piece on top of longer piece so bottom ends meet. Stitch up the sides and bottom with slip stitches, tie off and weave ends through work. When finished, it will hang over the arm of a couch or chair, with the pockets on the outside.

- Use slip stitches to create individual pockets. Measure out 3 sections that are 3" wide, and sew along that line. You now have 3 compartments.

February

This is the month for romance, so we have added some fun and easy Valentine's Day patterns for you. Make your own greeting cards, garlands, and all kinds of other cute items that are decorated with hearts In addition to romantic craft projects, be on the lookout for more winter projects to keep you busy and warm throughout the month.

February 1

Little Girl's Heart Purse

Materials

- Scrap red yarn, 4-ply
- 2-3 feet of ¼" wide white satin ribbon
- Crochet hook size 5.5 mm

Directions

Hearts (make 2)
- Crochet a chain of 5 stiches, join with slip stitch to create a ring.
- Round 1: Chain 2, 14 double crochet in middle of ring. Join with slip stitch. Work in double crochet for 2 more rounds.
- Round 4: Chain 1, half double crochet in next stitch, 1 double crochet in next 2 stitches, 2 double crochet in next stitch, 1 double crochet in next stitch, 2 double crochet in next stitch, 1 double crochet in next stitch, 2 double crochet in next stitch, 1 double crochet in next stitch, 2 double crochet in next stitch, 1 double crochet in next stitch, 1 half double crochet in next stitch (first half of heart). Follow pattern backwards for the second half of heart. Single crochet in first stitch of round.
- Round 5: Chain 1, half double crochet in next stitch, * 1 double crochet, 2 double crochet in next stitch. Repeat from * 3 more times, 1 double crochet in next stitch, 1 half double crochet in next 2 stitches. Single crochet in next 9 stitches to the point. Follow pattern backwards for other side of heart

Finishing
- Sew two hearts together along sides, leaving top open.
- Attach ribbon to either side to make strap.

February 2

Heart Headband

Materials

- ½ skein white 4-ply yarn, scraps of red yarn to make small heart
- Crochet hook size 5 mm
- White button
- Needle and thread to sew button and heart to headband

Directions

Band
- Crochet a chain of 10 stitches.
- Row 1: Skip first stitch, single crochet to end of row. Chain 1 and turn.
- Row 2-desired length: Skip first stitch, single crochet to end of row. Work until piece is long enough to fit around your head, comfortable yet a bit snug so it will stay in place.
- Connect ends using slip stitches. Tie off and weave ends through work.

Heart

- Crochet a chain of 3 stitches, 3 triple crochet in the farthest chain from hook, 3 double crochet, chain 1, triple crochet, chain 1, 3 double crochet, 3 triple crochet. Chain 2 and slip stitch at first chain at start of piece.

Finishing

Place the heart where you want it on the headband. Place the button on top of the heart in the center, and sew both pieces to the band. You can leave it like this, or add more hearts, buttons, etc.

February 3

Choker with Heart Pendant

Materials

- 1 small skein red worsted weight yarn
- Crochet hook size 4 mm
- Beads and other embellishments
- Heart pendant (in jewelry findings at craft stores)
- Necklace clasp and jump rings (also with jewelry findings)
- Needle and red thread
- Needle nose pliers

Directions

- Crochet a chain long enough to go around your neck.
- Row 1: Single stitch in second chain from hook to end of round. Chain 1 and turn.
- Row 2: Repeat row 1.
- Row 3: Skip first stitch, 2 single crochet in every stitch to end of round. Do not turn. Round corner with 2 single crochet in 2 stitches, and then 2 single crochet in every stitch until you are back at the starting point. Tie off but leave tails hanging for now.

Finishing

Attach jump rings to clasp (if it doesn't already have them) by opening sideways with pliers. Close, and thread loose ends through rings, then weave through work. Attach the heart pendant to the center of the choker with another jump ring.

February 4

Heart Garland

Materials

- 1 skein Red Heart yarn, red
- 40 feet white Red Heart Yarn
- Crochet hooks sizes 5 mm and 10 mm
- Tapestry needle

Directions

- With white yarn and 10 mm hook, crochet a 5' chain. Tie off but leave ends so you have something for tying the garland to doorways, archways, etc. Set aside.

Heart (make 11)

- Follow the same directions for the hearts as for the Little Girl's Heart Purse (February 1). Tie off each heart, but leave enough yarn at end to make 6" chains.
- Crochet a 5" chain on 6 of the hearts, and an 8" chain on the remaining five.

Finishing

- Tie the first heart with the 5" chain to one end of the white chain. Tie the rest of the 5" chain hearts every 12".
- Tie the first heart with the 8" chain at the 6" mark on the chain. Tie the remaining hearts every 12" after that.

February 5

Heart Coasters

Materials

- Scraps of red and white yarn
- Crochet hook size 5 mm

Directions

- Crochet a chain of 15 stitches with white yarn.
- Row 1: Single crochet in second stitch from hook. Single stitch to end of row. Chain 1 and turn at end of all rows.
- Row 2: Skip first stitch, single crochet next 7 stitches. Join red, single crochet 1 stitch. Single crochet remaining stitches in white.
- Row 3: Skip first stitch, single crochet in next 6 stitches, 3 red, white to end of row.
- Rows 4-7: Continue to work in this pattern, increasing red stitches on either side until there are 9 red stitches. Repeat the last row.
- Row 8-9: Skip first stitch, 1 single crochet in white, 11 red, 1 white.
- Row 10: Skip first stitch, 13 red, 1 white.
- Row 11: Skip first stitch, 6 single crochet in red, 1 white, 6 red, 1 white.
- Row 12: Skip first stitch, 1 single crochet in white, 5 red, 1 white, 5 red, 2 white.
- Row 13: Skip first stitch, 1 single crochet in white, 4 red, 3 white, 4 red, 2 white.
- Row 14: Skip first stitch, 2 single crochet in white, 2 red, 5 white, 2 red, 3 white.
- Row 15: Slip first stitch, single crochet in white to end of round. Tie off and weave ends through work.

February 6

Heart Earrings

Materials

- Scraps of red crochet cotton
- Crochet hook size 1.5 mm
- Earring hooks (available at craft stores)

Directions

- Crochet a chain of 4 stitches.
- Round 1: 11 triple crochet in farthest chain from hook. The 3 chains count as 1 triple crochet. Slip stitch to join at top of third chain.
- Round 2: Slip stitch into next triple crochet, 1 double and 2 triple crochet in next triple crochet, 2 triple and 1 double crochet in next triple crochet, slip stitch into next stitch, 1 double crochet and 2 triple crochet in next stitch, 2 triple and 1 double crochet in next stitch, slip stitch into next 3 stitches, 1 double followed by 1 triple and another double in next stitch, slip stitch in next three stitches. Tie off and weave ends through work.

Finishing

Attach earring hooks to the top of the hearts in the center point.

February 7

Crochet Candy Kiss

Materials

- Scraps of worsted weight yarn
- Crochet hook size 4.5 mm
- Fiberfill stuffing
- Tapestry needle
- Strip of paper
- Glue

Directions

- Crochet a chain of 5 stitches, join with slip stitch to create a ring. Chain 1.
- Round 1: 4 single crochet in ring.
- Round 2: 2 single crochet in each stitch.
- Round 3: 1 single crochet in each stitch.
- Round 4: 2 single crochet in next stitch, 1 single next 3. Repeat once.
- Round 5: 2 single crochet in next stitch, 1 single 4. Repeat once.
- Round 6: 2 single crochet in next stitch, 1 single next 3. Repeat twice.
- Round 7: 2 single crochet in next stitch, 1 single next 4. Repeat twice.
- Round 8: 2 single crochet in next stitch, 1 single next 5. Repeat twice.
- Round 9: 2 single crochet in next stitch, 1 single next 6. Repeat twice.
- Rounds 10-11: Single crochet in each stitch.
- Round 12: Single crochet 2 stitches together, 1 single next 6. Repeat twice.
- Round 13: (work in back loops) single crochet 2 stitches together, 1 single crochet in next 5 stitches. Repeat twice.
- Round 14: Single crochet 2 stitches together, 1 single crochet in next 4 stitches, repeat twice, stuff with fiberfill.
- Round 15: Single crochet 2 stitches together, 1 single crochet in next stitch. Repeat to end of round.
- Round 16: Single crochet 2 stitches together, pull thread tight, tie off and weave ends through work. Glue paper tag to top of candy kiss.

February 8

Valentine's Day Heart Card

Materials

- Scraps of red worsted yarn
- Crochet hook size 5 mm
- 1 sheet 8.5 X 11 card stock or construction paper
- Gathered lace
- Glue gun and glue stick

Directions

- Follow same pattern for heart as in Little Girl's Heart Purse (February 1). Tie off and weave ends through work.

Putting the Card Together
- Fold the card stock in half lengthwise, so you have a card that is 8.5" X 5.5".
- Decide where you want the heart to go on the front of the card, and glue in place with the glue gun.
- Measure enough lace to go completely around the heart. Glue in place with the glue gun.
- You can leave the card as is, or add other embellishments such as stickers or glitter.

February 9

Heart Scarf

Materials

- 1 skein red worsted weight yarn, 1 skein white worsted weight yarn
- Crochet hook size 5.5 mm

Directions

- Use same heart pattern as the Heart Coasters from February 4.
- Crochet a chain of 30 stitches.
- Rows 1-15: Follow heart pattern for first half of scarf, and continue to the end of the row with single crochet in white. Chain 1 and turn at end of each row.
- Rows 16-30: Skip first stitch, single crochet next 14 stitches in white, follow heart pattern.
- Continue working in this manner so you have hearts going up either side of the scarf, finishing when the scarf is at the desired length. Tie off and weave ends through work.

Finishing

Make fringes for either end of scarf.

February 10

Stuffed Heart Sachet

Materials

- Red worsted yarn
- Crochet hook size 5.5 mm
- Fiberfill stuffing
- Essential oil

Directions

- Make 2 hearts as with the Little Girl's Heart Purse from February 1.
- Sew hearts together using a slip stitch, leaving the top open. Do not tie off.
- Put a couple of drops of your favorite essential oil on the stuffing.
- Stuff the heart, and sew it shut with slip stitches.
- Add a tassle to the bottom point of heart, and a chain at the top so you can hang it.

February 11

Valentine's Day Dishcloth

Materials

- Red and white worsted weight yarn
- Crochet hook size 5.5 mm

Directions

- Crochet a chain of 45 stitches.
- Row 1: Single crochet in second chain from hook, single crochet to end of row. Chain 1 and turn.
- Rows 2-10: Skip first stitch, single crochet in each stitch to end of row. Chain 1 and turn.
- Rows 11-25: Work same pattern as for Heart Coasters from February 5.
- Row 26-35: Skip first stitch, single crochet in each stitch to end of row. Chain 1 and turn. When piece is completed, tie off.
- Edging: 2 single crochet in each stitch all the way around dish cloth. Tie off and weave ends through work.

February 12

Crochet Heart Pin and Necklace

Materials

- Scraps of red crochet cotton
- Crochet hook size 1.5 mm
- Pin backing (available at craft stores in jewelry findings)
- Glue gun and glue
- Jump ring (in jewelry findings)
- Necklace clasp

Directions

- Follow same directions as heart earrings for both the pin and the pendant. Tie off ends and weave through work.
- Glue the pin backing to one of the hearts.
- Crochet a chain measuring 18 inches. Attach clasp by tying yarn ends to rings on clasp.
- Attach a jump ring to the top middle of the heart, and attach the pendant to the crochet chain.

February 13

Valentine's Day Poster to Make with the Kids

Materials

- Scraps of red worsted weight yarn
- Crochet hook size 5 mm
- 1 sheet of white Bristol board
- Craft glue
- Red and silver glitter
- Pencil
- 2" wide ruffled lace (eyelet lace is ideal for this project)

Directions

- Crochet a chain that is at least 10 feet in length.
- Mix craft glue with red glitter.
- Print the words "Happy Valentine's Day" on Bristol board in big letters.
- Get the kids to soak the crochet chain in the glue/glitter mixture.
- Place the chain on the various letters. You will need to cut out pieces of the crochet chain to fit the letters. Don't worry about them unraveling, because the glue will hold them together. If you don't have enough chain, make some more.
- Draw some dots with glue in random spots around the message, and sprinkle red and silver glitter on the dots.
- Glue ruffled lace all the way around the poster.
- Allow everything to dry for at least 2-3 hours.

February 14

Heart Shoulder Bag

Materials

- 2 skeins worsted weight yarn, 1 red and 1 light pink
- Crochet hook size 5.5 mm
- Tapestry needle
- Red, heart-shaped button
- Needle and thread

Directions

- Make 2 Valentine's Day Dishcloths from February 11. Add an extra 4 inches of length to one of the cloths in light pink yarn. Only add ruffled edge to the top of the long piece.
- Crochet a chain of 10 stitches.
- 1 single crochet in second stitch from hook, single crochet to end of row. Chain 1 and turn. Repeat this row until piece is long enough to go around three sides of the small dishcloth and create a shoulder strap. Tie off and weave ends through work.
- Using a slip stitch, attach both larger pieces to the panel to form a purse, with the rest of the panel at the top as the strap. The top 4 inches of the longer dish cloth piece will serve as the flap.
- 2 single crochet in each stitch all the way around flap. When you reach the center, make a chain of ten, and then repeat the 2 single crochet in each stitch to complete the ruffle on the flap. The chain is for the button.
- Using the needle and thread, attach the button to the front of the purse.
- Weave all ends through work.

February 15

Soft Baby Blanket

Materials

- 3 large skeins Red Heart yarn (pastel color)
- 1 large skein Red Heart yarn, white
- Crochet hooks sizes 5 mm and 5.5 mm

Directions

- Crochet a chain of 129 stitches with 5 mm hook.
- Row 1: 5 double crochet in 6ᵗʰ chain from hook. *Skip 2 stitches, double crochet in next stitch, skip 2, 5 double crochet in next stitch. Repeat from * to last 3 stitches. Skip 2 stitches, 1 double crochet in last stitch. Chain 3 and turn.
- Rows 2-50: Repeat row 1.

Finishing

With 5.5 mm hook and white yarn, join with a slip stitch at the top right-hand corner. 2 double crochet in every stitch all the way around. Tie off and weave ends through work.

February 16

Baby Ballet Slippers (Infant Girl)

Materials

- White worsted weight yarn
- Crochet hook size 3.5 mm
- ¼" ribbon, pale pink

Directions

- Crochet a chain of 11 stitches.

- Row 1: Half double crochet in 3rd chain from hook, 7 half double crochet, 6 half double crochet in last stitch. Turn piece so you are stitching on the opposite side of the chain. 7 half double crochet, 5 half double crochet in next stitch, join at top of original chain.
- Row 2: Chain 2, 7 half double crochet, 2 half double crochet in each of next 5 stitches, 7 half double crochet, 2 half double crochet in each of next 5 stitches, join at top of first chain.
- Row 3: Chain 2, 7 half double crochet, 10 double crochet, 1 half double crochet, join at top of beginning chain.
- Row 4: Chain 2, 7 half double crochet, double crochet 2 stitches together twice, 6 double crochet, double crochet 2 stitches together twice, half double crochet to end, join with slip stitch. Tie off and weave ends through work.

Finishing

Weave pink ribbon through top part of ballet slippers, tie in a little bow at the front.

February 17

Easy-Peasy Scarf

Materials

- 1 large skein Red Heart yarn, light green
- Crochet hook size 6 mm

Directions

- Crochet a chain of 19 stitches.
- Row 1: 2 double crochet, chain 1, 2 double crochet in 5th chain from hook. *Skip next 3 stitches, 2 double crochet, chain 1, 2 double crochet in next stitch. Repeat 3 times, skip 1 stitch, 1 double crochet in last stitch. Chain 3 and turn.
- Row 2: 2 double crochet, chain 1, 2 double crochet in each chain space all the way across. Finish row with 1 double crochet at top of first chain. Chain 3 and turn.
- Row 3-end: Repeat row 2 until piece reaches the desired length.

Finishing

1 double crochet in each stitch all the way around scarf to make a border. Tie off and weave ends through work.

February 18

Cozy Doggie Sweater (Small Dogs)

Materials

- 2-3 ounces 4-ply worsted weight yarn
- Crochet hook size 4.5

Directions

- Crochet a chain of 70 stitches, join with a slip stitch to create a ring (do not twist chain).
- Round 1: Chain 2, 1 half double crochet in each chain all the way around ring. Join with slip stitch.
- Rounds 2-12: Chain 2, 1 half double crochet in each stitch all the way around. Join with slip stitch.
- Round 13: 20 slip stitches, chain 2, 39 half double crochet.
- Rounds 14-20: Chain 2, half double crochet all the way around. Chain 2 and turn.
- Round 21: Half double crochet in each stitch. Chain 16, don't turn. Join with slip stitch to the other end of the row you just finished.
- Round 22: Chain 2, half double crochet all the way around. Join with slip stitch at top of first chain 2. Don't turn. Repeat round 2 more times, tie off and weave ends through work.

February 19

Sparkly Beaded Crochet Bracelet

Materials

- Metallic crochet thread, any color
- Beads to match color of thread (make sure holes are large enough for the crochet thread)
- Clasp (available at craft stores in jewelry findings)
- Crochet hook size 3.5 mm

Directions

- Crochet a chain long enough to fit comfortably around your wrist.
- Row 1: Skip first chain, single crochet to end of row. Chain 1 and turn.
- Row 2: Thread beads onto crochet thread (about 10-15 beads should do). *Pull 1 bead close to work, single crochet in next stitch. Repeat to end of row.

Finishing

Attach clasp by tying crochet thread ends to each end. Tie off and weave ends through work.

February 20

Pocket Patches (Sew on shirts, bags, skirts, aprons, etc.)

Materials

- 1 skein 4-ply worsted weight yarn
- Crochet hook size 5 mm

Directions

- Crochet a chain of 25 stitches.
- Row 1: Skip first chain, single crochet to end of row. Chain 1 and turn.
- Rows 2-12: Skip first stitch, single crochet to end of row. Chain 1 and turn.
- Row 13: 1 single crochet in 2 stitches (decrease stitch). Single crochet to end of row. Chain 1 and turn.
- Row 14: 1 single crochet in 2 stitches. Single crochet to end of row. Chain 1 and turn.

- Row 15-end: Continue with this decreasing pattern until the top comes to a point. Tie off and weave ends through work.

February 21

Baby Doll Blanket and Pillow

Materials

- 1 skein Red Heart yarn, light pink
- 1 skein Red Heart yarn, white
- Crochet hook size 5 mm
- Fiberfill stuffing

Directions

Doll Blanket
- Using pink yarn, crochet a chain of 70 stitches.
- Row 1: Skip first chain, single crochet in each stitch to end of row. Chain 2 and turn.
- Row 2: Skip first chain, double crochet in each stitch to end of row. Chain 1 and turn.
- Rows 3-end: Alternate rows 1 and 2 until pieces reaches desired size. Tie off and weave ends through work.

Finishing

2 double crochet in each stitch all the way around blanket with white to create a ruffle.

Doll Pillow
- Crochet a chain of 35 stitches with pink yarn.
- Row 1: Skip first chain, single crochet in each stitch to end of row. Chain 1 and turn. Repeat row 1 until piece measures 8 inches.
- Make another piece the same as the first.

Finishing

Place one piece on top of the other, and stitch 3 sides together with a slip stitch. Stuff with fiberfill stuffing, and stitch final side closed. Go all the way around the edge with white yarn, 2 double crochet in each stitch to create a ruffle.

February 22

Nap Mat with Built-In Pillow

Materials

- 2 large skeins Red Heart yarn, any color
- Crochet hook size 6 mm
- Fiberfill stuffing

Directions

- Crochet a chain measuring 36 inches.
- Row 1: Skip first chain, double crochet in each chain to end of row. Chain 2 and turn.

- Row 2: Skip first stitch, double crochet in each stitch to end of row. Chain 2 and turn.
- Row 3-end: Repeat row 2 until piece reaches 8 feet in length.

Finishing
- Fold work over at top 12 inches. Stitch down each side with a slip stitch, leaving part open.
- Stuff pillow section, stitch closed.
- You can leave the mat like this, or go all the way around with single crochet to give the edge a neat finish.

February 23

Glittery G-Clef Chain Earrings

Materials

- Crochet thread, any color
- Crochet hook size 3 mm
- Earring hooks (available at craft stores in jewelry findings)
- Fabric stiffener (equal parts craft glue and water)
- Glitter

Directions

- Crochet 2 chains 4 inches long.
- Form into G-clef symbols.
- Lay flat in a dish lined with waxed paper, and cover with just enough stiffener to soak the G-clefs.
- Sprinkle on some glitter, and let dry for a couple of hours.
- Peel G-clefs off waxed paper, and attach to earring hooks.

You can make more G-clefs and use them for pendants, bracelet charms, and brooches. They can also be used to decorate various items of clothing.

February 24

Roll-Up Crochet Hook Case

Materials

- 1 skein 4-ply worsted weight yarn
- Crochet hook size 5 mm
- Tapestry needle

Directions

Outside
- Crochet a chain measuring 10 inches in length.
- Row 1: Skip first chain, single crochet to end of row. Chain 1 and turn.
- Row 2: Skip first stitch, single crochet to end of row. Chain 1 and turn.
- Row 3-end: Repeat row 2 until piece measures 10 inches tall.

Pocket
- Crochet a chain measuring 10 inches in length.

- Follow same pattern as for outside, but finish at 8 inches tall.

Finishing
- Lay both pieces together so 3 ends meet. With tapestry needle, stitch three sides, leaving top open.
- About every inch or so across, stitch a line from the bottom to the top of the pocket, going through both pieces.
- Crochet a chain measuring 12 inches.
- Attach one end of chain half-way up one side of the case. This is your tie, so you can roll up the case and tie it shut.

February 25

Tube Bracelet

Materials

- 4-ply worsted weight yarn, any color
- Crochet hook size 4 mm
- Bracelet clasp (available at craft stores in jewelry findings)

Directions

- Crochet a chain of 4 stitches. Join with a slip stitch to create a ring.
- Round 1: Chain 1, skip first stitch, single crochet to end of round.
- Round 2: Single crochet to end of round.
- Keep working in rounds until piece measures long enough to fit comfortably around your wrist.
- Pull ends tight to gather the ends.
- Tie each end to clasp, weave ends through work.

You can leave the bracelet as it is, or have a bit of fun decorating it with beads, charms, etc. One fun idea is to wrap yarn around the bracelet a few times, every inch or so, and hang charms or beads from each of these wrapped sections.

February 26

Crochet Doggie Tug-O-War Toy

Materials

- Heavy cotton yarn
- Crochet hook size 5 mm
- Fiberfill stuffing

Directions

- Crochet a chain of 5 stitches. Join with a slip stitch to create a ring.
- Round 1: Chain 1, 6 single crochet. Chain 1.
- Rounds 2-5: 2 single crochet in each stitch. Chain 1.
- Rounds 6-end: Work in rounds, with single crochet all the way around until piece measures 10" long.
- Stuff pull toy with fiberfill stuffing.

- Decrease round 1: Single crochet in 2 stitches together all the way around. Continue decreasing until there are 2 stitches left, draw yarn through. Tie off and weave ends through work.

February 27

11" Fashion Doll Sleeping Bag and Pillow

Materials

- 4-ply worsted weight yarn, pink
- Crochet hook size 5 mm
- Fiberfill stuffing

Directions

- Crochet a chain of 20 stitches.
- Row 1: Skip first chain, double crochet all the way across. Chain 2 and turn.
- Row 2: Skip first stitch, double crochet all the way across. Chain 2 and turn. Repeat this row until piece measures 20 inches.

Finishing

Measure 8 inches, and fold. Stitch up both sides with slip stitches. Tie off ends and weave through work.

Pillow
- Crochet a chain of 20 stitches.
- Row 1: Skip first chain, double crochet all the way across. Chain 2 and turn. Repeat this row until piece measures 5 inches.

Finishing

Stitch up three sides. Stuff with fiberfill stuffing. Stith last side closed, tie off and weave ends through work.

February 28

Keyboard Wrist Rest

Materials

- 1 skein 4-ply worsted weight yarn
- Crochet hook size 5.5 mm
- Fiberfill stuffing

Directions

- Make 2 pieces
- Crochet a chain of 25 stitches.
- Row 1: Skip first chain, single crochet in each stitch to end of row. Chain 1 and turn.

- Row 2: Skip first stitch, single crochet in each stitch to end of row. Chain 1 and turn. Repeat this row until piece measures 18".
- With a slip stitch, sew together both long sides and one short side. Stuff with fiberfill stuffing, and close the end with slip stitches. Tie off and weave ends through work.

You can make a smaller version to be a wrist rest to use with your mouse.

February 29 (Leap Year Bonus Pattern)

Hair Bun Cover

Materials

- 4-ply worsted weight yarn
- Crochet hook size 4 mm
- 5mm ribbon, same or contrasting color

Directions

- Crochet a chain of 5 stitches. Join with slip stitch to create a ring.
- Round 1: 12 double crochet in ring. Join to first double crochet with a slip stitch.
- Round 2: Chain 5, skip first stitch, * double crochet, chain 2. Repeat from * to end of round. Join all rounds with a slip stitch.
- Round 3-4: Chain 5, double crochet in chain space, chain 2, double crochet in same chain space. *Double crochet, chain 2, double crochet, chain 2 double crochet in next chain space. Repeat from * to end of round.
- Round 5: Chain 5, double crochet in chain space, chain 2, double crochet in next chain space. *Double crochet, chain 2, double crochet in next chain space. Chain 2, double crochet in next chain space. Repeat from * to end of round.
- Round 6-8: Chain 4, double crochet in chain space, chain 1, double crochet in next chain space. *Double crochet, chain 1, double crochet in next chain space. Chain 1, double crochet in next chain space. Repeat from * to end of round.
- Round 9: Chain 1, 2 half double crochet in each chain space around. Tie off and weave ends through work.

Finishing

Weave ribbon between the stitches in round 8.

March

March is a fun month, with spring break and St. Patrick's Day. This month you will find some great patterns that will help take you into the spring, as well as some awesome shamrock patterns for the Irish in all of us.

March 1

Green Scarf with Fringes

Materials

- 1 large skein Green Variegated Red Heart Yarn
- Crochet hook size 5.5 mm

Directions

- Crochet a chain measuring 10 inches.
- Row 1: Skip first stitch, single crochet in each stitch across. Chain 2 and turn.
- Row 2: Skip first stitch, double crochet in each stitch across. Chain 2 and turn.
- Row 3: Skip first stitch, double crochet in each stitch across. Chain 1 and turn.
- Row 4: Skip first stitch, single crochet in each stitch across. Chain 1 and turn.
- Rows 5-end: Repeat rows 2-4 until piece reaches desired length. Tie off ends and weave through work.

Finishing

Add fringes to each end of the scarf.

March 2

Leprechaun Brooch

Materials

- Scraps of black and yellow 4-ply worsted weight yarn
- Crochet hook size 5 mm
- Pin backing (available at craft stores in jewelry findings)
- Hot glue gun and glue

Directions

- Crochet a chain with black yarn measuring 3 inches.
- Row 1: Skip first stitch, single crochet in each stitch across. Chain 1 and turn.
- Row 2: Skip first stitch, single crochet in each stitch across. Chain 1 and turn.
- Row 3: Single crochet first 2 stitches together, and single crochet the next 2 stitches together. Single crochet until there are 4 stitches left, and single crochet in 2 stitches twice. Attach yellow yarn, chain 1 and turn
- Row 4: Skip first stitch, single crochet in each stitch. Chain 1 and turn.
- Row 5: Skip first stitch, single crochet to end of row. Switch to black yarn, chain 1 and turn.
- Row 6-9: Repeat row 5. Tie off ends and weave through work.

Finishing

Glue pin back to one side of the piece.

March 3

Shamrock Mug Cozy

Materials

- Scraps of green, white, and black 4-ply worsted weight yarn
- Crochet hook size 5 mm
- Tapestry needle

Directions

Cozy
- Crochet a chain of 30 stitches with black yarn. Slip stitch in first chain to create a ring.
- Round 1: Chain 2, half double crochet in each chain around. Join with slip stitch at top of chain 2.
- Round 2: Switch to white yarn. Chain 2, half double crochet in each stitch. Join with slip stitch at top of chain 2.
- Rounds 3-6: Repeat round 2. Switch back to black yarn at end of round 6.
- Round 7: Repeat last round. Tie off and weave ends through work.

Shamrock

With green yarn, crochet a chain of 3 stitches, 2 double crochet in first chain, chain 2, slip stitch in same chain. * Chain 2, 2 double crochet, chain 2, slip stitch in same chain. Repeat from * twice. Chain 7, single crochet in third chain from hook, slip stitch in next 4 chain stitches, slip stitch in same chain as petals. Fasten off and weave ends through work. Using the tapestry needle, stitch the shamrock to the cozy.

March 4

Shamrock Garland

Materials

- Scraps of light and dark green yarn
- Crochet hook size 5.5 mm

Directions

Shamrocks (make as many as you want in both shades of green, depending on how long you want the garland to be)
- Crochet a chain of 3 stitches, join with slip stitch to create a ring.
- Round 1: Chain 3, 1 triple crochet, 1 double crochet, 1 triple crochet, chain 3, slip stitch (all in loop). Repeat 3 times.
- Stem: Chain 5 with tail of yarn, skip first chain, single crochet in rest of stitches. Tie off and weave ends through work.

Finishing

Attach yarn to one of the shamrocks, chain 10. Slip stitch into another shamrock, chain 10. Continue until pieces reaches desired length.

March 5

Shamrock Dishcloth

Materials

- 1 skein white Red Heart yarn
- Scraps of green yarn
- Crochet hook size 5 mm
- Tapestry needle

Directions

- Crochet a chain measuring 8 inches.
- Row 1: Skip first stitch, single crochet in each stitch across. Chain 1 and turn.
- Row 2-end: Skip first stitch, single crochet in each stitch across. Chain 1 and turn. Tie off ends and weave through work.
- Edging: Switch to green yarn, 2 single crochet in each stitch all the way around cloth. Tie off ends and weave through work.

Finishing

Make a shamrock (follow instructions from Shamrock Garland, March 4). Using tapestry needle, stitch shamrock to dishcloth.

March 6

St. Patty's Day Shades of Green Necklace

Materials

- Embroidery thread in several shades of green
- Crochet hook size 3 mm or smaller
- A chain necklace (or make one with a chain and clasp you can get at craft stores in jewelry findings)
- Jump rings

Directions

Large Circles
- Crochet a chain of 3 stitches. Slip stitch in first chain to create a ring.
- Round 1: 6 single crochet in ring.
- Round 2: 2 single crochet in each stitch around.
- Round 3: 1 single crochet in first stitch, 2 single crochet in next stitch. Repeat to end of round. Tie off and weave ends through work.

Small Circles

Crochet a chain of 3 stitches. Slip stitch in first chain to create a ring.

- Round 1: 7 single crochet in ring.
- Round 2: 2 single crochet in each stitch around.
- Round 3: 1 single crochet in each stitch around. Tie off and weave ends through work.

Make several large and small circles, and attach them to the chain using the jump rings.

March 7

Shades of Green Earrings

Materials

- Light and dark green embroidery thread
- Crochet hook size
- Earring hooks (available in craft stores in jewelry findings)
- Jump rings

Directions

Make 2 large and 2 small circles identical to the ones in the Shades of Green Necklace pattern from March 6. Tie off ends and weave through work.

Finishing
- Attach each of the smaller circles to the earring hooks.
- Attach jump rings to bottom of smaller circles, and attach larger circles.

March 8

St. Patrick's Day Granny Square Shamrock Coaster

Materials

- 1 skein white Red Heart yarn
- Scraps of emerald green yarn
- Crochet hook size 5 mm
- Tapestry needle

Directions

This pattern uses a shell stitch: 3 double crochet, chain 2, 3 double crochet in one space.
- Crochet a chain of 8 stitches with white yarn. Join with a slip stitch to create a ring.
- Round 1: Chain 3, 2 double crochet in ring. Chain 2, 3 double crochet in ring. Chain 1, 3 double crochet in ring. Chain 2, 3 double crochet in ring. Chain 2, 3 double crochet in ring. Chain 1, 3 double crochet in ring. Chain 2, join at top of chain 3 with a slip stitch.
- Round 2: Slip stitch in next 2 double crochet. Slip stitch in next chain 2 space. Chain 3, 2 double crochet, chain 2, 3 double crochet in same space. Chain 1, 3 double crochet, chain 2, 3 double crochet in next chain 2 space. Chain 1. Shell in next chain 2 space. Chain 1, 3 double crochet in next chain 1 space. Chain 1. Shell in next 2 chain spaces. Chain 1 and join with slip stitch at top of chain 3.
- Round 3: Slip stitch in 2 stitches and in next chain 2 space. Chain 3, 2 double crochet, chain 2, 3 double crochet in next chain 2 space. * Chain 1, 3 double crochet in next chain space, repeat. Shell in next chain 2 space, chain 1, 3 double crochet in next chain 1 space, chain 1. Shell in next chain 2 space. Repeat from * once, join with slip stitch at top of chain 3.

Finishing
- Switch to green yarn, and single crochet all the way around coaster.
- Make a shamrock (follow instructions from Shamrock Garland, March 4). Using tapestry needle, stitch shamrock to front of coaster.

March 9

Lucky Bracelet

Materials

- Scraps of variegated green 4-ply double worsted yarn
- Crochet hook size 4 mm
- Shamrock charm and jump ring (available in craft stores in jewelry findings)
- Green ¼ inch satin ribbon (about 12-14 inches)

Directions

- Crochet a chain long enough to fit comfortably around your wrist.
- Row 1: Skip first stitch. Single crochet to end of row. Chain 1 and turn.
- Row 2: Skip first stitch *half double crochet, chain 1, half double crochet to end of row. Chain 1 and turn.
- Row 3: Skip first stitch, single crochet to end of row. Tie off ends and weave through.

Finishing
- Weave ribbon through open spaces in bracelet, leaving ends long enough to tie instead of using a clasp.
- Use the jump ring to hang the shamrock charm from the bracelet.

March 10

Sparkly Shamrock Necklace, Earrings, and Bracelet

Materials

- Green metallic crochet thread
- Crochet hook size 3 mm or smaller
- Earring hooks (available in craft stores in jewelry findings)
- Silver chain
- Jump rings
- 2 necklace/bracelet clasps

Directions

- Make 7 of the small shamrocks and 1 large shamrock from the Shamrock Garland pattern from March 4.

Necklace
- Put clasp on chain.
- Attach large shamrock to jump ring and put on the chain.

Earrings
- Attach 2 small shamrocks to the earring hooks.

Bracelet

- Cut chain long enough to make a bracelet (about 7").
- Attach clasp.
- Attach 5 small shamrocks all the way around bracelet with jump rings.

March 11

Pot O' Gold Coasters

Materials

- Scraps of black, yellow, red, green blue, and gold 4-ply worsted weight yarn
- Crochet hook size 5 mm

Directions

- Crochet a chain of 7 stitches in black.
- Round 1: Skip first chain, single crochet in next chain, 4 single crocket, 3 single crochet in last chain. Continue to work around to other side with 4 single crochet, 3 single crochet in last chain, and slip stitch to join.
- Round 2: * Chain 1, single crochet in same stitch, 4 single crochet, 2 single crochet in next stitch. Repeat from * 3 times. 5 single crochet, 2 single crochet in next stitch (repeat 3 times). Join with slip stitch.
- Round 3: Chain 1, single crochet in same stitch, 4 single crochet. * 2 single crochet in next stitch, 1 single crochet. Repeat from * 4 times. 5 single crochet. Repeat from * again 3 times, slip stitch to join.
- Round 4: Chain 1, single crochet in same stitch, 4 single crochet. * 2 single crochet in next stitch, 1 single crochet. Repeat from * 5 times. 4 single crochet, repeat from * again 4 times. 2 single crochet in next stitch, slip stitch to join. Tie off and weave ends through work.
- Attach gold yarn 4 stitches in, 11 single crochet, 1 slip stitch, chain 1 and turn.
- Row 2: Slip stitch in first stitch, 9 single crochet, 1 slip stitch. Chain 1 and turn.
- Row 3: Slip stitch in first stitch, 7 single crochet, 1 slip stitch, chain 1, tie off and weave ends through work.
- Attach blue with slip stitch, and single crochet all around gold. Switch colors and keep going around until you have a rainbow. Tie off ends and weave through work.

March 12

Pot O' Gold Candy Dish

Materials

- Black 4-ply worsted weight yarn
- Crochet hook size 5.5 mm
- Chocolate coins with gold foil wrappers

Directions

- Round 1: Chain 2, 6 single crochet in second chain.
- Round 2: 2 single crochet in each stitch.
- Round 3: 2 single crochet in each stitch.
- Round 4: Single crochet in next 2 stitches, 2 single crochet in next stitch. Repeat 6 times.
- Round 5: Single crochet in next 3 stitches, 2 single crochet in next stitch. Repeat 6 times.

- Round 6: Single crochet in next 4 stitches, 2 single crochet in next stitch. Repeat 6 times.
- Round 7: Single crochet in next 5 stitches, 2 single crochet in next stitch. Repeat 6 times.
- Round 8: Single crochet in next 6 stitches, 2 single crochet in next stitch. Repeat 6 times.
- Round 9: Single crochet in next 7 stitches, 2 single crochet in next stitch. Repeat 6 times.
- Rounds 10-19: Single crochet each stitch.
- Round 20: Single crochet in next 7 stitches, decrease (single crochet 2 stitches together). Repeat 6 times.
- Rounds 21-23: Single crochet in each stitch.

Finishing
- Crochet a chain measuring 6 inches, and attach to either side of the pot o' gold.
- Fill pot o' gold with chocolate coins.

March 13

Little Girl's Shamrock Purse with Fringes

Materials

- Green and white scrap yarn, 4-ply worsted weight
- Crochet hook size 5.5 mm
- Tapestry needle

Directions

- Make 2 granny squares in white yarn that are about 8" square. Use the March 8 St. Patrick's Day Granny Square Shamrock Coaster as a guide. Go around edges of each square with 2 single crochet in each stitch all the way around in green yarn.
- Crochet a chain measuring 24" in length.
- Row 1: Skip first stitch, single crochet all the way across. Tie off.
- Using tapestry needle and white yarn, stitch around 3 sides of the granny squares, between the white and green yarn.
- Attach chain strap to either side of bag
- Crochet 1 shamrock the same as that of the Shamrock Garland from March 4. Using tapestry needle, stitch shamrock to front of purse.
- Using white yarn, add fringes to bottom of purse.

March 14

Lucky Heart Brooch

Materials

- Green and black 4-ply worsted weight yarn
- Small gold buckle
- Crochet hook size 5 mm
- Pin backing (available at craft stores in jewelry findings)
- Glue gun and glue

Directions

- Make a heart identical to the one from the Little Girl's Heart Purse pattern from February 1.

- Attach black yarn to one side of heart, and crochet a chain long enough to reach the other side. Attach at side with slip stitch.
- Row 1: Single crochet to end of row. Chain 1 and turn.
- Row 2: Skip first stitch, single crochet to end of row. Tie off and weave ends through work.

Finishing
- Attach pin back to back of heart with glue.
- Attach gold buckle to the middle of the black strap with glue.

March 15

Round Emerald Afghan

Materials

- 2 large skeins emerald green Red Heart yarn
- 1 large skein light green Red Heart yarn
- Crochet hook size 10 mm

Directions

- Crochet a chain of 5 stitches. Join with slip stitch to create a ring.
- All Rounds: Double crochet in each stitch all the way around. Continue working in rounds until afghan reaches desired size. Don't worry about using a stitch marker, because you will be working around and around without making any changes. Tie off and weave ends through work.

Finishing

Using the light green yarn, create fringes all the way around afghan.

March 16

Shamrock Headband

Materials

- 1 skein white 4-ply worsted weight yarn
- Scraps of emerald green yarn, 4-ply worsted weight
- Crochet hook size 5 mm
- Tapestry needle
- Sewing needle and thread
- 1" wide elastic, white

Directions

- Crochet a chain measuring 2'.
- Row 1: Skip first stitch, single crochet to end of row. Chain 1 and turn.
- Row 2: Skip first stitch, single crochet to end of row. Chain 1 and turn.
- Rows 3-end: Repeat row 2 until piece measures 8". Tie off ends and weave through work.
- Crochet 3 small shamrocks like the ones used for the Sparkly Shamrock Necklace, Earrings, and Bracelet from March 10.

Finishing

- With sewing needle and thread, sew the elastic to either end of the headband.
- With the tapestry needle, stitch the 3 shamrocks to the white section of the headband.

March 17

Lucky Leprechaun Doggie Hat

Materials

- Green 4-ply worsted weight yarn
- Black and yellow felt
- Glue gun and glue

Directions

- Chain 2, 10 double crochet in second chain. Join with a slip stitch and chain 2.
- Round 1: 1 double crochet in the second chain stitch. 2 double crochet in each stitch to end of round. Join and chain 2.
- Round 2: 1 double crochet in second chain stitch. * 3 double crochet, 2 double crochet in next stitch. Repeat from * to end of round and join.
- Round 3: Chain 2, 1 double crochet in each stitch (back loops only). Join and chain 2.
- Round 4-6: 1 double crochet in each stitch to end of round. Join and chain 2.
- Round 7: 1 double crochet in each stitch. Join and chain 2.
- Round 8: 1 double crochet in second chain stitch. * 1 double crochet, 2 double crochet in next stitch. Repeat from * to end of round. Join and chain 2.
- Round 9: 1 double crochet in second chain stitch. * 1 double crochet, 2 double crochet in next stitch. Repeat from * to end of round. Join and tie off, weaving ends through work.

Finishing

Straps
- Crochet 2 chains measuring 8-12" each. Attach one chain to each side of hat with slip stitch, tie off and weave ends through work.

Decorations
- Cut a strip of felt ½" wide and long enough to go all the way around the hat. Glue to hat.
- Cut a piece of yellow felt to look like a buckle. Glue to middle of black felt hat band.

March 18

Mobile Phone Case

Materials

- White fingering weight yarn
- Pink sport weight yarn
- Black sport weight yarn

- Crochet hook size 4 mm
- Pink button
- Needle and thread

Directions

- Working with 1 strand of black and 1 strand of white, crochet a chain of 17 stitches.
- Round 1: Single crochet in second chain from hook, 14 single crochet, 3 single crochet in last chain. Instead of turning, work around the other side (upside down). 14 single crochet, 2 single crochet in last chain. Slip stitch to join in first chain. Make sure that there are a total of 34 stitches, and that this number stays the same throughout the work.
- Rounds 2-21: Chain 1, single crochet all the way around. Slip stitch to join at first chain.
- Rounds 22-32: Repeat the same round, but using pink and white instead of black and white yarn. Fasten off and weave ends through work.

Finishing

Crochet a chain of 15 stitches using black and white yarn. Connect the chain to one side of the case to form a loop for the button hole. Using the needle and thread, sew the button to the other side of the case.

March 19

Fresh Orange/Clove Pomander

Materials

- 4-ply worsted weight yarn
- Crochet hook size 5
- 1 orange
- Whole cloves

Directions

- Crochet a chain of 5 stitches, join to create a ring.
- Round 1: 10 single crochet in ring. Do not turn. Continue to work around in single crochet until piece measures about 3-4" across.
- Next round: Chain 2, 1 double crochet in each stitch all the way around. Slip stitch to join at chain space. Continue in this manner until piece looks like a bag, and measures about 4" tall.
- Edging: 2 single crochet in each stitch all the way around. Crochet a chain measuring 12", and thread through top of bag to create a drawstring (between last double crochet round and edging). Tie ends of drawstring together.

Finishing

Poke whole cloves into an orange. Place orange into crochet bag, pull drawstring tight and hang bag in a closet for fresh-smelling clothes. Change the orange weekly.

March 20

Kitty Cat Toy

Materials

- Red Heart yarn
- Crochet hook size 5 mm
- Toilet paper tube
- Jingle bell
- Needle and thread

Directions

- Crochet a chain of 20 stitches. Join with a slip stitch to create a ring, do not twist stitches.
- Round 1: Chain 2, skip first stitch, double crochet in each stitch around. Repeat for 7 rounds or until piece is as long as one half of a toilet paper roll (cut roll in half). Join with a slip stitch.
- Last round: Slip stitch in each stitch all the way around. Tie off, but do not cut yarn.
- Chain 30 where last stitch is. 2 double crochet in third chain from hook. 3 double crochet in each chain to end. Join with a slip stitch, tie off and weave ends through work.

Finishing
- Sew jingle bell onto chain with the needle and thread.
- Slip other end over the toilet paper tube half.

March 21

Spring Sunshine Placemats

Materials

- 1 skein Red Heart yarn, bright yellow
- 1 skein Red Heart yarn, white
- 1 skein Red Heart yarn, bright green
- Crochet hook size 5.5 mm

Directions

- With white yarn, crochet a chain measuring 12".
- Row 1: Skip first stitch, single crochet to end of row. Chain 1 and turn.
- Row 2-end: Repeat row 1 until piece measures 10" tall. Tie off and weave ends through work.
- Edging row 1: Join bright green yarn with a slip stitch to one corner. Chain 1, double crochet in each stitch all the way around. Join and tie off, weaving ends through work.
- Edging row 2: Switch to bright yellow yarn, chain 1, double crochet in each stitch all the way around. Join and tie off, weaving ends through work.

March 22

Pony Bead Crochet Choker

Materials

- Crochet thread, lavender

- Crochet hook size 3 mm
- White pony beads
- Necklace clasp (available at craft stores in jewelry findings)

Directions

- Crochet a chain long enough to fit snugly but comfortably around your neck.
- Row 1: Skip first stitch, single crochet in each stitch to end of row. Chain 2 and turn.
- Row 2: Skip first stitch, double crochet in next stitch. *Chain 1, skip a stitch, 1 double crochet. Repeat from * to end of row. Chain 1 and turn.
- Row 3: Skip first stitch, single crochet in each stitch to end of row. Tie off but leave ends.

Finishing
- Attach a piece of yarn to one end of the choker at the double crochet row. Crochet a chain that is equal to the length of the piece.
- Slide a pony bead onto chain. Weave chain through double crochet, placing a pony bead in each space.
- Attach chain at other end. Tie off and weave ends of chain through work.
- Attach necklace clasp by tying each end of chocker to clasp. Weave ends through work.

March 23

Pretty Spring Shawl

Materials

- 1 large skein Red Heart yarn, lavender
- 1 skein Red Heart yarn, white
- Crochet hook size 8 mm

Directions

- Crochet a chain with lavender yarn measuring 48".
- Row 1: Skip first stitch, double crochet to end of row. Chain 2 and turn.
- Row 2: Skip first stitch, double crochet to end of row. Chain 2 and turn.
- Row 3: Double crochet 2 stitches together (decrease). Double crochet in each stitch until last 2 stitches, and decrease again. Chain 2 and turn.
- Row 4: Repeat row 3.
- Rows 5-end: Continue with the pattern, decreasing every third row until piece looks like a triangle.

Finishing
- Attach white yarn, and single crochet all the way around piece. Tie off.
- Now you have 2 options. You can either put a fringe on the 2 shorter sides, or 2 crochet in each stitch all the way around to create a little ruffled edge.

March 24

Book Cover

Materials

- Red Heart yarn, any color
- Crochet hook size 5 mm

Directions

- Crochet a chain measuring 8-10".
- Row 1: Skip first stitch, single crochet in each stitch to end of row. Repeat row 1 until piece measures 16". Tie off but do not weave ends through.

Finishing
- Mark 3" at each end, and fold over at this spot. Slip stitch together at short ends. Tie off and weave ends through work.
- Place cover over your favorite book, and slip the covers into the pockets.

March 25

Belt Loop Change Purse

Materials

- 4-ply worsted weight yarn
- Crochet hook size 5 mm
- Velcro (1" piece)
- Needle and thread

Directions

- Crochet a chain measuring 4 inches.
- Row 1: Skip first stitch, single crochet to end of row. Repeat row 1 until piece measures 5".

Back Loop
- Crochet a chain measuring 4".
- Row 1: Skip first stitch, single crochet to end of row. Chain 1 and turn.
- Row 2: Skip first stitch, single crochet to end of row. Tie off, leaving ends.

Finishing
- On main piece, mark the 2" line, and fold at this space. There should be 1" overhang. Using ends, slip stitch sides together to form a little purse.
- Attach Velcro with needle and thread to front of change purse, and to the inside part of the flap.
- Attach back loop to back of change purse, vertically.

March 26

Eyeglasses Idiot Chain with Beads

Materials

- Crochet thread
- Crochet hook size 3 mm
- Beads (with holes large enough for crochet chain to thread through.

Directions

Crochet a chain measuring 26".

Make a loop at each end with a slip stitch in the 5th chain from hook and the 5th chain from the end. Tie off and weave ends through work.

Finishing

Tie a knot at one end of the chain, as close to the loop as possible. Add 1 bead, tie another knot so the bead fits snugly. Continue to do this to the end of the chain.

March 27

Barbie Wrap and Skirt

Materials

- Crochet thread
- Crochet hook size 2.5 mm
- 1/8" satin ribbon

Directions

Wrap
- Crochet a chain measuring 5".
- Row 1: Skip first stitch, single crochet to end of row. Chain 2 and turn.
- Row 2: Skip first stitch, double crochet to end of row. Chain 1 and turn.
- Repeat rows 1 and 2 until piece is 2-3" long.

Finishing

Put a short fringe on each end of the wrap.

Skirt
- Crochet a chain measuring 4".
- Row 1: Skip first stitch, single crochet in each stitch to end of row. Chain 1 and turn. Repeat row 1 until piece measures 2-3".
- Last row (skirt bottom): 2 single crochet in each stitch to end of row.

Finishing
- Fold in half and sew up the side with a slip stitch.
- Turn inside out so front is facing, and weave ribbon through the top of the skirt to make a drawstring so it fits tightly at the doll's waist.

March 28

Scarf Organizer

Materials

- Red Heart yarn, any color
- Crochet hook size 5 mm

Directions

Make at least 3 rings, more depending on how many scarves you have.

First Ring
- Crochet a chain measuring 6".
- Row 1: Skip first stitch, single crochet to end of row. Chain 1 and turn.
- Row 2-3: Repeat row 1.
- Using a slip stitch, sew ends together to make a ring and set aside.

Other Rings

Follow the same pattern as for the first ring. Before closing the ring, loop it through the first ring. Continue to do this with all of the rings until you have a chain. Loop scarves through the various chains to keep them from getting tangled together.

March 29

Braided Chain Necklace

Materials

- 4-ply worsted weight yarn, 3 colors
- Crochet hook size 8 mm
- Necklace toggle clasp (available at craft stores in jewelry findings)

Directions

With 3 strands of each color yarn, crochet a chain measuring 16-18". Tie off ends, and cut so there is a 2-3" fringe at each end.

Finishing

Attach toggle clasp to each end by tying the loose end of one strand of yarn to each part of the clasp. Weave ends through work. Wear necklace with clasp in front so fringes are showing.

March 30

Pompom Necklace, Bracelet, and Earrings

Materials

- 4-ply worsted weight yarn
- Crochet hook size 6 mm
- Necklace toggle clasp (available at craft stores in jewelry findings)

Directions

- Using the yarn, make 5-10 1" pompoms, leaving 6" of yarn on each pompom.
- Crochet a chain measuring 16-18".

Finishing
- Tie ends of chain to each end of toggle clasp, then weave ends through chain.
- Tie pompoms to the chain all the way around.

You can also make a matching bracelet in the same manner, but make the chain about 7". To make earrings, tie 1 pompom to each earring hook.

March 31

Cleavage Cover

Materials

- 4-ply worsted weight yarn
- 2 buttons
- Crochet hook size 5 mm
- ¼" elastic
- Needle and thread

Directions

- Crochet a chain measuring about 8".
- Row 1: Skip first stitch, double crochet to end of row. Chain 2 and turn. Repeat row 1 until piece measures 4".
- Decrease row 1: Decrease 1 stitch on either end (double crochet over 2 stitches). Chain 2 and turn.
- Next row: Skip first stitch, double crochet to end of row. Repeat these two rows for about 2". Tie off and weave ends through work.

Finishing

At the top corners (wider end), attach elastic loops on one side, and buttons on the opposite side. Loops will go around your bra strap, and connect to buttons to hold the cleavage cover in place. You may have to play with this pattern a bit to get the perfect size.

April

Spring is finally here, and that means new spring outfits for Easter, not to mention warmer weather, flowers, and sunshine. This month we have loads of fun and easy patterns for spring, including baby clothes, a lacy scarf, and crochet flowers, not to mention some awesome patterns for Easter.

April 1

Round Porch Pillow

Materials

- 2 skeins Red Heart yarn
- Crochet hook size 4mm
- 12" foam pillow form (round)

Directions

Front
- Crochet a chain of 2 stitches with main color.
- Round 1: 6 single crochet in second stitch from hook. Slip stitch to join. Chain 1.
- Round 2: 2 single crochet in each stitch all the way around. Add second color by joining with a slip stitch to the first single crochet. Chain 1.
- Round 3: 2 single crochet in first stitch. * Single crochet, 2 single crochet in next stitch. Repeat from * to end of round.
- Round 4-end: Repeat round 3 until piece measures about 13 inches.

Back

Repeat same pattern as for front.

Finishing
- Lay front and back pieces together, and slip stitch half way around.
- Slide pillow form between the front and back, and continue stitching with a slip stitch the rest of the way around.

April 2

Kitty Cat Bed

Materials

- 2 balls bulky yarn
- 1 ball bulky yarn in another color
- Crochet hook size 6mm
- Stitch marker
- Tapestry needle

Directions

- Crochet a chain of 2 stitches.
- Round 1: 6 single crochet in second stitch from hook. Put a stitch marker here.
- Round 2: 2 single crochet in each stitch.
- Round 3: 2 single crochet in next stitch, 2 single crochet. Repeat pattern to end of round.
- Round 4: 2 single crochet in next stitch, 3 single crochet. Repeat pattern to end of round.
- Round 5: 2 single crochet in next stitch, 4 single crochet. Repeat pattern to end of round.

- Round 6: 2 single crochet in next stitch, 5 single crochet. Repeat pattern to end of round. Continue in this pattern until there are 19 rounds.
- Round 20: 2 single crochet in next stitch, 18 single crochet. You can add more rounds if you want the bed to be bigger.
- Rounds 21-28: 1 single crochet in each stitch.
- Rounds 29-30: Switch colors, and single crochet in each stitch for both rounds. Tie off ends and weave through work.

April 3

Baby Bunny Hat (3-6 months)

Materials

- 2 colors of chunky weight yarn (white and light pink)
- Crochet hook size 8 mm

Directions

Hat
- Crochet a chain of 3 stitches with white yarn. Join with slip stitch to create a ring.
- Round 1: 6 single crochet in ring, slip stitch to join.
- Round 2: 2 single crochet in each stitch to end of round.
- Round 3: Single crochet, 2 single crochet in next stitch. Repeat 6 times.
- Round 4: 2 single crochet, 2 single crochet in next stitch. Repeat 6 times.
- Round 5: 3 single crochet, 2 single crochet in next stitch. Repeat 6 times.
- Round 7: Single crochet all the way around. Repeat for 7-8 more rows. Tie off and weave ends through work.

Ears (make 2)
- Crochet a chain of 10 stitches with pink yarn.
- Row 1: Skip first 2 stitches, double crochet in next stitch. Double crochet to end of row. Attach white yarn and chain 2.
- Row 2: Double crochet in each stitch to end of round, and continue to double crochet all the way around. Do not crochet in white at bottom end of ears.
- Squeeze ears together at bottom. Using hook, attach ears to hat with slip stitches. Tie off and weave ends through work.

April 4

Striped Fashion Doll Dress

Materials

- ¼ oz each 3 colors of sport yarn
- Crochet hook size 4 mm

Directions

Back
- With first color, crochet a chain of 40 stitches.
- Row 1: Skip first stitch, single crochet to end of round. Chain 1 and turn.
- Row 2: Skip first stitch, single crochet to end of round. Chain 1 and turn.
- Rows 3-4: Switch to second color, and repeat round 2.
- Rows 5-6: Switch back to first color, and repeat round 2.
- Rows 7-8: Switch to third color, and repeat round 2.
- Rows 9-10: Switch back to first color, and repeat round 2.
- Rows 11-12: Switch to second color, and repeat round 2.
- Rows 13-14: Switch back to first color, and repeat round 2.
- Row 15: End with third color, repeating round 2. Tie off.

Front

Work same as back.

Finishing
- With a slip stitch, sew up each side, leaving enough space at the top for arm holes.
- Stitch along the top, leaving enough space for the neck hole. Tie off and weave ends through work.
- Crochet a chain measuring 6" in any of the three colors to make a belt.

April 5

Fringed Bookmark

Materials

- Sport weight crochet cotton
- Crochet hook size 8mm

Directions

- Crochet a chain of 8 stitches.
- Row 1: Skip first stitch, single crochet to end of row. Chain 1 and turn.
- Row 2: Single crochet in same stitch as first chain 1. Single crochet to end of row. Chain 1 and turn.
- Rows 3-36: Repeat row 2. Tie off and weave ends through work.

Finishing

Add a fringe to one or both ends of the bookmark. You can also glue a metal clip-style book mark to the back to give it stability and make it actually attach to the pages so you never lose your place again.

April 6

Granny Square Spring Purse

Materials

- 3 colors Red Heart yarn
- Crochet hook size 5.5 mm
- Button
- Needle and thread

Directions

Front and back
- Crochet a chain of 4 stitches. Slip stitch to join.
- Round 1: Chain 3, 2 triple crochet in ring, chain 2. Repeat so there are 4 clusters of 3 stitches. Switch to next color.
- Round 2: Chain 3, 2 triple crochet in first chain space, chain 2, 3 triple crochet in same space. Chain 2, 3 triple crochet in next chain space, chain 2. * 3 triple crochet in next chain space, chain 2, 3 triple crochet in next chain space, chain 2, 3 triple crochet in same chain space. Repeat from * to end of round, making sure that there are 2 clusters of 3 triple crochet in each corner. Switch to next color.
- Rounds 3-end: Repeat pattern until piece measures desired size, making sure that there are always 2 clusters in each corner, and 1 cluster in each of the rest of the chain spaces.

Finishing
- Using a slip stitch, sew the front and back sections together on 3 sides.
- Crochet a chain of 10 stitches, and sew to the center of the back section as a loop.
- Using the needle and thread, stitch button to the front.

Strap
- Crochet a chain measuring 36'.
- Row 1: Skip first stitch, single crochet to end of row. Chain 1, turn.
- Row 2: Skip first stitch, single crochet to end of row. Tie off and attach strap to purse.

April 7

Granny Purse of Many Colors

Materials

- Multiple colors of Red Heart yarn
- Crochet hook size 5mm
- Button
- Needle and thread

Directions

Front and back

Follow the same directions as above for the Granny Purse, but make squares that are 4 inches wide, in multiple colors. You will want a total of 40 squares.

Sides

Using the same granny square pattern, make 28 smaller squares that are 2 inches wide. Stitch together to make one long row of squares.

Finishing
- Stitch side pieces to front and back using a slip stitch.
- Crochet a chain of 10 stitches, attach to center of back section to make a loop.
- Sew button to front of purse.
- Make more of the small granny squares and stitch together to make a strap. Attach strap to sides of purse.

April 8

Easter Egg Coasters

Materials

- Scraps of 10-ply worsted weight yarn
- Crochet hook size 5.5 mm

Directions

- Crochet a chain of 5 stitches. Join with slip stitch to create a ring.
- Round 1: Chain 3, 8 double crochet in loop. Join with a slip stitch.
- Round 2: Chain 1, single crochet in each stitch (make stitches loose). Join with a slip stitch.
- Round 3: Change color, chain 1, 2 single crochet in same stich, 3 single crochet in next 2 stitches, 1 half double crochet, 2 double crochet in next stitch, 1 double crochet, 2 triple crochet in next stitch, 2 double crochet, 1 half double crochet, 3 single crochet. Join with slip stitch.
- Round 4: Chain 1, single crochet in each stitch. Tie off and weave ends through work.

April 9

Easter Bunny Head (table ornament)

Materials

- Scraps of Red Heart soft yarn
- Crochet hook size 3.75 mm
- 9mm googly eyes
- Embroidery thread
- Tapestry needle

Directions

Head
- Crochet a chain of 2 stitches.
- Round 1: 6 single crochet in first chain.
- Round 2: 2 single crochet in each stitch to end of round.
- Round 3: Single crochet in each stitch to end of round.
- Round 4: * 2 single crochet in first stitch, 1 single crochet. Repeat from * to end of round.
- Round 5: Single crochet in each stitch to end of round.
- Round 6: * 2 single crochet in first stitch, 2 single crochet. Repeat from * to end of round.
- Round 7: Single crochet in each stitch to end of round.
- Round 8: * 2 single crochet in first stitch, 3 single crochet. Repeat from * to end of round.
- Round 9-18: Single crochet in each stitch to end of round.
- Round 19: * Single crochet 2 stitches together, 3 single crochet. Repeat from * to end of round and pack in some stuffing until piece is firm.
- Round 20: * Single crochet 2 stitches together, 1 single crochet. Repeat from * to end of round. Finish stuffing and sew hole. Tie off and weave ends through work.

Ears (same as Baby Bunny Hat from April 3), attach in same manner.
- Stitch ears to bunny head.
- Stitch on eyes, and use embroidery thread to stitch on a face.

April 10

Easter Cross Bookmark

Materials

- Cotton crochet yarn
- Crochet hook size 4.5 mm

Directions

Middle Section
- Crochet a chain of 8 stitches.
- Row 1: Skip first chain, single crochet in each stitch to end of row. Chain 1 and turn.
- Rows 2-36: Single crochet in each stitch to end of row. Chain 1 and turn.
- Row 37: Single crochet in each stitch. Fasten off.

Left Side
- Row 1: Attach yarn at end of row 27. Single crochet at ends of rows 27 down to 21. Chain 1 and turn.
- Rows 2-6: Single crochet to end of row. Chain 1 and turn.
- Row 7: Single crochet in each stitch. Tie off.

Right Side

Work in same pattern as left side.

Finishing

Single crochet all the way around cross for a finishing edge.

April 11

Easter Cross Lapel Pin

Materials

- Cotton crochet yarn
- Crochet hook size 4.5 mm
- Pin back (available at craft stores in jewelry findings)
- Glue gun and glue

Directions

Long Section
- Crochet a chain of 15 stitches.
- Row 1: Skip 2 stitches, half double crochet in 3rd stitch. Half double crochet to end of row. 5 half double crochet at end of foundation chain. Go down the other side with 1 half double crochet in each unworked loop, and 5 half double crochet at end. Join with slip stitch, tie off and weave ends through work.

Short Section
- Crochet a chain of 10 stitches.
- Row 1: Skip first 2 chains, half double crochet in 3rd chain. Half double crochet in each stitch to end of row, and 5 half double crochet at end of foundation chain. Go down the other side with 1 half double crochet in each unworked loop, and 5 half double crochet at end. Join with slip stitch, tie off and weave ends through work.

Finishing
- Place shorter piece over longer piece to form a cross. Join yarn through both parts, chain 1, and single crochet all the way around the cross to create an edging.
- Glue pin back to back of cross.

April 12

Easter Egg Cozy (Holds 6 Eggs)

Materials

- Worsted weight cotton yarn
- Crochet hook size 5 mm
- Tapestry needle

Directions

- Crochet a chain of 107 stitches.
- Row 1: Skip first chain, single crochet to end of row.
- Row 2: Single crochet in each stitch to end of row.
- Row 3: Single crochet to end of row. Tie off and leave a tail for stitching.

Finishing

- Fold piece in half lengthwise. Stitch short edges together to create a large ring, tie off and weave ends through work.
- With tapestry needle, beginning from sewn end, count 8 stitches, and sew through both sides at the 9th stitch. Repeat 4 times. Tie off and weave ends through work.

April 13

Easter Candy Basket

Materials

- Stiff cotton yarn
- Crochet hook size 4 mm

Directions

Bottom
- Crochet a chain of 3 stitches. Join with slip stitch to create a ring.
- Round 1: 10 single crochet in ring.
- Round 2: Single crochet, 2 single crochet in next stitch. Repeat 5 times.
- Round 3: 2 single crochet, 2 single crochet in next stitch. Repeat 5 times.
- Round 4: 3 single crochet, 2 single crochet in next stitch. Repeat 5 times.
- Round 5: 4 single crochet, 2 single crochet in next stitch. Repeat 5 times.
- Round 6: 5 single crochet, 2 single crochet in next stitch. Repeat 5 times.
- Rounds 7-8: 6 single crochet, 2 single crochet in next stitch. Repeat 5 times.
- Rounds 9-10: 7 single crochet, 2 single crochet in next stitch. Repeat 5 times.
- Rows 11-12: 3 single crochet, 2 single crochet in next stitch. Repeat 5 times. Piece should measure about 6 inches across. You may need to add or decrease a row to get the right size.

Sides
- Crochet a chain of 15 stitches.
- Row 1: Skip first 4 stitches, double crochet in next stitch. * Chain 1, skip a stitch, 1 double crochet. Repeat from * 5 times. Continue making the same row until piece measures long enough to go all the way around the bottom part.
- Edging row 1: In each chain space, 1 single crochet, 2 double crochet, 1 single crochet.
- Edging row 2: Slip stitch in first single crochet of first edging row. Chain 3, slip stitch in next double crochet, chain 3, slip stitch in next double crochet. Chain 3, slip stitch in single crochet. Slip stitch between stitch groups. Tie off and weave ends through work.

Finishing

Using tapestry needle. Sew side part to bottom of basket.

April 14

Sparkly Ankle Bracelet

Materials

- Silver or gold crochet thread
- Crochet hook size 3mm
- Rod/ring style bracelet clasp (available at craft stores in jewelry findings)

Directions

- Crochet a chain long enough to loosely fit around your ankle.
- Row 1: Skip the first stitch, single crochet to end of row.
- Row 2: Chain 2, 2 double crochet in first stitch, chain 2. * 3 double crochet in next stitch, chain 2, 3 double crochet in next stitch. Repeat from * to end of row. Tie off.

Finishing

Tie the ends of the ankle bracelet to each end of the bracelet clasp. Tie off and weave ends through work.

April 15

Checkerboard Mat

Materials

- 2 large skeins Red Heart yarn, different colors
- 1 skein in a different color for border
- Crochet hook size 5.5mm

Directions

Squares (make 4 in main color and 5 in other color)
- Crochet a chain measuring 12".
- Row 1: Skip first stitch, single crochet to end of row. Chain 1 and turn.
- Rows 2-end: Skip first stitch, single crochet to end of row. Repeat row until piece is square. Tie off and weave ends through work.

Finishing
- Using border color, stitch squares together using a slip stitch.
- Go around entire mat with 2 rows of single crochet in border color.

April 16

Fast and Easy Baby Booties

Materials

- Baby yarn
- Crochet hook size 3.75mm
- 1/8" ribbon (2 pieces measuring 14")

Directions

- Crochet a chain of 26 stitches.
- Row 1: Skip first stitch, single crochet in each stitch to end of row. Chain 1 and turn.
- Rows 2-4: Single crochet in each stitch. Chain 1 and turn.
- Row 5: 11 single crochet, single crochet 3 stitches together, 11 single crochet. Chain 1 and turn.
- Row 6: 10 single crochet, single crochet 3 stitches together, 10 single crochet. Chain 1 and turn.
- Row 7: 9 single crochet, single crochet 3 stitches together, 9 single crochet. Chain 3 and turn.
- Row 8: Skip first stitch, half double crochet, chain 1. Repeat to end of row, join to second chain of beginning chain 3 with a slip stitch. Chain 1 and turn.
- Row 9: Single crochet in chain space. * Chain 3, single crochet in next space. Repeat from * to end of row. Chain 3, join with slip stitch. Tie off, leaving a tail for stitching.

Finishing
- Turn booties inside out, sew heel and bottom sections.
- Turn right side out, weave ribbon through the half double crochet row and tie ribbon into little bows.

April 17

Teddy Bear Hat for Newborns

Materials

- Worsted weight yarn, use a second color for ears
- Crochet hook size 5mm

Directions

- Crochet a chain of 3 stitches. Join with a slip stitch to create a ring.
- Round 1: Chain 2, 9 double crochet in ring. Join with a slip stitch at the top of chain 2.
- Round 2: 2 double crochet in each stitch. Join with a slip stitch at the top of chain 2 (do this for each round)
- Round 3: * 2 double crochet in first stitch, 2 double crochet. Repeat from * to end of round.
- Round 4: * 2 double crochet in first stitch, 3 double crochet. Repeat from * to end of round.
- Rounds 5-7: Double crochet in each stitch all the way around.
- Round 8: * double crochet in first stitch, front post double crochet in next stitch. Repeat from * to end of round. Tie off and weave ends through work.

Ears (make 2)
- Using other color, crochet a chain of 2 stitches.
- Round 1: 9 half double crochet in ring. Join with slip stitch at the top of chain 2.

- **Round 2:** Join first color, chain 1, 2 single crochet in each stitch around. Join with slip stitch at the top of chain 2. Fasten off, sew ears to sides of hat, and weave ends through work.

April 18

Easy Crochet Head Kerchief

Materials

- 50g cotton yarn
- Crochet hook size 3.75mm

Directions

- Crochet a chain of 4 stitches.
- Row 1: In 4th chain from hook, 2 double crochet, chain 1, 3 double crochet. Turn.
- Row 2: Chain 3, 2 double crochet in first stitch, chain 1. 3 double crochet, chain 1, 3 double crochet in next chain space. Chain 1, 3 double crochet in last stitch. Turn.
- Row 3: Chain 3, 2 double crochet in first stitch, chain 1, 3 double crochet in next chain space, chain 1. 3 double crochet, chain 1, 3 double crochet in corner chain space, chain 1, 3 double crochet in next chain space, chain 1, 3 double crochet in last stitch. Turn.
- Rows 4-18: Chain 3, 2 double crochet in first stitch. * Chain 1, 3 double crochet in next chain space. Repeat from * to corner chain space. * 3 double crochet, chain 1, 3 double crochet in corner chain space. Repeat from * to last stitch. 3 double crochet in last stitch. Fasten off and weave ends through work.

April 19

Lacy Scarf

Materials

- Worsted weight yarn with metallic threads
- Crochet hook size 5.5mm

Directions

- Crochet a chain of 139 stitches.
- Row 1: Skip first 5 stitches, double crochet in 6th stitch. * Chain 1, skip next stitch, double crochet in next stitch. Repeat from * to end of row. Chain 4 and turn.
- Row 2: Skip first chain, double crochet in next chain. * Chain 1, double crochet in next double crochet. Repeat from * to end of row. Chain 2 and turn.
- Rows 3-end: Repeat row 2 until piece measures desired length. Tie off and weave ends through work.

Finishing

Add fringes to both ends of the scarf.

April 20

Tooth Fairy Pillow

Materials

- 1 large skein 4-ply worsted weight yarn
- Crochet hook size 5.5 mm
- Fiberfill stuffing

Directions

Front and Back
- Crochet a chain measuring 14".
- Row 1: Skip first stitch, double crochet to end of row. Chain 1 and turn.
- Row 2: Skip first stitch, double crochet to end of row. Chain 1 and turn.
- Rows 3-end: Repeat row 2 until piece measures 11".

Pocket
- Crochet a chain measuring 4 inches.
- Row 1: Skip first stitch, single crochet to end of row. Chain 1 and turn.
- Row 2: Skip first stitch, single crochet to end of row. Chain 1 and turn.
- Rows 3-8: Repeat row 2.

Finishing
- Stitch pocket to the outside of the center of the back piece using a slip stitch. Tie off and weave ends through work.
- Place front and back sides together, and slip stitch all the way around, leaving an opening about 4" wide.
- Stuff pillow, and stitch the rest of the way.

April 21

Fashion Doll Clothes Hangers

Materials

- Crochet thread
- Crochet hook size 3 mm
- Fabric stiffener (equal parts water and white glue)

Directions

- Crochet a chain measuring 9". Tie off and remove tails.
- Soak in fabric stiffener until entire chain is completely soaked.
- Lay chain on a piece of waxed paper, and form into the shape of a coat hanger.
- At the top section, wrap longer end around shorter end and tie in a knot to secure.
- Curve rest of longer end into a hook.
- Allow to sit and dry for at least 4-5 hours.

April 22

Gingham Dish Cloth

Materials

- 3 balls yarn: white, light pink, dark pink
- Crochet hook size 4 mm

Directions

- Crochet a chain of 36 stitches with color A.
- Row 1: Skip first stitch, 3 single crochet with color A. Switch to color b, 4 single crochet. Keep going back and forth with colors A and B to end of row. Chain 1 and turn.
- Rows 2-4: Repeat row 1.
- Row 5: Skip first stitch, 3 single crochet with color A, 4 single crochet with color B. Chain 1 and turn.
- Rows 6-8: Repeat row 5.
- Row 9-12: Repeat rows 1-4.
- Rows 13-16: Repeat rows 5-8.
- Continue with the gingham pattern until piece has 49 squares, or until piece is square.

Finishing

Go around the entire cloth with single crochet using color A. Tie off and weave ends through work.

April 23

Baby Octopus Amigurumi Toy

Materials

- Worsted weight yarn scraps
- Crochet hook size 3.5 mm
- Fiberfill stuffing
- Black beads
- Needle and black thread

Directions

- Crochet a chain of 2 stitches.
- Round 1: 6 single crochet in loop.
- Round 2: 2 single crochet in each stitch.
- Round 3: * single crochet, 2 single crochet in next stitch. Repeat from * to end of round.
- Round 4: * single crochet, 2 single crochet in next stitch, single crochet. Repeat from * to end of round.
- Rounds 5-8: Single crochet in each stitch all the way around.
- Round 9: * single crochet 2 stitches together, single crochet. Repeat from * 8 times. Join round with slip stitch.
- Round 10: Chain 1. Work in back loops now. * Single crochet, single crochet 2 stitches together, single crochet. Repeat from * 4 times. This gives you the little ridge that is the beginning of the legs.
- Round 11: Skip first chain, single crochet two stitches together 6 times.
- Stuff body and sew hole together.

Legs

- Attach yarn with a slip stitch to the row of ridged stitches.
- Round 1: 5 half double crochet in next stitch, slip stitch in next stitch. Repeat from * 8 times. Join with a slip stitch. Tie off and weave ends through work.

Finishing

With the needle and thread, sew beads to the head to create eyes.

April 24

Baby Rattle

Materials

- 4-ply worsted weight yarn
- Crochet hook size 5 mm
- Pony beads
- Plastic egg or ball that comes apart into 2 halves
- Fiberfill stuffing

Directions

- Crochet a chain of 3 stitches. Join with slip stitch to create a ring.
- Round 1: Chain 1, 5 single crochet in ring.
- Round 2: Chain 1, 2 single crochet in each stitch around.
- Round 3: Chain 1, single crochet in each stitch around.
- Round 4: Repeat round 2.
- Round 4: Repeat round 3. Continue in this manner until egg or ball fits loosely inside, and work is half way up the egg or ball (put some pony beads inside first) wrapped in stuffing (to make rattle softer and avoid injuries).
- Decrease round 1: Single crochet 2 stitches together all the way around with ball inside.
- Round 2: Single crochet all the way around.
- Round 3: Repeat round 1.
- Round 4: Repeat round 2. Continue in this manner until there is a space about 1" wide. Now you will add the handle.
- Round 5: Single crochet all the way around. Continue doing this until handle measures 4'5". Pack handle tightly with fiberfill stuffing, pull end thread tight, tie off, and weave ends through work.

April 25

Spring Flowers

Materials

- Scraps of 4-ply worsted weight yarn, 2 colors
- Crochet hook size 4 mm
- Button in a different color from both yarns
- Needle and thread

Directions

- Crochet a chain of 5 stitches. Join with slip stitch to create a ring.
- Round 1: Chain 1, 9 single crochet in ring. Join with a slip stitch, and tie off.
- Round 2: Switch to second color. * Chain 1, 3 double crochet in next stitch, 1 single crochet. Repeat from * 4 times. Skip last stitch and join with slip stitch. Tie off and weave ends through work.

Finishing

Using the needle and thread, sew buttons to the center of each flower.

April 26

Spring Flower Garland

Materials

- Scraps of 4-ply worsted weight yarn
- Crochet hook size 4 mm
- Buttons of various colors
- Needle and thread

Directions

- Make 24 flowers from the Spring Flower pattern.
- Crochet a chain measuring 72".
- Row 1: Skip first stitch, single crochet in each stitch across. Chain 1 and turn.
- Row 2: Skip first stitch, single crochet in each stitch across. Leave tails on for hanging garland.

Finishing

Attach a flower to the chain every few inches. Stitch a button in each space between the flowers.

April 27

Simple Lacy Spring Wrap

Materials

- 1 lb 4-ply worsted weight yarn
- Crochet hook size 10 mm

Directions

- Crochet a chain of 159 loose stitches.
- Row 1: Skip first 3 chains, double crochet 3 stitches together, chain 1. Triple crochet, chain 1, two times. Triple crochet, chain 1, triple crochet in next stitch. Chain 1, triple crochet, two times. * Double crochet 7 stitches together, chain 1, triple crochet, chain 1 twice. Triple crochet, chain 1, triple crochet in next stitch. Chain 1, triple crochet twice, chain 1. Repeat from * to last four stitches. Double crochet these stitches together.
- Row 2: Chain 3, double crochet in next chain 1 space. Double crochet in next stitch, double crochet in next chain space, 5 times, double crochet in next stitch. * Double crochet 2 stitches together (skip 7 double crochet together between stitches), double crochet in next stitch and in next chain 1 space, 5 times. Double

crochet in next stitch. Repeat from * to last chain 1 space. 2 double crochet together in next chain space, double crochet last 3 stitches together. Turn.

- Row 3: Chain 3, skip first stitch, double crochet 3 stitches together, chain 1. Triple crochet in next stitch, chain 1, twice. Triple crochet, chain 1, triple crochet. Chain 1, triple crochet, twice, chain 1. * Double crochet 7 stitches together, chain 1. Triple crochet, chain 1, twice. Triple crochet, chain 1, triple crochet. Chain 1, triple crochet, twice, chain 1. Repeat from * to last 4 stitches. Double crochet these stitches together. Turn.
- Repeat rows 2 and 3 until piece measures desired width.

Finishing

Add fringes to either end of scarf.

April 28

Triangle-Shaped Shawl

Materials

- 1 large skein Red Heart yarn
- Crochet hook size 5 mm
- Tapestry needle

Directions

- Crochet an adjustable ring.
- Row 1: Chain 2, 2 half double crochet, chain 2, 3 half double crochet in ring. Turn, tighten ring (do not close ring).
- Row 2: Chain 2, 2 half double crochet in first stitch, chain 2. 3 half double crochet, chain 2, 3 half double crochet (this makes a corner). Chain 2, 3 half double crochet in top of beginning chain. Turn.
- Row 3: Chain 2, 2 half double crochet in first stitch, chain 2. 3 half double crochet in next chain 2 space, chain 2, 3 half double crochet, chain 2, three half double crochet in corner chain 2 space. Chain 2, 3 half double crochet in next chain 2 space. Chain 2, three half double crochet in top of first chain. Turn.
- Row 4: Chain 2, 2 half double crochet in first stitch. * Chain 2, three half double crochet in next chain 2 space. Repeat from * to corner chain 2 space. Chain 2, 3 half double crochet, chain 2, 3 half double crochet in center chain 2 space. Repeat from * across, chain 2, 3 half double crochet at the top of beginning chain.
- Rows 5-30: Repeat row 4 without turning at the end of the last row.

Finishing

Add fringes to the 2 shorter sides of shawl.

April 29

Simple Shoulder Shrug

Materials

- 1 large skein Red Heart yarn
- Crochet hook size 8 mm

Directions

- Crochet a chain of 93 stitches.
- Row 1: Skip first 3 chains, 1 double crochet in 4th chain. * Chain 1, skip next chain, double crochet. Repeat from * to end of row. Chain 4 and turn.
- Row 2: * Double crochet in next chain 2 space, chain 1. Repeat from * to last 2 double crochet. Chain 1, double crochet. Chain 3 and turn.
- Row 3: * Double crochet in chain 1 space, chain 1. Repeat from * to end of row, ending with 1 double crochet in last stitch.
- Rows 4: Repeat rows 2 and 3 until piece measures 14", ending with the row 3 section. Tie off.

Finishing

- At sides, stitch foundation chain and last row together, 8 inches. This makes the sleeves.
- Join yarn to body at seam for sleeve. Chain 1, single crochet in each stitch around. Join with slip stitch, fasten off and weave ends through work. This part can be a different color for a bit of contrast.

April 30

Tube Necklace

Materials

- Variegated worsted weight yarn
- Crochet hook size 5 mm
- Necklace toggle clasp (available at craft stores in jewelry findings)

Directions

- Crochet a chain of 5 stitches. Join with slip stitch to create a ring.
- Round 1: 6 single crochet in ring.
- Round 2: Single crochet in each stitch. Repeat this round until piece measures 16-18". Leave ends.

Finishing

- Tie the two parts of the clasp to either end of the necklace. Tie off and weave ends through work.
- Make 2 tassels, attach one to each end of the necklace. Wear necklace with clasp in the front.

May

This month, we are sharing all kinds of fun and easy Mother's Day patterns. You will also find more patterns for spring, including jewelry, dishcloths, hats, and baby items. Have fun with these easy projects. Some of them are so easy you can teach your kids how to make them, and they can have nice gifts to give to you and their grandmothers.

May 1

Bath Pouf for Mom

Materials

- Worsted weight yarn
- Crochet hood size 5.5 mm

Directions

Crochet a chain of 5 stitches. Join with a slip stitch to create a ring. Chain 30 and slip stitch in ring. This is the loop for hanging the bath pouf when it is not being used.

- Round 1: Chain 1, 25 single crochet in ring. Join with slip stitch.
- Round 2: Chain 2, 3 double crochet in each stitch. Join with slip stitch.
- Round 3: Chain 2, 3 double crochet in each stitch. Join with slip stitch.
- Round 4: Chain 2, 3 double crochet in each stitch. Join with slip stitch. Tie off and weave ends through work.

May 2

Mom's Relaxing Flax Seed Eye Bag

Materials

- Worsted weight yarn
- Crochet hook size 4 mm
- Flax seeds

Directions

Front and back
- Crochet a chain measuring 7".
- Row 1: Skip first chain, single crochet in each stitch to end of row (make sure stitches are tight so there are no spaces). Chain 1 and turn.
- Row 2: Skip first stitch, single crochet in each stitch to end of row. Chain 1 and turn.
- Row 3 to end: Repeat row 2 until piece measures 4". Tie off.

Finishing
- Stitch 3 sides together using a slip stitch.
- Fill bag with flax seeds, and stitch the end shut. Tie off and weave ends through work.

May 3

Pocket Facecloth

Materials

- Cotton yarn
- Crochet hook size 5 mm

Directions

- Crochet a chain of 19 stitches.
- Row 1: Skip first stitch, single crochet in next stitch. * 1 single crochet, 1 double crochet. Repeat from * to end of row. Chain 1 and turn.
- Row 2: * 1 double crochet in first stitch, 1 single crochet. Repeat from * to end of row. Chain 1 and turn.
- Row 3: * 1 single crochet in first stitch, 1 double crochet. Repeat from * to end of row. Chain 1 and turn.
- Rows 4-20: Repeat rows 2 and 3.

Pocket
- Crochet a chain of 3 stitches.
- Row 1: 3 double crochet in 2nd chain from hook. Chain 1 and turn.
- Row 2: 1 single crochet and 1 double crochet in first stitch, 1 single crochet, 1 double crochet and 1 single crochet in last stitch. Chain 1 and turn.
- Row 3: 1 double crochet and 1 single crochet in first stitch, 1 double crochet, 1 single crochet, 1 double crochet, 1 single crochet and 1 double crochet in next stitch, 1 double crochet in last stitch. Chain 1 and turn.
- Row 4: Repeat row 3.
- Row 5: 1 double crochet and 1 single crochet in first stitch, double crochet, single crochet, double crochet, single crochet, double crochet along row, 1 single crochet and 1 double crochet in last stitch. Chain 1 and turn.
- Round 6: Repeat round 4.
- Round 7: 1 single crochet in each stitch to end of row, 1 single crochet in corner, single crochet to end of row, 2 single crochet in corner, single crochet to end of row, 2 single crochet in corner. Tie off.

Finishing
- Place corner pocket in one corner of the face cloth, and stitch in place with a slip stitch.
- Single crochet around all sides of the face cloth, with 3 single crochet in each corner. Tie off and weave ends through work.

May 4

Hand Sanitizer Pump Bottle Cover

Materials

- Cotton worsted weight yarn
- Crochet hook size 4.5 mm
- Tapestry needle

Directions

- Crochet a chain of 28 stitches. Join with a slip stitch to create a ring.
- Round 1: Chain 1, single crochet in each chain. Slip stitch in first chain to join.
- Rounds 2-17: Chain 1, single crochet in each stitch around. Slip stitch in first chain to join.
- Round 18: Chain 1. * Single crochet 2 stitches together (4 times), 6 single crochet. Repeat from * twice. Slip stitch in first chain to join.
- Round 19: Chain 1. * Single crochet 2 stitches together (twice), six single crochet. Repeat from * twice. Join, tie off, and weave ends through work.

May 5

Mom's Flip-Flop Slippers

Materials

- Cotton yarn
- Crochet hook size 4 mm
- Tapestry needle
- Foam insoles

Directions

Soles (make 4)
- Crochet a chain of 30 stitches.
- Row 1: Skip first 3 chains, double crochet in next chain. 1 double crochet in next 25 chains, 5 double crochet in last chain. Working around the opposite side, double crochet in next 25 chains, 3 double crochet in last chain. Slip stitch on top of chain 3 to join.
- Row 2: Chain 3, 1 double crochet in same space as slip stitch, 2 double crochet in next stitch, 25 double crochet, 2 double crochet in each of the next 5 stitches, 25 double crochet, 2 double crochet in last 3 stitches. Join with a slip stitch.
- Row 3: Chain 3, 1 double crochet in slip stitch, 2 double crochet in next 3 stitches, 4 double crochet, 4 half double crochet, 13 single crochet, 4 half double crochet, 2 half double crochet in next 10 stitches (heel section), 4 half double crochet, 4 double crochet, 2 double crochet in next 6 stitches, slip stitch to join. Tie off.

Uppers (make 2)
- Crochet a chain of 23 stitches.
- Row 1: Skip first 3 chains, double crochet in 4th chain until end of row.
- Row 2: Chain 3, double crochet in each stitch.
- Rows 3-4: Repeat row 2.
- Row 5: Chain 3, double crochet in each stitch. Do not turn.
- Row 6: Chain 1, single crochet all the way around piece. Tie off.

Assembly

Sandwich 1 insole between 2 soles (you may need to trim insoles to fit). Single crochet all the way around.

Fasten uppers to soles. Tie off and weave ends through work.

May 6

A Dozen Roses for Mom

Materials

- Soft yarn in pinks, reds, etc.
- Crochet hook size 5.5 mm
- Tapestry needle
- Green felt
- Green pipe cleaners
- Glue gun and glue

Directions

- Crochet a chain of 21 stitches. Leave a long tail for stitching.
- Row 1: Skip first chain, 2 single crochet in next chain and in each stitch to end of row. Chain 3 and turn.
- Row 2: 1 double crochet in first stitch, 2 double crochet in each stitch to end of row. Tie off, leave tail.
- Roll piece so it looks like a rose, pinching at the bottom and stitching together with the tapestry needle. Tie off and weave ends through work.

Finishing
- Put a bit of glue on the end of each pipe cleaner, and stick them into the bottom of each rose in the center.
- Cut felt in the shape of leaves, attach to the bottom of each rose with the glue gun.

May 7

Crochet Vase

Materials

- Cotton yarn
- Crochet hook size 3.5 mm

Directions

- Crochet a chain of 4 stitches. Join with a slip stitch to create a ring.
- Round 1: 6 single crochet in ring.
- Round 2: 2 single crochet in each stitch. Place stitch marker, and move after each round so you know where you are in the work.
- Round 3: * 1 single crochet, 2 single crochet in next stitch. Repeat from * to end of round.
- Round 4: * 2 single crochet, 2 single crochet in next stitch. Repeat from * to end of round.
- Round 5: * 3 single crochet, 2 single crochet in next stitch. Repeat from * to end of round.
- Rounds 6-10: Single crochet in each stitch to end of round.
- Round 11: * Single crochet 2 stitches together, 3 single crochet. Repeat from * to end of round.
- Round 12: Single crochet in each stitch to end of round.
- Round 13: * 2 single crochet, single crochet 2 stitches together. Repeat from * to end of round.
- Round 14: Single crochet in each stitch to end of round.
- Round 15: * Single crochet 2 stitches together, 1 single crochet. Repeat from * to end of round.
- Rounds 16-18: Single crochet in each stitch to end of round.

- Round 19: * 2 single crochet in next stitch, 2 single crochet. Repeat from * to end of round.
- Round 20: * 3 single crochet, 2 single crochet in next stitch. Repeat from * to end of round.
- Rounds 21-22: Single crochet in each stitch to end of round. Tie off and weave ends through work.

May 8

Fancy Flower Brooch

Materials

- Scraps of worsted weight yarn
- Crochet hook size 5 mm
- Pin back (available at craft stores in jewelry findings.
- Glue gun and glue stick

Directions

- Crochet a circle of 5 stitches. Join with a slip stitch to create a ring.
- Round 1: 12 half double crochet in ring. Join with slip stitch.
- Round 2: 2 half double crochet in next stitch, 1 half double crochet. Repeat to end of round.
- Round 3: Chain 9, slip stitch in back loop of next stitch. Repeat to end of round.
- Round 4: Chain 6, slip stitch in front loop of next stitch. Repeat to end of round. Tie off and weave ends through work.

Finishing

Glue pin back to back of flower.

May 9

Soap Holder/Scrubber

Materials

- Cotton blend yarn
- Crochet hook size 3.5 mm
- Tapestry needle

Directions

- Crochet a chain of 19 stitches.
- Row 1: Skip first stitch, single crochet to end of row. Chain 1 and turn.
- Rows 2-4: Repeat row 1.
- Row 5: Chain 5, skip stitch, 1 single crochet. * Chain 2, skip 2 stitches, double crochet, chain 2, skip 2 stitches, 1 single crochet. Repeat from * once. Chain 2, skip 2 stitches, 1 double crochet.
- Row 6: Chain 3, 1 double crochet. * Chain 2, 1 single crochet, chain 2, 1 double crochet. Repeat once, chain 2, single crochet in 3rd chain.
- Row 7: Chain 5, 1 single crochet. * Chain 2, 1 double crochet, chain 2, 1 single crochet. Repeat once, chain 2, double crochet in 2nd chain.

- Row 8: Chain 3, 1 double crochet. * Chain 2, 1 single crochet, chain 2, 1 double crochet. Repeat once, chain 2, single crochet in 3rd chain.
- Rows 9-16: Repeat rows 6 and 7 four times.
- Row 17: Repeat row 6.
- Rows 18-20: Chain 1, single crochet to end of row. Tie off.

Finishing

Fold piece in half, stitch short ends together with tapestry needle.

May 10

Eyeglasses Case

Materials

- Red Heart yarn
- Crochet hook size 4 mm
- Button
- Needle and thread

Directions

- Crochet a chain of 25 stitches. Join with a slip stitch to create a ring.
- Row 1: Chain 1, single crochet in same chain, and in each stitch. Place a stitch marker.
- Row 2-end: Single crochet in back loop of each stitch in round. Move stitch marker at the end of each round to mark your place. Work until piece measures 6.5". Join with slip stitch, chain 1 and turn to start making flap.

Flap

- Row 1: 10 single crochet. Chain 1 and turn.
- Row 2: Single crochet 2 stitches together (decrease). 6 single crochet, decrease. Chain 1 and turn.
- Row 3: Decrease. 4 single crochet, decrease. Chain 1 and turn.
- Row 4: Decrease. 2 single crochet, decrease. Chain 1 and turn.
- Row 5: Decrease twice. Chain 1 and turn.
- Row 6: Decrease over remaining stitches. Do not tie off.

Finishing

- Chain 10. Join to last row to create a loop. Tie off and weave ends through work.
- Sew button to front of eyeglasses case.

May 11

Microwavable Heating Pad

Materials

- Cotton yarn
- Crochet hook size 5 mm
- Uncooked rice (not instant)

Directions

Front and back
- Crochet a chain measuring 12".
- Row 1: Skip first chain, single crochet to end of row. Chain 1 and turn. Make sure all stitches are tight.
- Row 2: Skip first stitch, single crochet to end of row. Chain 1 and turn.
- Rows 3-end: Repeat row 2 until piece measures 8". Tie off, leave tail for stitching.

Finishing
- Stitch 3 sides together with a slip stitch.
- Fill heating pad with rice.
- Stitch heating pad closed.

May 12

Toy Blocks for Babies

Materials

- 2 colors of Red Heart Super Saver yarn
- Crochet hook size 4 mm
- Fiberfill stuffing

Directions

Make 6 pieces for each block.
- Crochet a chain of 7 stitches.
- Row 1: Skip first chain, single crochet to end of row. Chain 1 and turn.
- Rows 2-6: Single crochet to end of row. Tie off, leave ends for stitching.

Finishing
- Assemble squares to form a block.
- Join second color of yarn, and single crochet each side together, leaving one side open.
- Fill block with fiberfill stuffing.
- Single crochet last side closed. Tie off and weave ends through work.

May 13

Baby Bottle Cover

Materials

- Soft baby yarn
- Crochet hook size 3.75 mm

Directions

- Crochet a chain of 27 stitches. Join with a slip stitch to create a ring. Do not twist the chain.
- Round 1: Chain 2, 1 half double crochet, 1 triple crochet. * 2 half double crochet, 1 triple crochet. Repeat from * to end of round. Join with slip stitch.
- Round 2: Chain 2, half double crochet to end of round. Join with slip stitch.
- Rounds 3-6: Repeat row 3.
- Round 7: Repeat row 2.
- Rounds 8-12: Repeat row 3.
- Round 13: Repeat row 2.
- Round 14: Repeat row 3.
- Round 15: Chain 2. * Skip next stitch, single crochet, chain 4. Repeat from * to end of round, with a single crochet in the last stitch. Repeat this pattern in next round so you fill in the skipped stitches and chains.

Finishing

Attach yarn at opposite end, chain 2, repeat round 15.

May 14

Kitty Cat Harness/Leash

Materials

- Worsted weight yarn
- Crochet hook size 5 mm
- Key ring

Directions

Forearm Section
- Crochet a chain long enough to fit your cat's forearms (approx. 45 stitches).
- Slip first 2 chains, half double crochet to end of row. Tie off and make a second piece.
- Hold 2 loops together one on top of the other so the tops of the stitches are on the outside. Insert hook through both loops, chain 2, 5 half double crochet, turn.
- Chain 1, skip first stitch, 3 half double crochet. Do nothing with last stitch.
- Chain 1, 3 half double crochet, turn.
- Chain 4, slip stitch in last stitch (key ring loop). Tie off and weave ends through work.

Leash
- Crochet a chain of 200 stitches.
- Skip first 9 chains, half double crochet until there are 10 stitches remaining. 10 slip stitches.
- Slip stitch to last half double crochet, creating a loop. Tie off and weave ends through work.

Finishing
- Join yarn to any stitch of harness.
- Slip stitch all the way around harness edges. Tie off and weave ends through work.
- Join yarn to any base chain stitch.
- Slip stitch around foreleg holes. Tie off and weave ends through work.

- Join yarn to any stitch on lead.
- Slip stitch all the way around, except end loops.
- Attach loop of harness to lead with a key ring.

May 15

Floor Sweeper Cover

Materials

- Cotton yarn
- Crochet hook size 5 mm

Directions

- Crochet a chain of 17 stitches.
- Row 1: Skip first chain, single crochet to end of row and turn.
- Rows 2-9: Chain 1, single crochet to end of row and turn.
- Row 10: Chain 2, half double crochet across in front loops only and turn.
- Rows 11-38: Chain 2, double crochet to end of row and turn.
- Row 39: Chain 2, half double crochet to end of row in front loops only and turn.
- Rows 40-48: Chain 1, single crochet to end of row and turn. Fasten off, leaving long tail for sewing.

Finishing

Fold each end at the half double crochet row. Stitch the sides of each end with slip stitches so there are little pockets. Tie off and weave ends through work.

May 16

Guitar Strap

Materials

- Worsted weight yarn
- Crochet hook size 5 mm

Directions

- Crochet a chain of 19 stitches.
- Row 1: Skip first chain, double crochet to end of row. Chain 3 and turn.
- Rows 2-110: Double crochet to end of row. Chain 3 and turn. You can make this longer or shorter, depending on the length you need. Tie off and weave ends through work.

First End

- Row 1: Attach yarn to one end of strap with a slip stitch. Chain 1, half double crochet to end of row and turn.
- Rows 2-4: Chain 1, half double crochet to end of row.
- Rows 5-8: Skip first stitch, slip stitch, half double crochet to second to last stitch. Turn and chain 1.
- Row 9: 3 half double crochet, chain 10, 3 half double crochet, and turn.

- Row 10: 2 half double crochet, single crochet across chains, 2 half double crochet. Tie off and weave ends through work.

Other End

- Repeat rows 1-8 as with first end.
- Row 9: 3 half double crochet, chain 75, 3 half double crochet and turn.
- Row 10: 2 half double crochet, single crochet in each chain, 2 half double crochet. Tie off and weave ends through work.

May 17

Yoga Socks

Materials

- Red Heart Super Saver yarn (2 colors)
- Crochet hook size 10 mm

Directions

Make 2
- Working with 1 strand of each color, Crochet a chain of 20 stitches. Join with a slip stitch to create a ring.
- Round 1: Half double crochet to end of round.
- Rounds 2-7: Chain 2, half double crochet 2 stitches together, half double crochet to end of round.
- Round 8: Chain 2, 1 half double crochet, chain 10, skip 5 stitches, half double crochet in 6th stitch to end of round.
- Round 9: Chain 2, 6 half double crochet in chain 10 space, half double crochet to end of round.
- Round 10: Chain 2, half double crochet 2 stitches together, half double crochet to end of round.
- Rounds 11-17: Half double crochet to end of round. Tie off and weave ends through work.

May 18

Brimmed Cap

Materials

- 1 large skein worsted weight yarn
- Crochet hook size 5 mm
- Stitch marker

Directions

- Crochet a chain of 4 stitches. Join with slip stich to create a ring.
- Round 1: 6 single crochet in ring.
- Round 2: 2 single crochet in each stitch (increase). Place stitch marker to mark beginning of round.
- Round 3: 2 single crochet in next stitch, 1 single crochet. Repeat to end of round.
- Round 4: 2 single crochet in next stitch, 2 single crochet. Repeat to end of round.
- Round 5: 2 single crochet in next stitch, 3 single crochet. Repeat to end of round.

- Round 6: 2 single crochet in next stitch, 4 single crochet. Repeat to end of round, move marker to this spot.
- Continue working in this pattern until there are 22 single crochet between each increase.
- Single crochet next 4 rounds.
- Decrease rounds (6): 11 single crochet, skip next stitch. Repeat to end of round. Chain 1 and turn.

Brim
- Rows 1-2: 28 single crochet. Chain 1 and turn.
- Rows 3-4: Skip first stitch, single crochet to end of row. Chain 1 and turn.
- Row 5: 26 single crochet. Chain 1 and turn.
- Repeat row 5 until there are 18 stitches left. Chain 1 and turn.
- Next 2 rows: Skip first 2 stitches, single crochet to end of row. Chain 1 and turn.
- Single crochet around brim and edge of hat. Tie off and weave ends through work.

May 19

Hanging Cat Toy

Materials

- 3 colors worsted weight yarn
- Crochet hook size 4 mm
- Stitch markers
- Tapestry needle
- Fiberfill stuffing
- Jingle bell

Directions

Hanger
- Crochet a chain of 41 stitches.
- Row 1: Skip first chain, single crochet to end of row, 2 single crochet on side edge, single crochet across opposite side of chain until second to last stitch. 2 single crochet in last stitch, slip stitch to first stitch to create a loop. Tie off.

Curly-Q
- With 2nd color, crochet a chain of 31 stitches.
- Row 1: Skip first chain, 3 single crochet in each stitch to end of row. Tie off.

Ball
- With 3rd color, crochet a chain of 2 stitches.
- Round 1: 6 single crochet in first chain. Place stitch marker to mark beginning of round, moving marker as you finish each round.
- Round 2: 2 single crochet in each stitch.
- Round 3: 2 single crochet in next stitch, 1 single crochet. Repeat to end of round.
- Round 4: 2 single crochet in next stitch, 2 single crochet. Repeat to end of round.
- Rounds 5-9: Single crochet to end of round. Fill ball with stuffing at end of round 9.
- Round 10: Single crochet 2 stitches together (decrease), 2 single crochet. Repeat to end of round.
- Round 11: Single crochet 2 stitches together all the way around.
- Round 12: Repeat round 11. Tie off and weave ends through work.

Finishing

- Sew hanger ends together.
- Stitch curly-q to hanger.
- Stitch ball to other end of curly-q. Tie off and weave ends through work.

May 20

Baby Shawl

Materials

- 6 balls of soft baby yarn
- Crochet hook size 3.25 mm

Directions

- Crochet a chain of 316 stitches.
- Row 1: Skip first chain, single crochet to end of row. Chain 1 and turn.
- Row 2: (Reverse side) Skip first stitch, 2 single crochet. * Chain 3, skip 2 stitches, 1 double crochet, chain 3, 1 double crochet in next stitch (V stitch). Chain 3, slip 3 stitches, 3 single crochet. Repeat from * to end of row. Chain 4 and turn.
- Row 3: * 7 double crochet in chain 3 space of V stitch, chain 3, skip next stitch, 1 single crochet, chain 3, skip next stitch. Repeat from * to end of row, ending with 1 single crochet in last stitch. Chain 6 and turn.
- Row 4: * 7 single crochet, chain 3. Repeat from * to end, ending with double crochet in first chain of turning chain. Chain 6 and turn.
- Row 5: * Skip 2 stitches, 3 single crochet, chain 3, skip 2 stitches and next chain, V stitch in next chain, chain 3, skip next chain. Repeat to end of row, ending with skip 2 stitches. 3 single crochet, skip 3 stitches, 1 double crochet in 3rd chain, chain 6 and turn.
- Row 6: Slip stitch, slip in chain 3, 2 slip stitches, chain 4. * 7 double crochet in chain 3 space of V stitch, chain 3, skip next stitch, 1 single crochet, chain 3, skip next stitch. Repeat from * ending with 7 double crochet in chain 3 space of last V stitch. Chain 3, skip next stitch, 1 single crochet, chain 6 and turn.
- Row 7: * 7 single crochet, chain 3. Repeat from * to end, ending with 1 double crochet in top of last stitch. Chain 6 and turn.
- Row 8: Repeat row 5.
- Repeat rows 6-8 36 times.
- Repeat row 6, leaving off turning chain. Tie off.

Edging
- Row 1: Wrong side facing, join yarn with slip stitch in first chain. Chain 1, single crochet in same chain space, single crochet in rest of chain stitches. Chain 1 and turn.
- Rows 2-3: 2 single crochet in each stitch around. Tie off and weave ends through work.

May 21

Sunshine Dish Cloth

Materials

- Yellow worsted weight yarn

- Crochet hook size 5 mm

Directions

- Crochet a chain of 3 stitches.
- Round 1: 10 half double crochet in 3rd chain from hook. Join each round with slip stitch.
- Round 2: Chain 2, 2 half double crochet to end of round.
- Round 3: Chain 2. * 2 half double crochet in next stitch, 1 half double crochet. Repeat from * to end of round.
- Round 4: Chain 2. * 2 half double crochet in next stitch, 2 half double crochet. Repeat from * to end of round.
- Round 5: Chain 2. * 2 half double crochet in next stitch, 3 half double crochet. Repeat from * to end of round.
- Round 6: Chain 2. * 2 half double crochet in next stitch, 4 half double crochet. Repeat from * to end of round.
- Round 7: Chain 2. * 2 half double crochet in next stitch, 5 half double crochet. Repeat from * to end of round.
- Round 8: Chain 2. * 2 half double crochet in next stitch, 8 half double crochet. Repeat from * 7 times. 2 half double crochet in next stitch, 6 half double crochet. Join with slip stitch.

Finishing

Chain 1, 1 single crochet in same space as slip stitch. * Chain 7, skip a stitch, single crochet in next stitch, 1 half double crochet in next chain, 1 double crochet in next chain, 1 triple crochet in next chain, 1 double triple crochet in next chain (yoh) 4 times. Draw up loop from next chain (yoh and draw yarn through 2 loops on hook) 5 times, slip next 5 stitches of 9th round, single crochet. ** 1 single crochet. Repeat from * 11 times, and from * to *8 once. Join with slip stitch. Tie off and weave ends through work.

May 22

Striped Baby Blanket

Materials

- 6 skeins of worsted weight yarn, different colors
- Crochet hook size 5.5 mm

Directions

- Crochet a chain measuring 36 inches.
- Row 1: Skip first chain, double crochet to end of row. Chain 1 and turn.
- Row 2: Skip first stitch, single crochet to end of row. Chain 2 and turn.
- Row 3: Repeat row 1.
- Row 4: Repeat row 2.
- Rows 5-8: Switch colors, repeat rows 1 and 2 twice.
- Rows 9-12: Switch colors, repeat rows 1 and 2 twice. Continue in this pattern with all the colors until piece is desired length.

Finishing

2 single crochet in each stitch all the way around blanket.

May 22

Flower Paper Clips

Materials

- Size 10 crochet thread
- Crochet hook size 2 mm
- Paper clips
- Glue gun and glue stick

Directions

- Crochet a chain of 6 stitches. Join with slip stitch to create a ring.
- Round 1: Chain 1, 16 single crochet in ring. Join with slip stitch in first single crochet of round.
- Round 2: Chain 1. In same stitch as join, * 1 single crochet, chain 3, 1 single crochet, skip next stitch. Repeat from * 7 times. Join with a slip stitch in first single crochet of round.
- Round 3: Chain 1, 5 single crochet in each chain space. Join with slip stitch in first single crochet of round. Tie off and weave ends through work.

Finishing

Glue flowers to paper clips.

May 23

Princess Crown with Long Braids

Materials

- Pink and white #4 medium weight yarn
- Yellow worsted weight yarn
- Crochet hook size 5.5 mm

Directions

Crown
- Crochet a chain of 55 stitches. Join with a slip stitch to create a ring, being careful not to twist chain.
- Rounds 1-2: Single crochet in each stitch to end of round.
- Round 3: 16 slip stitches, 22 single crochet, turn.
- Round 4: Skip first stitch, (2 half double crochet, chain 2, half double crochet in next stitch). Skip next stitch, 1 slip stitch. Skip 2 stitches, (3 double crochet, chain 2, 3 double crochet in next stitch). Skip next stitch, 1 slip stitch. Skip next stitch, (2 half double crochet, chain 2, 2 half double crochet in next stitch). Skip next stitch, 1 slip stitch. Skip next stitch, (2 half double crochet, chain 2, 2 half double crochet in next stitch). Skip next stitch, 1 slip stitch. Turn.

- Slip stitch to back of crown. When you get to the chain 2 spaces at each point, slip stitch in space, chain 2, puff stitch (yarn over, put hook in stitch, yarn over, pull through, repeat twice for a total of 7 loops to pull yarn through), chain 2, slip stitch in same chain 2 space. Tie off and weave ends through work.

Braids
- Cut 108 strands of yarn measuring 4'.
- Attach yarn by folding in half to create tassels and joining to 18 stitches on either side of crown.
- Braid yarn strands, tie with ribbons.

May 24

Plant Hanger

Materials

- Worsted weight yarn
- Crochet hooks sizes 3.5 mm and 5 mm

Directions

- Crochet a chain of 6 stitches with smaller hook. Join with slip stitch to create a ring.
- Round 1: Chain 1, 12 single crochet in ring.
- Round 2: Chain 1, 1 single crochet. * Chain 5, skip next stitch, 1 single crochet. Repeat from * 4 times. Chain 3, double crochet into fist stitch of round to join.
- Rounds 3-5: * Chain 6, 1 single crochet in next loop. Repeat from * 4 times. Chain 4, triple crochet in fist stitch of round to join.
- Round 6: * Chain 5, 1 single crochet in next chain loop. Repeat from * 5 times.
- Round 7: 6 single crochet in each loop. Slip stitch in first single crochet to join.

Chains to hang planter

Attach yarn to one of the top loops, chain 25-35 stitches. Pull through a large loop and tie off. Repeat in 2 more loops so you have 3 chains that are evenly spaced. Using the size 5 mm crochet hook, put hook through the 3 large loops, pull up the tails, chain 1 with the 3 tails. Tie off and weave ends through work.

May 25

Curtain Tiebacks

Materials

- Worsted weight yarn
- Crochet hook size 5.5 mm

Directions

- Crochet a chain measuring 4 inches.
- Row 1: Skip first chain, single crochet to end of row. Chain 1 and turn.

- Row 2-end: Skip first stitch, single crochet to end of row. Continue in this pattern until piece measures 18".

Finishing
- Pull each end tight so they are pinched. Tie off and weave ends through work.
- Add a tassel to each end.
- Crochet a chain measuring 18". Skip first chain, single crochet to end of row. Tie off and weave ends through work. This is the tie to attach the tiebacks to hooks.

May 26

Wine Glass Lanyard

Materials

- Bulky yarn
- Crochet hook size 6.5 mm

Directions

Cup section
- Crochet a chain of 18 stitches. Join with slip stitch to form a ring.
- Round 1: * Chain 4, skip 2 stitches, 1 single crochet. Repeat from * to last 3 stitches. Slip stitch to join.
- Round 2: * Chain 3 (single crochet, chain 3, single crochet) around chain 4 space. Repeat from * to end of round. Do not join.
- Round 3 to end: * Chain 3, 1 single crochet around chain 3 space. Repeat from * to end of round. Repeat round until cup part reaches desired size (about 4" is good). Do not fasten off.

Strap
- Crochet a chain of 70 stitches (or desired length for strap).
- Row 1: Skip first 2 chains, double crochet in each stitch to end of row.
- Attach strap with single crochet stitches to a chain 3 space at each side of the cup section. Tie off ends and weave through work.

May 27

Doggie Bandana

Materials

- 4-ply worsted weight yarn
- Crochet hook size 4 mm
- 2 buttons
- Needle and thread

Directions

- Crochet a chain of 70 stitches.
- Row 1: Skip first chain, single crochet to end of row. Chain 1 and turn.
- Row 2: Single crochet in first stitch. * Chain 1, skip next stitch, 1 single crochet. Repeat from * to end of row. Chain 1 and turn.

- Row 3: Single crochet in each stitch and in each chain space to end of row. Tie off.
- Row 4: Attach yarn 20 stitches from where you fastened off. Chain 1, single crochet in same stitch. * Chain 2, skip next stitch, 1 single crochet. Repeat from * to last 20 stitches. Chain 1 and turn.
- Row 5: 1 single crochet in next chain 2 space. * Chain 2, single crochet in next chain 2 space. Repeat from * to end.
- Row 6: Repeat row 5 until there is only 1 chain 2 space remaining. Chain 1 and turn.
- Final row: 1 single crochet, chain 1, 1 single crochet in next chain 2 space. Slip stitch in next stitch. Tie off and weave ends through work.

Finishing

Sew buttons onto band.

May 28

Crochet Finger Ring

Materials

- Silver crochet thread
- Crochet hook size 3.25 mm
- Stitch marker
- Sewing needle

Directions

Special Stitches:
- Cluster – Yarn over, insert hook in stitch or space, yarn over, draw up a loop, yarn over, draw through 2 loops on hook, (yarn over, insert hook in same stitch or space, yarn over, draw up loop, yarn over, draw through 2 loops on hook twice), yarn over, draw through 4 loops on hook.

Ring
- Crochet a chain of 5 stitches. Join with slip stitch to create a ring.
- Round 1: Chain 3, 1 double crochet in ring, chain 3, cluster in ring, chain 3. Repeat 7 times. Join with slip stitch at the top of beginning chain.
- Round 2: Chain 3, slip stitch in top of next double crochet, chain 4, (slip stitch, chain 3, slip stitch in next Cluster), chain 9. First half of ring is completed. (Slip stitch, chain 3, slip stitch in next cluster), (chain 4, slip stitch, chain 3, slip stitch in next cluster 3 times). Chain 4, slip stitch in 5th chain of first half of ring band, chain 4. (Slip stitch, chain 3, slip stitch in next cluster, chain 4, twice). Join with slip stitch in first slip stitch. Tie off and weave ends through work.

May 29

Water Bottle Holder

Materials

- 2 ounces worsted weight yarn
- Crochet hook size 5.5 mm

Directions

- Crochet a chain of 2 stitches.
- Round 1: 6 single crochet in first chain. Join with slip stitch in first single crochet at end of each round.
- Round 2: Chain 1, 2 single crochet in each stitch around.
- Round 3: Chain 1, * 2 single crochet in next stitch, 1 single crochet. Repeat from * to end of round.
- Round 4: Chain 1, * 2 single crochet in next stitch, 2 single crochet. Repeat from * to end of round.
- Round 5: Chain 1, * 2 single crochet in next stitch, 3 single crochet. Repeat from * to end of round.
- Rounds 6-8: Chain 1, single crochet in each stitch to end of round.
- Rounds 9-17: Chain 2, double crochet in each stitch to end of round.
- Round 18: Chain 1, single crochet in each stitch to end of round. Do not tie off.

Strap

- Row 1: Pick up yarn from end of last round, chain 1, 5 single crochet. Chain 1 and turn.
- Rows 2-100: Single crochet in each stitch to end of row. Chain 1 and turn. Do not chain at end of last row. Do not tie off.

Finishing

Attach working end of strap to other side of bottle holder with slip stitches. Tie off and weave ends through work.

May 30

3-Chain Headband

Materials

- Cotton worsted weight yarn
- Crochet hook size 4 mm

Directions

- Crochet a chain of 100 stitches.
- Row 1: Skip first chain, single crochet in next 29 stitches. Chain 80, single crochet in 30th chain from the beginning of first chain loop, and in the next 29 chains. Chain 1 and turn.
- Row 2: Single crochet in first 30 stitches, chain 80, single crochet in 30 stitches of previous row. Tie off ends tightly and snip excess yarn.

May 31

No-Scratch Newborn Mittens

Materials

- Baby fingering weight yarn
- Crochet hook size 3.75 mm
- Tapestry needle
- 1/8" ribbon

Directions

- Crochet a chain of 30 stitches. Join with slip stitch to create a ring, being careful not to twist chain. Chain 1, do not turn.
- Round 1: Single crochet in each chain to end of round. Do not join. Place stitch marker, move after each round.
- Rounds 2-9: Single crochet in each stitch around, in back loops only.
- Round 10: Single crochet 2 stitches together (decrease) to end of round. Join with slip stitch to first decrease. Tie off, leaving long tail. Thread tail through tapestry needle, and weave through stitches on last round. Pull tight, fasten off, and weave ends through work.

Cuff

- Round 1: Attach yarn at foundation chain. Chain 2, double crochet in each unworked chain. Join with slip stitch to beginning chain 2. Slip stitch around post of beginning chain 2. Chain 3.
- Round 2: Back post double crochet in next double crochet (yarn over hook, insert hook into back of work across the front of stitch, through work again, finish stitch as normal). * Front post double crochet in next double crochet (reverse of back post double crochet). Back post double crochet around post of next double crochet. Repeat from * to end of round. Join with slip stitch at top of first chain 3.
- Round 3: Chain 4, single crochet in back loop of next stitch. Repeat to end of round. Join with slip stitch. Tie off and weave ends through work.

Finishing

Weave ribbon between cuff and hand section, tie in little bows.

June

Summer is finally here, and so is wedding season and Father's Day. This month, we have some fun patterns to make gifts for dad, and even a fun toy for your feline friends. There are also patterns for wedding favors, hair accessories, and an adorable mini-bride dress for baby girls that you can make in a few hours.

June 1

An Apple Paperclip for the Teacher

Materials

- Scraps of red and green yarn
- Crochet hook size 4 mm
- Glue gun and glue
- Large colored paperclips

Directions

Apple
- Crochet a chain of 4 stitches. Join with slip stitch to create a ring.
- Round 1: Chain 2, 10 double crochet in ring. Join with slip stitch.
- Round 2: Chain 2, 2 double crochet in each stitch.
- Round 3: Chain 2, slip stitch in last double crochet. Tie off and weave ends through work.

Leaves
- Crochet a chain of 6 stitches.
- Row 1: Skip first stitch, 1 single crochet, 1 half double crochet, 1 double crochet, 1 half double crochet, 1 single crochet. Tie off and slip stitch to top of apple. Weave ends through work.

Stem
- Crochet a chain of 5 stitches.
- Row 1: Skip first stitch, 1 single crochet, 3 slip stitches. Tie off and attach stem to top off apple. Weave ends through work.

Finishing

Glue apple to the top of the paperclip, leaving the clip end open.

June 2

Bridal Garter Belt

Materials

- #3 cotton crochet thread
- Crochet hook size 2.75 mm
- ½" elastic

Directions

- Crochet a chain of 198 stitches. Join with slip stitch to create a ring, being careful not to twist chain.
- Round 1: Chain 1, 1 single crochet in each stitch to end of round. Join to chain 1 with slip stitch.
- Round 2: Chain 3, triple crochet in each stitch to end of round. Join with slip stitch at top of chain 3.
- Round 3: Chain 1, single crochet in each stitch to end of round. Join with slip stitch to chain 1.
- Round 4: Chain 2, 3 half double crochet in same stitch. * Skip 2 stitches, 4 half double crochet in next stitch. Repeat from * to end of round. Join with slip stitch. Tie off and weave ends through work.

- Turn work upside down and repeat last row on opposite side of work.

Finishing
- Mark the desired length on the elastic with a marker (try the elastic on for size to get the right length). Attach one end of the garter, and weave it through the open spaces.
- Embellish garter with beads, charms, etc.

June 3

Ring Bearer's Pillow

Materials

- White worsted weight yarn
- Crochet hook size 5 mm
- White pipe cleaners
- White ½" satin ribbon
- 10" square white pillow
- Needle and thread

Directions

Front and Back
- Crochet a chain measuring 10".
- Row 1: Skip first stitch, double crochet to end of row. Chain 2 and turn.
- Row 2: Skip first stitch, double crochet to end of row. Chain 2 and turn.
- Rows 3-end: Repeat row 2 until piece measures 10". Tie off and weave ends through work.

Finishing
- Stitch front and back along 3 sides and half of the last side using a slip stitch.
- Fill pillow with fiberfill stuffing.
- Stitch last side closed.
- Attach yarn, chain 3, 3 double crochet in each stitch all the way around to make a little ruffle.
- Make little bows with the ribbon, and attach to each corner of the pillow.
- Cut pipe cleaner into 4" pieces. Form into "U" shapes, and press into pillow to hold rings in place.

June 4

Comfy Neck Pillow

Materials

- 5 oz worsted weight yarn
- Crochet hook size 5 mm
- Fiberfill stuffing

Directions

- Crochet a chain of 49 stitches.
- Row 1: 7 single crochet, 2 single crochet in next chain. Repeat 5 times. Chain 1 and turn at end of each round unless otherwise stated.
- Row 2: 8 single crochet, 2 single crochet in next stitch. Repeat 5 times.

- Rows 3-11: Repeat row 2, adding 1 single crochet each time until round 11 has a pattern of 17 single crochet and 2 single crochet in the next stitch.
- Rows 12-16: Single crochet in each stitch in round.
- Round 17: 17 single crochet, 1 single crochet over 2 stitches (decrease). Repeat 5 times.
- Rounds 18-20: Repeat round 17, decreasing in each round until there is a pattern of 9 single crochet and 1 decrease.
- Stuff pillow with fiberfill stuffing.
- Rounds 21-27: Repeat round 17, decreasing in each round until there is a pattern of 7 single crochet and 1 decrease. Stitch ends shut, tie off, and weave ends through work.

June 5

Simple Round Baby Afghan

Materials

- Soft worsted weight yarn (2 colors)
- Crochet hook size 8 mm

Directions

- Crochet a chain of 5 stitches. Join with a slip stitch to create a ring.
- Round 1: 10 double crochet in ring. Chain 2.
- Round 2: 2 double crochet in each stitch. Switch colors and chain 2.
- Rounds 3-end: Repeat row 2, switch colors every 2 rows until piece measures 36" or more across. Tie off and weave ends through work.

Finishing

Add a fringe all the way around the blanket.

June 6

Bow Tie for Dad

Materials

- Red Heart Super Saver yarn
- Crochet hook size 5 mm
- Clip
- Glue gun and glue

Directions

- Crochet a chain of 33 stitches.
- Row 1: Skip first chain, single crochet to end of row, working only in back loops. Chain 1 and turn.
- Rows 2-7: Single crochet in each stitch across, working in both loops.

Center section
- Crochet a chain of 8 stitches.
- Row 1: Work in the back loops, and do 1 single crochet in second chain from hook and in each stitch across (11 stitches). Chain 1 and turn.

- Row 2: Single crochet in each stitch. Tie off.

Finishing
- Pinch center of main piece in the middle, and wrap center section around this spot. Secure in place with slip stitch.
- Glue clip to back of bow tie.

June 7

Pretty Ponytail Elastics

Materials

- Scraps of worsted weight yarn
- Ponytail elastics

Directions

- Round 1: Put crochet hook through the middle of the ponytail elastic. Wrap yarn around one time, pull through. Single crochet all the way around until you can't see the elastic. Join to first single crochet with a slip stitch and chain 3.
- Round 2: Skip first stitch, single crochet in next stitch. Continue skipping a stitch and then 1 single crochet to end of round. Slip stitch to join. Tie off and weave ends through work.

June 8

Mason Jar Cozy

Materials

- Worsted weight yarn
- Crochet hook size 5 mm

Directions

- Crochet a chain of 5 stitches. Join with slip stitch to create a ring.
- Round 2: 6 single crochet in ring. Chain 1.
- Round 2: 2 single crochet in each stitch. Join with slip stitch. Chain 1.
- Round 3: * 1 single crochet, 2 single crochet in next stitch. Repeat from * to end of round. Join and chain 1.
- Round 4: * 2 single crochet, 2 single crochet in next stitch. Repeat from * to end of round. Join and chain 1.
- Round 5: * 1 single crochet, 2 single crochet in next stitch, 2 single crochet. Repeat from * to end of round. Join and chain 1.
- Round 6: Work this row in back loops. 14 single crochet, 2 single crochet in next stitch. Repeat once. Join and chain 1.
- Rounds 7-16: Work in both loops from here on in. * 1 single crochet and 1 double crochet in the same stitch. Skip next stitch. Repeat from * to end of round. Join and chain 1.
- Round 17: Single crochet to end of round. Tie off and weave ends through work.

June 9

Mason Jar Topper

Materials

- Worsted weight yarn
- Crochet hook size 3.75 mm
- ½" satin ribbon

Directions

- Crochet a chain of 3 stitches. Join with slip stitch to create a ring.
- Round 1: Chain 3, 11 double crochet in ring. Slip stitch to beginning of chain to join.
- Round 2: Chain 3, double crochet in first stitch, 2 double crochet in each stitch to end of round. Slip stitch at beginning of chain to join.
- Round 3: Chain 3, double crochet in first 2 stitches. * 2 double crochet in next stitch, 1 double crochet. Repeat from * 10 times. Slip stitch to beginning of chain to join.
- Round 4: Chain 1, single crochet to end of round (back loops only). Slip stitch in beginning chain to join.
- Rounds 5-7: Chain 1. * Skip next stitch, 2 single crochet in next stitch. Repeat from * to end of round. Slip stitch in first single crochet to join.
- Round 8: Chain 3. * Skip 2 stitches, 1 single crochet in next stitch, chain 2. Repeat from * to end of round. Slip stitch in beginning chain to join.
- Round 9: Slip stitch in first chain 2 space. 1 single crochet, 1 double crochet, 1 triple crochet, 1 double crochet, 1 single crochet in every chain 2 space. Slip stitch to join. Tie off and weave ends through work.

Finishing

Weave ribbon through ruffled edge.

June 10

Dad's Golf Club Covers

Materials

- 1 ounce of worsted weight yarn for each club head cover
- Crochet hook sizes 3.75 mm (irons) and 4.25 mm (woods)

Directions

- Crochet a chain of 4 stitches. Join with slip stitch to create a ring. Chain 1.
- Round 1: 12 single crochet in ring. Slip stitch at top of first single crochet to join. Chain 3. (Join and chain 3 at the end of every round).
- Round 2: 1 double crochet in stitch at bottom of chain 3. 2 double crochet in each stitch to end of round.
- Round 3: 1 double crochet in next stitch, 2 double crochet in next stitch. Repeat this pattern to end of round.
- Rounds 4-13: 1 double crochet in each stitch to end of round.
- Round 14: 1 double crochet in next stitch. Chain 1, skip next stitch, 1 double crochet, chain 1. Repeat pattern to end of round.
- Round 15: Double crochet in each double crochet stitch (skip chain stitches).

- Rounds 16-21: Double crochet in each stitch to end of round. Tie off and weave ends through work.

Finishing

Crochet a chain measuring 14". Tie a knot at each end, and weave through mesh row of cover.

June 11

Lacy Wedding Bell Ornament

Materials

- #10 crochet cotton
- Crochet hook size 2.5 mm
- ½" satin ribbon
- Fabric stiffener (equal parts of white glue and water)

Directions

- Crochet a chain of 8 stitches. Join with slip stitch to create a ring. Chain 5, 1 double crochet in fourth chain of the original 8 chains in ring. This is the hanging loop.
- Round 1: Chain 3, 19 triple crochet in ring. Slip stitch at top of chain 3 to join.
- Round 2: * Chain 4, skip next stitch, 1 double crochet. Repeat from * to end of round, ending with 1 chain and 1 triple crochet in first stitch of first chain 4.
- Rounds 3-5: * Chain 4, 1 double crochet in next loop. Repeat from * to last loop. End with chain 1, 1 triple crochet in first stitch of first chain 4.
- Rounds 6-8: Repeat round 4, but chain 5 instead of 4. End with chain 2 and 1 triple crochet.
- Rounds 9-12: Repeat round 4, but chain 6. Finish with chain 3, 1 double triple crochet.
- Rounds 13-14: Repeat round 4, but chain 7. Finish with chain 4, 1 double triple crochet.
- Round 15: Repeat round 4, but with chain 8. End with chain 4, 1 triple crochet.
- Round 16: Chain 4, 2 triple crochet, 1 half triple crochet, 1 double crochet in loop below hook. 8 In next loop, 1 double crochet, 1 half triple crochet, 2 triple crochet, 1 double triple crochet, 2 triple crochet, 1 half triple crochet, 1 double crochet. Repeat to end of round. End with 1 double crochet, 1 half triple crochet, 2 triple crochet, 1 slip stitch in last of fourth chain 4. Tie off and weave ends through work.

Finishing

Attach ribbon to top loop to hang bell.

June 12

Mesh Purse

Materials

- 200 grams cotton yarn
- Crochet hook size 5 mm

Directions

- Crochet a chain of 39 stitches.
- Row 1: Skip first stitch, single crochet to end of row. Chain 1 and turn.

- Rows 2-4: Single crochet to end of row. Turn.
- Row 5: Chain 7, yarn over twice. Draw up next loop, yarn over (YO) and draw through 2 loops, twice. Yarn over and draw through all loops. * Chain 5, YO twice, draw up next loop, YO, draw through 2 loops twice. YO and draw through all 3 loops. Repeat from * to last stitch. Chain 3, 1 triple crochet. Turn.
- Row 6: Chain 5, skip next 3 chain, 1 triple crochet. * Chain 5, YO twice. Draw up loop in same stitch as before. YO, draw through 2 loops twice. Skip next chain 5 space. YO twice, draw loop from next stitch. YO, draw through 2 loops twice. YO and draw through all 3 loops. Repeat from * to last stitch. Triple crochet 2 stitches together and turn.
- Row 7: Chain 7. Triple crochet 2 stitches together. * Chain 5, triple crochet 2 stitches together over stitch just worked and next stitch. Repeat from * to last triple crochet. Chain 3, 1 triple crochet in fourth chain of chain 5 and turn.
- Rows 8 and beyond: Repeat rows 6 and 7 until piece measures 20", ending with third row.
- Next row: Chain 1, single crochet in first stitch. * 2 single crochet in chain 5 space. Repeat from * to turning chain 7. 1 single crochet in chain 7 space, 1 single crochet in fourth stitch of chain 7 and turn.
- Next 3 rows: Chain 1, single crochet to end of row. Tie off and weave ends through work.

Handles
- Attach yarn to top left corner. Chain 1, work 30 single crochet across side of bag. Turn.
- Chain 57, skip first chain, 55 single crochet, single crochet in each single crochet to end of row. Turn.
- Next 2 rows: Chain 1, single crochet to end of row. Sew end of handle in place. Repeat procedure for other handle.

You can make a cloth bag to line this lacy bag to keep smaller items from falling out.

June 13

Wedding Favor Bags

Materials

- Scraps of worsted weight yarn
- Crochet hook size 6 mm
- ¼" ribbon

Directions

- Crochet a chain of 12 stitches.
- Row 1: Skip first chain, single crochet to end of row. Chain 1 and turn.
- Row 2: Chain 1. * 1 single crochet, 1 half double crochet. Repeat from * to end of row. Chain 1 and turn.
- Rows 3-end: Repeat row 2 until piece measures 8".
- Last Row: Chain 1, single crochet in each stitch across. Tie off and leave a tail for stitching.

Finishing
- Fold piece in half and stitch up the long sides, leaving top open.
- Weave ribbon through top section to use as a drawstring.

June 14

Catnip Mouse Toy

Materials

- Scraps of worsted weight yarn
- Crochet hook size 3.5 mm
- Catnip

Directions

- Crochet a chain of 17 stitches.
- Row 1: Skip first chain, single crochet to end of row. This is the tail.
- Row 2: 7 single crochet in last loop of tail.
- Row 3: 2 single crochet in each of the 7 stitches from row 2.
- Row 4: * 1 single crochet, 2 single crochet in next stitch. Repeat from * 6 times.
- Rows 5-7: Single crochet in each stitch to end of row.
- Row 8: 5 single crochet, single crochet next 2 stitches together (decrease). Repeat until you can just get your finger into the top. Fill with stuffing and a jingle bell if you want.
- Row 9: 1 single crochet, 1 decrease until 7 stitches remaining. Then decrease until there are 3 stitches. Pull tight, tie off, and weave ends through work.

June 15

The Next Best Thing to a Sock Bun

Materials

- Scraps of worsted weight yarn
- Crochet hook size 5 mm

Directions

- Crochet a chain of 29 stitches.
- Row 1: Skip first 2 chains, double crochet in each chain to end of row. Chain 2 and turn.
- Rows 2-16: Double crochet in each stitch across. Tie off and leave tail for stitching.

Finishing
- Roll piece so it looks like a long tube, and stitch down the side.
- Fold over ends so piece looks like a donut, and stitch ends together.

June 16

Pretty Butterfly

Materials

- Scraps of worsted weight yarn
- Crochet hook size 4.25 mm
- Tapestry needle

Directions

- Crochet a chain of 4 stitches. Join with slip stitch to form a ring.
- Round 1: Chain 4, 3 double triple crochet in ring. Chain 4. Slip stitch into ring. Repeat once.
- Round 2: Chain 3, 3 triple crochet in ring, chain 3, slip stitch into ring. Repeat once. Tie off and weave ends through work.

Finishing

With a contrasting yarn color, stitch along center to create an abdomen and antennae.

June 17

Bride's Handkerchief

Materials

- #10 cotton crochet yarn
- Crochet hook size 1.5 mm

- ¼" satin ribbon

Directions

- Crochet a chain of 51 stiches.
- Row 1: Sip first chain, single crochet to end of row. Chain 1 and turn.
- Rows 2-63: Single crochet in each stitch to end of row. Chain 1 and turn.
- Row 64: Single crochet in each stitch to end of row. Do not turn because you are now going to work the border.
- Border: * Chain 3. Skip next stitch or row (row counts as 1 stitch), single crochet to end of row. Repeat from * all the way around.
- Next row: Chain 5, double crochet in same space. 1 double crochet, chain 2, 1 double crochet in each chain 3 space all the way around. Join with slip stitch in the third chain of first chain 5.
- Next row: 2 slip stitches, chain 5, double crochet in same space. 1 double crochet, chain 2, 1 double crochet in each chain 2 space around. Join with a slip stitch in the third chain of first chain 5. Tie off and weave ends through work.

Finishing

Beginning at a corner, weave ribbon through border. Tie in a bow at corner.

June 18

Soda Bottle Bangle Bracelet

Materials

- #10 cotton crochet thread
- Crochet hook size 2 mm
- Plastic soda bottle
- Tapestry needle
- Glue gun and glue

Directions

- Cut a strip from plastic bottle measuring about ¼" or narrower.
- Crochet a chain of 3 stitches. Join with slip stitch to create a ring.
- 6 single crochet in ring. Continue with a single crochet in rounds until piece measures about 7". Slide plastic strip in to see how much more you need to crochet. Finish crocheting, tie off but leave tail end.
- Once you are done crocheting, slide plastic strip back inside tube.
- Overlap ends of plastic about ¼", and secure with a bit of glue.
- Stitch tube closed.

Now you can embellish the bracelet with charms, or leave it as it is.

June 19

Little Girl's Hair Bows

Materials

- Scraps of worsted weight yarn
- Crochet hook size 5 mm
- Hair clip
- Glue gun and glue

Directions

- Crochet a chain of 6 stitches.
- Row 1: Skip first chain, half double crochet to end of row. Chain 1 and turn.
- Rows 2-18: Half double crochet in each stitch across. Chain 1 and turn.

Center
- Crochet a chain of 4 stitches.
- Row 1: Skip first chain, 3 half double crochet. Chain 1 and turn.
- Rows 2-6: 3 half double crochet. Chain 1 and turn.

Finishing
- Pinch bow section in middle. Wrap center section around, stitch in the back to hold it in place.
- Attach bow to hair clip.

June 20

Bi-Fold Wallet for Dad

Materials

- Worsted weight yarn
- Crochet hook size 4 mm

Directions

Outer section
- Crochet a chain measuring 9".
- Row 1: Skip first chain, single crochet to end of row. Chain 1 and turn.
- Row 2: Skip first stitch, single crochet to end of row. Repeat row 2 until piece measures 3.5". Tie off and weave ends through work.

Inside section
- Crochet a chain measuring 9".
- Row 1: Skip first chain, single crochet to end of row. Chain 1 and turn.
- Row 2: Skip first stitch, single crochet to end of row. Repeat row 2 until piece measures 3". Tie off, leave tail for stitching.

Finishing

Go around outside of top edge with a slip stitch.

Finishing

Place both pieces together so that the larger piece is on the bottom, and there is ½" overhang. Stitch up the short sides and bottom long side. Place money inside and fold in half.

June 21

Baby Flower Girl Dress

Materials

- Medium weight yarn
- Crochet hook size 3.25 mm
- Tulle

Directions

- Crochet a chain of 26 stitches. Check to see if this is large enough by wrapping around the baby's belly. Add or remove stitches as necessary.
- Row 1: Skip first 3 chains, triple crochet to end of row. Chain 3 and turn.
- Rows 2-20: Triple crochet in each stitch to end of row. Tie off and leave long tail for stitching.

Attach tulle
- Cut tulle into 12" strips that are 3" wide. Make at least 25 strips.
- Fold each tulle strip in half, and attach to the bottom edge of crocheted piece in the same manner as making a fringe. Place a strip every second space all the way around.
- Using tail end from top section, stitch up back of top with slip stitch. Turn right side out.

June 22

Baby Headband with Flowers

Materials

- Scraps of worsted weight yarn (2 or more colors)
- Crochet hook size 5 mm

Directions

- Crochet a chain of 8 stitches.
- Row 1: Skip first 2 chains, half double crochet to end of row. Chain 2 and turn.
- Row 2: Half double crochet in back loop of each stitch to last stitch. Half double crochet in both loops of last stitch. Repeat this row until piece is long enough to fit around baby's head. Tie off and weave ends through work.

Flowers
- Crochet a chain of 5 stitches. Join with slip stitch to create a ring.
- Round 1: 10 single crochet in ring. Join to first chain stitch with a slip stitch.
- Round 2: Chain 1, 5 double crochet in first single crochet. Chain 1, slip stitch in same stitch. Repeat this pattern in each stitch around to form petals. Tie off. Use tail to stitch flowers to headband.

June 23

#1 Dad Scarf

Materials

- Worsted weight variegated yarn
- Crochet hook size 5 mm
- Felt
- Needle and thread

Directions

- Crochet a chain measuring 9".
- Row 1: Skip first chain, single crochet to end of row. Chain 1 and turn.
- Row 2: Skip first stitch, single crochet to end of row. Chain 1 and turn.
- Rows 3-end: Repeat row 2 until piece reaches desired length. Tie off and weave ends through work.

Finishing
- Cut out felt so you have letters that spell #1 DAD (make 2 sets). Attach with needle and thread to either end of scarf.
- Add fringes to both ends of scarf.

June 24

Flapper Hat (Cloche)

Materials

- Worsted weight yarn
- Crochet hook sizes 9 mm and 10 mm

Directions

- Crochet a chain of 3 stitches with smaller hook. Join with slip stitch to create a ring.
- Round 1: 6 single crochet in ring. Place stitch marker at beginning of round.
- Round 2: 2 single crochet in each stitch.
- Round 3: * 1 single crochet, 2 single crochet in next stitch. Repeat from * to end of round.
- Round 4: * 2 single crochet, 2 single crochet in next stitch. Repeat from * to end of round. Continue in this manner, increasing the amount of single crochet, until round 9 (you will have 7 single crochet, 2 single crochet in next stitch).
- Round 10: Single crochet in each stitch to end of round. Repeat this round until piece measures 3.5" from last increase round.
- Next round: Work in front loops only. 5 single crochet, 2 single crochet in next stitch. Repeat pattern to end of round. Switch to larger hook.
- Next round: Work in single crochet for another 2.5".
- Last round: Slip stitch in back loop of each stitch. Tie off and weave ends through work.

Add a flower

- Crochet a chain of 5 stitches. Join with slip stitch to create a ring.
- Round 1: 10 single crochet in ring. Join to first chain stitch with a slip stitch.
- Round 2: Chain 1, 5 double crochet in first single crochet. Chain 1, slip stitch in same stitch. Repeat this pattern in each stitch around to form petals. Tie off. Use tail to stitch flower to hat.

June 25

Lacy Blue Bridal Garter

Materials

- #10 crochet thread, light blue
- Crochet hook size 1.5 m006D
- 48" ¼" satin ribbon

Directions

- Crochet a chain of 150 stitches.
- Row 1: Skip first chain, single crochet in each chain to end of row.
- Row 2: Chain 1, single crochet in each stitch to end of row.
- Row 3: Chain 7, skip 2 stitches, 1 triple crochet. * Chain 2, skip 2 stitches, triple crochet. Repeat from * to end of row.
- Row 4: Chain 1. Single crochet with 2 stitches in each chain space.
- Row 5: Chain 1. Single crochet in each stitch to end of row.

- Row 6: Chain 2, skip first stitch, 1 single crochet. * Chain 1, skip next stitch, 1 single crochet. Repeat from * to end of row.
- Row 7: Chain 1, 1 single crochet. * Chain 3, skip next stitch, 1 single crochet. Repeat from * to end of row.
- Row 8: Chain 1. *In first chain 3 space, 1 single crochet, 1 half double crochet, 1 double crochet, chain 2, 1 double crochet, 1 half double crochet, 1 single crochet. 1 single crochet in next chain 3 space, chain 3 and single crochet at bottom of chain (picot stitch), 1 single crochet. Repeat from * to end of row. Tie off and weave ends through work.

Finishing

Weave ribbon through garter, leaving enough ribbon to tie around leg.

June 26

Dangly Rosette Earrings

Materials

- #10 crochet thread
- Crochet hook size 2 mm
- Earring hooks (available at craft stores in jewelry findings)
- Chain (available at craft stores)
- Jump rings (available at craft stores)
- Needle and thread

Directions

- Crochet a chain measuring 1.5".
- Row 1: Skip first chain, single crochet in each stitch to end of row.
- Row 2: Chain 1, single crochet in next stitch. 2 single crochet in each stitch to end of row. Tie off and weave ends through work.

Finishing
- Roll crochet roll and pinch at the bottom, sew tight with needle and thread. You have a rosette.
- Tie each rosette to 1" of chain.
- Attach chains with to earring hooks with jump rings.

June 27

Chunky Yarn Basket

Materials

- 1 skein chunky yarn
- Crochet hook size 15 mm

Directions

- Crochet a chain of 7 stitches.
- Round 1: 1 half double crochet in third chain from hook. 2 half double crochet, 5 half double crochet in last chain. Rotate to opposite side of chain. 3 half double crochet, 4 half double crochet in next chain. Join with slip stitch at the top of beginning chain 2.

- Round 2: Chain 2, 4 half double crochet, 2 half double crochet in next stitch, 1 half double crochet, 2 half double crochet in next stitch, 5 half double crochet, 2 half double crochet in next stitch, 1 half double crochet, 2 half double crochet in next stitch. Join with slip stitch at top of beginning chain 2.
- Round 3: Chain 2, 4 half double crochet, 2 half double crochet in each of the next 2 stitches, 1 half double crochet, 2 half double crochet in each of the next 2 stitches, 5 half double crochet, 2 half double crochet in each of the next 2 stitches, 1 half double crochet, 2 half double crochet in each of the next 2 stitches. Join with slip stitch at top of beginning chain 2.
- Round 4: Chain 2, half double crochet in each stitch (back loops only). Join with slip stitch at top of beginning chain 2.
- Rounds 5-7: Chain 2, half double crochet in each stitch to end of round. Join with slip stitch at top of beginning chain 2.
- Round 8: Slip stitch in each stitch around. Tie off and weave ends through work.

June 28

Mini Wedding Cake Ornament

Materials

- Scraps of worsted weight yarn
- Crochet hook size 4 mm
- Fiberfill stuffing

Directions

Base
- Crochet a chain of 2 stitches.
- Round 1: 6 single crochet in second chain from hook. Place a stitch marker, and move after each round.
- Round 2: 2 single crochet in each stitch around.
- Round 3: * 2 single crochet in next stitch, 1 single crochet. Repeat from * to end of round.
- Round 4: * 2 single crochet in next stitch, 2 single crochet. Repeat from * to end of round.
- Round 5: * 2 single crochet in next stitch, 3 single crochet. Repeat from * to end of round.
- Round 6: * 1 single crochet, 1 half double crochet in each stitch. 1 half double crochet and 1 single crochet in next stitch. Slip stitch in next stitch. Repeat from 8 to end of round. Tie off and weave ends through work.

Bottom Layer
- Crochet a chain of 2 stitches.
- Rounds 1-5: Same as rounds 1-5 of base.
- Round 6: Single crochet in each stitch around, back loops only.
- Rounds 7-8: Single crochet in each stitch, both loops. Tie off, stuff with fiberfill, and stitch to base with slip stitch. Tie off and weave ends through work.

Middle Layer
- Same as bottom layer to round 4.
- Rounds 5-7: Work rounds 6-8 of bottom layer. Tie off, stuff, and stitch to bottom layer.

Top Layer
- Same as bottom layer to round 3.

- Round 4: Work rounds 6-8 of bottom layer. Tie off, stuff, and stitch to bottom layer. Weave all ends through work.

June 29

Bridal Head Chain with Beads

Materials

- Worsted weight yarn
- Crochet hook size 5 mm
- Beads
- Needle and thread

Directions

- Crochet a chain long enough to go around the top of your scalp (make sure there is a multiple of 10 stitches). Join with slip stitch to create a ring, being careful not to twist chain.
- Chain 20, skip 9 stitches, slip stitch in 10th chain. Skip 9 stitches, chain 20, slip stitch in next chain. Repeat all the way around. Tie off.

Finishing

With the needle and thread, stitch beads to the center of each chain loop so the loops hang down in points.

June 30

Wedding Favor Lacy Basket

Materials

- Crochet cotton
- Crochet hook size 1.5 mm
- Fabric stiffener (equal parts white glue and water)

Directions

- Crochet a chain of 11 stitches. Join with slip stitch to create a ring.
- Round 1: Chain 4, 39 double triple crochet in ring. Join with slip stitch in fourth chain.
- Round 2: Chain 5. * Double triple crochet in next stitch, chain 1. Repeat from * to end of round. Finish with a slip stitch in fourth chain of first chain 5.
- Round 3: (front loops only) Chain 4, 1 double triple crochet in each stitch to end of round. End with slip stitch in fourth chain of chain 4.
- Round 4: 1 double crochet between chain 4 and first stitch. * 3 triple crochet between next 2 stitches, 1 double crochet between next 2 stitches. Repeat from * to end of round. End with 1 double crochet in first double crochet. Do not tie off.

Handle

Chain 50, join with slip stitch between shells on opposite side of basket. Double crochet in each chain stitch. Tie off and weave ends through work.

Finishing

Soak basket in fabric stiffener. Allow to dry at least 3-4 hours.

July

here is so much going on right now. Summer vacations, barbecues, 4th of July celebrations, and more. So, we have some fun and easy patterns for summer stuff, including beach bags, beach mats, freezie holders, bags, and even cute baby barefoot sandals. Grab your crochet hook and yarn, and you'll have something to do while hanging out and relaxing at the beach or in your yard. These are also great patterns to work on while you are traveling, to keep long drives from getting boring.

July 1

Combination Beach Bag and Mat

Materials

- 32 ounces worsted weight yarn
- Crochet hook size 4.5 mm

Directions

Front
- Crochet a chain of 71 stitches.
- Row 1: Skip first 2 chains, half double crochet to end of row. Chain 3 and turn.
- Row 2: Double crochet in each stitch to end of row. Chain 2 and turn.
- Row 3: Half double crochet to end of row. Chain 3 and turn.
- Rows 4-end: Repeat rows 2 and 3 until piece measures 14". Tie off and weave ends through work.

Back

Repeat same pattern as for front of bag, but work until the piece measures 64" (or as long as you want the mat to be). Tie off and weave ends through work.

Bottom/Side Panel
- Crochet a chain of 18 stitches.
- Row 1: Skip first 2 chains, half double crochet to end of row. Chain 3 and turn.
- Row 2: Double crochet in each stitch to end of row. Chain 2 and turn.
- Row 3: Half double crochet in each stitch to end of row. Chain 3 and turn.
- Rows 4-end: Repeat rows 2 and 3 until piece measures 45". Tie off and weave ends through work.

Straps (2)
- Crochet a chain of 113 stitches.
- Row 1: Skip first chain, single crochet to end of row. Chain 1 and turn.
- Rows 2-5: Single crochet to end of row. Chain 1 and turn.
- Fold strap in half lengthwise and stitch along edge.

Finishing

Stitch panels to sides and bottom of front and back sections. Attach straps to the front and back. Tie off all ends and weave through work.

July 2

4ᵗʰ of July Picnic Placemats

Materials

- Red, white, and blue worsted weight yarn
- Crochet hook size 5 mm

Directions

- Crochet a chain of 47 stitches with red yarn.
- Row 1: Skip first 3 chains, double crochet to end of row. Turn.
- Rows 2-3: Chain 3, double crochet in each stitch to end of row. Switch to white yarn and turn.
- Rows 4-6: Chain 3, double crochet in each stitch to end of row. Switch to blue yarn and turn.
- Rows 7-9: Chain 3, double crochet in each stitch to end of row.
- Repeat pattern in red, white, and blue twice. Tie off and weave all ends through work.

Utensil Pocket

- Crochet a chain of 20 stitches with white yarn.
- Row 1: Skip first 4 chains. Double crochet to end of row. Turn.
- Rows 2-9: Chain 3, double crochet in each stitch to end of row. Tie off and weave ends through work.

Finishing

- Stitch pocket to one of the lower corners of the placemat, leaving top open to slide a knife and fork into.
- Tie (to hold it together when rolled up): Crochet a chain of 21 stitches. Skip first stitch, single crochet to end of row. Chain 1 and turn, repeat row, tie off.

July 3

Patriotic Dishcloth

Materials

- Red, white, and blue worsted weight yarn
- Red, white, and blue variegated yarn
- Crochet hook size 5.5 mm

Directions

- Crochet a chain measuring 10" with red yarn.
- Row 1: Skip first chain, double crochet to end of row. Chain 2 and turn.
- Row 2: Skip first stitch, double crochet to end of row. Turn.
- Row 3: Switch to white yarn, chain 2, double crochet to end of row. Chain 2 and turn.
- Row 4: Skip first stitch, double crochet to end of row. Turn.
- Row 5: Switch to blue yarn, chain 2, double crochet to end of row, Chain 2 and turn.
- Row 6: Skip first stitch, double crochet to end of row. Turn.
- Rows 7-12: Repeat pattern using all 3 colors. You may need to go a bit longer to make it a full square. Tie off and weave ends through work.

Edging

- Attach variegated yarn.
- Row 1: Chain 1, single crochet all the way around.
- Row 2: 2 single crochet in each stitch all the way around. Tie off and weave ends through work.

July 4

Patriotic Pot Holders

Materials

- Red, white, and blue variegated yarn
- White worsted weight yarn
- Crochet hook size 5 mm

Directions

- Crochet a chain measuring 9" with variegated yarn.
- Row 1: Skip first chain, single crochet to end of row. Chain 1 and turn.
- Rows 2-end: Skip first stitch, single crochet to end of row. Chain 1 and turn. Tie off when piece is a perfect square. Leave a tail.

Finishing
- With the tail of yarn, crochet a chain of 15 stitches. Join with a slip stitch to create a ring. This is the hanger for your potholder.

July 5

Freezie Holder/Lanyard

Materials

- Scraps of cotton worsted weight yarn
- Crochet hook size 5 mm

Directions

- Crochet a chain of 5 stitches. Join with a slip stitch to create a ring.
- Round 1: Chain 2, 5 double crochet in ring. Place stitch marker and move as you finish each round.
- Round 2: 2 double crochet in each stitch to end of round. Continue working rounds in double crochet until piece measures 6". Leave tail for strap.

Strap
- Crochet a chain measuring 36"
- Row 1: Skip first chain, single crochet to end of row. Attach to other side of holder. Tie off and weave ends through work.

July 6

Tea Light Flower Coasters

Materials

- Scraps of worsted weight yarn (2 colors)

- Crochet hook size 5.5 mm

Directions

- Crochet a chain of 5 stitches. Join with a slip stitch to create a ring.
- Round 1: 8 single crochet in ring.
- Round 2: * 1 single crochet, 2 single crochet in next stitch. Repeat from * to end of round.
- Rounds 3-4: Single crochet in each stitch around. Switch to second yarn color.
- Round 5: * 1 slip stitch, 4 double crochet in next stitch. Repeat from * 4 times. Tie off and weave ends through work.

July 7

Barefoot Sandals for Babies

Materials

- Light worsted weight yarn
- Crochet hook size 3.75 mm

Directions

- Crochet a chain of 5 stitches. Join with a slip stitch to create a ring.
- Round 1: Chain 3, 2 double crochet, chain 5, 3 double crochet, chain 5, 2 double crochet, chain 5. Join at top of chain 3 with slip stitch.
- Round 2: Chain 1, single crochet in same stitch, single crochet in each double crochet. In next chain 5 space, 2 single crochet, chain 6, 2 single crochet. 5 single crochet in each chain space, 1 single crochet in each double crochet. Tie off and weave ends through work.

Ties

Attach yarn at top corners, and make a chain of 30 stitches on each side. Tie off.

July 8

Bikini Top

Materials

- 3-4 skeins cotton yarn
- Crochet hook size 2.25 mm

Directions

Pattern is small. Larger sizes are in ( ).

Cups (2)
- Crochet a chain of 15 stitches (16-20)

- Row 1: Skip first chain, single crochet to last chain. 5 single crochet in last chain. Place stitch marker at center stitch. Do not turn. Work around to other side of chain, single crochet in each chain loop to end of row. Turn.
- Row 2: Chain 1, single crochet to end of row. Turn.
- Rows 3-4: Chain 1, single crochet in each stitch to center stitch. 5 single crochet in center stitch, single crochet in each stitch to end of row. Turn.
- Row 5: Chain 1, single crochet in each stitch to center stitch. 3 single crochet in center stitch, single crochet to end of row. Turn.
- Rows 6: Repeat rows 2-5 4 times (5-6), then repeat 2nd row once.
- Next row: (wrong side facing) 3 (4-5) single crochet. * Chain 1, skip next stitch, 2 single crochet. Repeat from * to last 1 (2-2) stitches. Single crochet to end. Turn.
- Next row: Chain 1, 1 (2-2) single crochet. * 5 double crochet in next chain 1 space, 1 single crochet in next chain 1 space. Repeat from * to last 3 (4-4) stitches. Single crochet to end. Tie off and weave ends through work.

Ties

- Crochet a chain of 95 stitches. Attach to bottom of first cup with wrong side facing, single crochet across. Chain 4, attach second cup, and single crochet across. Chain 96 and turn.
- Next row: Skip first chain, slip stich to end of chain. Single crochet across cups, slip stitch in each of the 95 chains. Tie off.

Neck ties

(right side facing) Join yarn with slip stitch to the top of the 5 double crochet group. Crochet a chain of 106 stitches. Slip stitch in 2nd chain from hook. Slip stitch in each chain to end. Tie off. Repeat for other side.

July 9

Bikini Bottom

Materials

- Cotton yarn
- Crochet hook size 2.25 mm
- Invisible elastic

Directions

Back
- Crochet a chain of 63 stitches.
- Row 1: Skip first stitch, single crochet to end of row. Turn.
- Rows 2-9: Chain 1, single crochet in each stitch to end of row. Turn.
- Shaping row 1: (right side facing) Draw up 1 loop in each of the first 2 stitches. YO and draw through all loops on hook. 1 single crochet in each stitch to last 2 stitches. Single crochet last 2 stitches together. Turn.
- Row 2: Chain 1, single crochet to end of row. Repeat rows 1 and 2 until there are 14 stitches remaining. Turn.
- Rows 3-22: Chain 1, single crochet to end of row. Turn.

- Front shaping row 1: Chain 1, 2 single crochet in first stitch, single crochet to last 2 stitches. 2 single crochet in last stitch. Turn.
- Rows 2-3: Chain 1, single crochet to end of row. Turn.
- Rows 4-18: Repeat rows 1-3. Tie off.

Back edging and side ties
- Crochet a chain of 55 stitches.
- Row 1: Slip in first chain of foundation chain on back. Chain 1, single crochet to end of foundation chain. Chain 56 and turn.
- Row 2: Skip first stitch, 55 slip stitches. Single crochet in each chain across back. Slip stitch in next 55 chains. Tie off. Repeat for front edging and side ties.

Leg edging
- Row 1: (right side facing) Join yarn to front side where tie is attached. Chain 1, single crochet along opening. Turn.
- Row 2: Chain 1, single crochet to end of row. Tie off and weave ends through work, and repeat on other side.

Finishing
Weave invisible elastic through last single crochet row of the edgings.

July 10

Striped Beach Mat

Materials
- Cotton yarn in 4 colors
- Crochet hook size 4.5 mm

Directions
- Crochet a chain of 99 stitches with main color.
- Row 1: Skip first 3 chains, double crochet to end of row. Join second color and turn.
- Row 2: Chain 1, single crochet in each stitch to end of row. Join main color and turn.
- Row 3: Chain 3, double crochet in each stitch to end of round. Join second color and turn.
- Row 4: Repeat row 2. Join third color and turn.
- Row 5: Repeat row 3. Join fourth color and turn.
- Row 6: Repeat row 2. Join third color and turn.
- Row 7: Repeat row 5.
- Row 8: Repeat row 2, join second color and turn.
- Row 9: Repeat row 3, join main color and turn.
- Row 10: Repeat row 2. Join second color and turn.
- Row 11: Repeat row 9. Join main color and turn.
- Row 12: Repeat row 2. Join fourth color and turn.
- Row 13: Repeat row 3. Join third color and turn.
- Row 14: Repeat row 2. Join fourth color and turn.
- Row 15: Repeat row 13. Join third color and turn.
- Row 16: Repeat row 2. Join main color and turn.

- Row 17: Repeat row 3. Join second color and turn.
- Repeat rows 2-17 until piece measures around 58". Tie off and weave ends through work.

Edging

Single crochet all the way around beach mat in main color. Tie off and weave ends through work.

July 11

X-Large Beach Mat

Materials

- Red Heart Super Saver yarn
- Crochet hook size 5.5 mm

Directions

- Crochet a chain measuring 36".
- Row 1: Skip first chain, half double crochet to end of row. Chain 2 and turn.
- Row 2: Skip first stitch, double crochet to end of row. Chain 1 and turn.
- Row 3: Skip first stitch, half double crochet to end of row. Chain 2 and turn.
- Rows 4-end: Repeat rows 2 and 3 until piece measures 72", or desired length. Tie off and weave ends through work.

Finishing

Single crochet all the way around beach mat to create a finished edge. Tie off and weave ends through work.

July 12

Barefoot Lace-Up Sandals

Materials

- Worsted weight cotton yarn
- Crochet hook size 5 mm

Directions

- Crochet a chain of 11 stitches. Join with a slip stitch to create a ring. This is the toe loop.
- Row 1: Chain 4, 2 double crochet in 3rd chain from hook. Turn.
- Row 2: Chain 2. Double crochet in same stitch as chain 2, and in each stitch to end of row. Double crochet in the chain 2 from the previous round. Turn.
- Row 3: Repeat last row 3 times or more, depending on the size of your foot. The piece should almost come to your ankle when loop is around toe.
- Chain 100 (1st strap to go around leg). Tie off.
- Attach yarn to other side of the triangle and chain 100 for 2nd strap. Tie off and weave ends through work.

July 13

Beach Party Hawaiian Lei

Materials

- 2 colors of worsted weight yarn
- Crochet hook size 5 mm
- Plastic straws (colors to match yarn or contrasting colors for a flashier lei)

Directions

- Make 36 flowers in the same manner as for the Tea Light Flower Coasters (July 6).
- Crochet a chain measuring 36".
- Cut the straws into 1" pieces.
- Thread 1 piece of straw onto the chain, followed by a flower (through the center of the flower). Continue stringing straws and flowers until lei is complete.
- Tie ends together, then tie off and weave ends through work.

July 14

Tank Top

Materials

- Light weight cotton yarn
- Crochet hook size 3.5 mm

Directions

- Crochet a chain of 180 stitches. Join with a slip stitch to create a ring, being careful not to twist the chain.
- Round 1: * 1 double crochet, chain 1, skip 1 chain. Repeat from * 90 times. Join with slip stitch.
- Rounds 2-3: * 1 double crochet, chain 1, skip next stitch. Repeat from * 90 times. Join with slip stitch.
- Round 4: * 1 single crochet, chain 1, skip next stitch. Repeat from * 90 times. Join with slip stitch.
- Rounds 5-7: * 1 double crochet, chain 1, skip next stitch. Repeat from * 90 times. Join with slip stitch.
- Round 8: * 1 single crochet, chain 1, skip next stitch. Repeat from * 90 times. Join with slip stitch. Repeat rounds 5-8 16 times.

Straps (make 2)
- Row 1: At the last stitch made, skip cluster of stitches, 1 single crochet chain 1, skip next stitch. Repeat 10 times. Insert hook in next stitch. * 1 double crochet, chain 1, skip next stitch. Repeat from * 3 times, double crochet in last stitch. Turn.
- Row 2: * 1 double crochet, chain 1, skip next stitch. Repeat from * 3 times, 1 double crochet in last stitch. Turn.
- Rows 3-32: Repeat row 2. Tie off and stitch to front. Repeat with second strap on other side.

July 15

Bean Bag Toss Game

Materials

- Scraps of worsted weight yarn
- Crochet hook size 5 mm
- Uncooked rice
- Cardboard (24" X 24")
- Cardboard box
- Scissors
- Paint or markers

Directions

Beanbags (make as many as you need)

Make 2 pieces for each beanbag
- Crochet a chain measuring 4".
- Row 1: Skip first chain, single crochet to end of row. Chain 1 and turn.
- Rows 2-end: Skip first stitch, single crochet to end of row. Chain 1 and turn. Tie off, leaving tail for stitching.

Finishing
- Stitch 3 sides of beanbags together with a slip stitch.
- Fill with uncooked rice.
- Slip stitch last side closed.
- Put designs on the cardboard, and cut out holes for beanbags to go through. Paint or draw numbers at each hole for scores.
- Lean cardboard against cardboard box so beanbags will go inside.

July 16

Popcorn Can Footstool

Materials

- Red Heart Super Saver yarn
- Crochet hook size 5.5 mm
- Large popcorn can
- Round foam cushion insert equaling the size of the top of the popcorn can

Directions

Cushion section (make 2)
- Crochet a chain of 5 stitches.
- Round 1: 10 double crochet in ring. Do not turn, as you will be working in rounds. You can use a stitch marker to mark the start of each round, moving it from round to round as you work.
- Round 2: 2 double crochet in each stitch to end of round.
- Round 3: 2 double crochet in each stitch to end of round.
- Round 4-end: Repeat round 3 until piece is just a bit larger than the foam cushion insert.
- Stitch both pieces together, 2/3 of the way around. Insert foam cushion, stitch the rest of the way to close.

- Next round: Double crochet in each stitch to end of round. Continue in this manner until piece is long enough to fit over can and reach to the bottom

July 17

Fringed Change Purse

Materials

- Scraps of worsted weight yarn
- Crochet hook size 5 mm
- Fringed ribbon
- Button
- Needle and thread

Directions

- Crochet a chain measuring 4".
- Row 1: Skip first chain, single crochet to end of row. Chain 1 and turn.
- Rows 2-end: Skip first stitch, single crochet to end of row. Repeat until piece measures 6". Tie off and leave end for stitching.

Finishing
- Fold piece at the first 2" mark, stitch up the sides.
- Using needle and thread, stitch button to the front section, near the bottom.
- Attach yarn at middle of flap, chain 10, and join with a slip stitch to create a loop for the button.
- Using needle and thread, stitch fringed ribbon to bottom of change purse.

July 18

Fringed Shoulder Bag

Materials

- Cotton worsted weight yarn, 2 colors
- Crochet hook size 6 mm
- Zipper (9")
- Needle and thread (or a sewing machine)

Directions

- Crochet a chain measuring 9" in main color.
- Row 1: Skip first chain, single crochet to end of row. Chain 2 and turn.
- Row 2: Skip first stitch, double crochet to end of row. Chain 1 and turn.
- Row 3: Skip first stitch, single crochet to end of row. Chain 2 and turn.
- Rows 4-end: Repeat rows 2 and 3 until piece measures 24". Tie off and weave ends through work.

Fold piece in half, and stitch up sides, leaving top open.

Strap
- Crochet a chain measuring 36".
- Row 1: Skip first chain, single crochet to end of row. Chain 1 and turn.
- Row 2: Skip first stitch, single crochet to end of row. Tie off and attach strap to either side of purse. Tie off and weave ends through work.

Finishing

Stitch the zipper to the top of the bag with the needle and thread or with your sewing machine.

July 19

Soda/Beer Can Cozy

Materials

- Worsted weight yarn
- Crochet hook size 5 mm

Directions

- Crochet a chain of 6 stitches. Join with slip stitch to create a ring.
- Round 1: Chain 1, 10 single crochet in ring. Join with slip stitch to first single crochet.
- Round 2: Chain 1, single crochet in same space as slip stitch. * 2 single crochet in next stitch, 1 single crochet in next stitch. Repeat from * to end of round, ending with 2 single crochet in last stitch. Join with slip stitch.
- Round 3: Repeat round 2, ending with 1 single crochet in last stitch.
- Round 4: Repeat round 2.
- Round 5: Chain 1, single crochet in back loop of each stitch. Join with slip stitch. This creates the base.
- Rounds 6-23: Chain 1, single crochet in same space as slip stitch. 1 single crochet in each stitch to end of round. Join with slip stitch. Tie off and weave ends through work.

July 20

Baby Doll Hat

Materials

- Worsted weight yarn
- Crochet hook size 4 mm

Directions

- Crochet a chain of 19 stitches.
- Rows 1-42: Single crochet in back loops of stitches to end of each row. Join sides with slip stitches to make a tube.
- Next Round: Chain 1, single crochet all the way around tube (60 stitches). Chain 4, 1 double crochet. * 3 single crochet, chain 2, 3 single crochet. Repeat from * to end of round. Tie off and weave ends through work.

Finishing

Cut a long piece of yarn, slip it at the top end of the tube (without the finishing edge). Weave yarn through, pull tight, tie off and weave ends through work.

July 21

Baby Doll Booties

Materials

- Worsted weight yarn
- Crochet hook size 4 mm

Directions

Make 2
- Crochet a chain of 4 stitches.
- Row 1: Skip first chain, single crochet in next 3. Do not turn, but work around to the other side.
- Row 2: 1 single crochet in same chain, and in next 2 chains, and add 3 more single crochet to equal 12 stitches. Join with slip stitch and chain 1.
- Rows 3-6: Work around oval in single crochet in each of the 12 stitches. Join each round with a slip stitch.
- Row 7: 6 half double crochet (heel), 6 slip stitches (front). Join with slip stitch and chain 1.
- Row 8: 6 half double crochet, 6 single crochet. Join with slip stitch and chain 1.
- Row 9: 6 half double crochet, 6 single crochet. Join with slip stitch and chain 1.
- Row 10: Half double crochet to end of row. Chain 1.
- Row 11: Single crochet to end of row. Tie off and weave ends through work.

July 22

Thong Sandals

Materials

- Red Heart Super Saver yarn
- Crochet hook size 4 mm

Directions

Pattern for small adult size. Larger sizes in ( ).

Soles (make 2)
- Crochet a chain of 25 stitches (add 2 or 4 stitches for larger sizes).
- Round 1: Skip first chain, 2 single crochet in next chain, 1 single crochet in each chain to last chain. 5 single crochet in last chain. Place stitch marker here and move it at the end of each round.
- Round 2: 2 single crochet in first stitch, 24 (26, 28) single crochet, 2 single crochet in next stitch, 1 single crochet, 2 single crochet in next stitch, 24 (26, 28) single crochet, 2 single crochet in next stitch, 2 single crochet.
- Round 3: 2 single crochet in next stitch, 26 (28, 30) single crochet, 2 single crochet in next stitch, 1 single crochet, 2 single crochet in next stitch, 26 (28, 30) single crochet, 2 single crochet in next stitch, 1 single crochet.

- Round 4: 2 single crochet in next stitch, 28 (30, 32)   single crochet, 2 single crochet in next stitch, 1 single crochet 2 single crochet in next stitch, 28 (30, 32)   single crochet, 2 single crochet in next stitch, 1 single crochet.
- Round 5: 2 single crochet in next stitch, 30 (32, 34)   single crochet, 2 single crochet in next stitch, 1 single crochet 2 single crochet in next stitch, 30 (32, 34)   single crochet, 2 single crochet in next stitch, 1 single crochet.
- Round 6: 2 single crochet in next stitch, 32 (34, 36)   single crochet, 2 single crochet in next stitch, 1 single crochet 2 single crochet in next stitch, 32 (34, 36)   single crochet, 2 single crochet in next stitch, 1 single crochet.
- Round 7: 2 single crochet in next stitch, 34 (36, 38)   single crochet, 2 single crochet in next stitch, 1 single crochet 2 single crochet in next stitch, 18 (19, 20) single crochet, slip stitch. Turn.
- Round 8: Skip first stitch, 18 (19, 20) single crochet, 2 single crochet in each of next 5 stitches, 18 (19, 20) single crochet, slip stitch. Turn.
- Round 9: Skip first stitch, half double crochet to end of row. Slip stitch into next slip stitch and turn.

Straps

Start straps from last slip stitch.
- Row 1: Skip first stitch, 2 single crochet, turn.
- Row 2: Chain 1, single crochet to end of row. Turn.
- Rows 3-end: Repeat row 2 until strap measures long enough to go from the middle of the sole to your toes, with the end sewn into the other side of the sole.

July 23

Beach Tote

Materials

- Worsted weight yarn, about 250 yards
- Crochet hook size 5 mm

Directions

- Crochet a chain of 3 stitches.
- Round 1: 12 double crochet in first chain from hook. Join with slip stitch at the top of the first double crochet.
- Round 2: Chain 2, 2 double crochet in each stitch to end of row. Join at top of first double crochet.
- Rounds 3-4: Chain 2. * 2 double crochet, 2 double crochet in next stitch. Repeat from * to end of round. Join with a slip stitch.
- Round 5: Chain 3. * 1 double crochet, chain 1. Repeat from * to end of round. Do not join, but insert hook in first chain 1 space of round 5 to begin round 6.
- Rounds 6-23: Double crochet and chain 1 in each chain 1 space to end of round.
- Round 24: Chain 2, double crochet in each chain 1 space.
- Round 25: Chain 2. Double crochet between each stitch of round 24.

Handles

- Row 1: Starting at last stitch, chain 2, 9 double crochet.
- Row 2: Chain 2 turn, 1 double crochet over next 2 stitches (decrease). 5 double crochet, decrease in last 2 stitches.

- Row 3: Chain 2, turn, decrease, 5 double crochet decrease.
- Rows 4-15: Chain 2, turn, 5 double crochet.
- Fold bag in half to determine where to place other side of handle. Work handle pattern backwards, finishing by attaching it to the other side of the bag.

July 24

Chair Pad

Materials

- Red Heart Super Saver yarn
- Crochet hook size 5 mm

Directions

Crochet a chain of 13 stitches.
- Row 1: Skip first chain, half double crochet in each chain to end of row. Chain 1 and turn.
- Rows 2-6: 2 half double crochet in next stitch, half double crochet to last stitch, 2 half double crochet in last stitch. Chain 1 and turn.
- Rows 7-10: Half double crochet in each stitch to end of row. Chain 1 and turn.
- Rows 11-15: 2 half double crochet next 2 stitches together (decrease), half crochet to last 2 stitches, decrease. Chain 1 and turn.
- Round 1: Now you are working all the way around the piece. Chain 3, double crochet end of row, 2 double crochet at end, single crochet to other end. Slip stitch to join at top of first chain 3.
- Row 2: Chain 3, 4 double crochet. * 2 double crochet in next stitch, 7 double crochet. Repeat from * to end of round. Slip stitch to join.
- Round 3: Chain 3, 4 double crochet. * 2 double crochet in next stitch, 8 double crochet. Repeat from * to end of round. Slip stitch to join.
- Round 4: Chain 3, double crochet to end of round. Slip stitch to join and turn.
- Rounds 5-6: Chain 3, 4 double crochet. * 2 double crochet in next stitch, 9 double crochet. Repeat from * to end of round. Slip stitch to join and turn.
- Round 7: Chain 3, 5 double crochet. * 2 double crochet in next stitch, 11 double crochet. Repeat from * to end of round. Slip stitch to join, tie off and weave ends through work.

July 25

Hacky-Sack Bag

Materials

- Cotton crochet thread
- Crochet hook size 4.5 mm
- Uncooked rice

Directions

- Crochet a chain of 5 stitches. Join with slip stitch to create a ring.

- Round 1: Chain 2, 9 single crochet in ring. Join with slip stitch at the top of first single crochet.
- Round 2: Chain 2, single crochet in same space. Single crochet to end of round. Join with slip stitch.
- Round 3: Chain 2, single crochet in same space, 1 single crochet. * 2 single crochet in next stitch, 1 single crochet. Repeat from * to end of round. Join.
- Round 4: Chain 2, single crochet in same space, 2 single crochet. * 2 single crochet in next stitch, 2 single crochet. Repeat from * to end of round. Join.
- Round 5: Chain 2, single crochet in same space, 3 single crochet. * 2 single crochet in next stitch, 3 single crochet. Repeat from * to end of round. Join.
- Round 6: Chain 2, single crochet in same space, 4 single crochet. * 2 single crochet in next stitch, 4 single crochet. Repeat from * to end of round. Join.
- Rounds 7-11: Chain 2, single crochet in next stitch and in each stitch to end of round. Join.
- Round 12: Chain 2, 4 single crochet. * Skip next stitch, 5 single crochet. Repeat from * to end of round. Join.
- Round 13: Chain 2, 3 single crochet. * Skip next stitch, 4 single crochet. Repeat from * to end of round. Join and fill with rice.
- Round 14: Chain 2, 2 single crochet. * Skip next stitch, 3 single crochet. Repeat from * to end of round. Join.
- Round 15: Chain 2, 1 single crochet. * Skip next stitch, 2 single crochet. Repeat from * to end of round. Join.
- Round 16: Repeat row 15. Close ball, tie off, and weave ends through work.

July 26

Shoulder Tote

Materials

- Worsted weight yarn
- Crochet hook size 4 mm
- 9.5 mm cording

Directions

- Crochet a chain of 77 stitches.
- Row 1: (right side facing) Skip 2 chains, half double crochet to end of row. Turn.
- Row 2: Chain 1, single crochet in each stitch to end of row. Turn.
- Row 3: Chain 2, half double crochet in each stitch to end of row. Turn.
- Rows 4-end: Repeat rows 2 and 3 until piece measures 40", ending with row 3. Tie off.

Finishing
- Fold side edges over 1", and sew in place. Run cording through this casing.
- Fold bag in half, sew side seams together. Pull cording to gather, and knot ends. Tie off yarn and weave ends through work.

July 27

Easy Apron

Materials

- Cotton yarn

- Crochet hook size 4 mm

Directions

- Crochet a chain of 52 stitches.
- Row 1: Skip first 2 chains, 2 half double crochet in next chain and in each stitch to last chain. 2 half double crochet in last chain. Turn.
- Rows 2-13: Chain 2, 2 half double crochet in first stitch, 1 half double crochet in each stitch to last stitch, 2 half double crochet in last stitch. Turn.
- Row 14: Chain 2, half double crochet in each stitch to end of row. Continue with edging.
- Edging row 1: Single crochet all the way around piece, with 3 single crochet in each corner. Tie off and weave ends through work.

Pocket

- Crochet a chain of 51 stitches.
- Row 1: Skip first 2 chains, half double crochet in next chain, and in each chain to end of row. Turn.
- Rows 2-end: Chain 2, half double crochet in each stitch to end of row. Turn. Repeat this row until piece measures about 7". Tie off and leave long tail for stitching.

Ties (make 2)

- Join yarn at top corner of apron. Crochet a chain of 28 stitches.
- Row 1: Skip first 2 chains, half double crochet in next chain and in each chain to end of row. Tie off and weave ends through work.

Finishing

Use a slip stitch to sew pocket to the front of the apron.

July 28

More Cute Baby Sandals (Size 3-6 Months)

Materials

- Worsted weight cotton yarn
- Crochet hook size 5 mm
- ½" buttons (2)
- Needle and thread

Directions

Soles (make 4)

- Crochet a chain of 9 stitches.
- Round 1: (work up chain and around other side to create a round). Skip first chain, 3 single crochet in next chain, 5 single crochet, 1 half double crochet. Chain 7, half double crochet in last chain. On other side, 1 half double crochet, 5 single crochet.
- Round 2: 2 single crochet in first stitch of previous round, and in each of the next 2 stitches. 7 single crochet, 2 single crochet in each if the next 5 stitches, 7 single crochet.
- Round 3: 1 single crochet in next stitch, 2 single crochet in next stitch. Repeat 3 times. 7 single crochet. * 1 single crochet, 2 single crochet in next stitch. Repeat from * 5 times. 7 single crochet. Join and tie off.
- Attach soles with wrong sides facing each other with slip stitches.

Sides

- Row 1: Join yarn at inside part of sole in the first slip stitch. Chain 1, 27 single crochet, don't work last 11 stitches. Turn.
- Row 2: Chain 1, single crochet 2 stitches together (decrease), 11 single crochet, decrease, 12 single crochet. Turn.
- Row 3: Chain 1, decrease, 10 single crochet, decrease, 11 single crochet. Turn.
- Row 4: Chain 1, single crochet in same stitch, 2 single crochet. In front loops only, 6 slip stitches, 5 single crochet, 6 slip stitches, 3 single crochet. Tie off.

Left Shoe

Join yarn at first row on left side of shoe with slip stitch, slip stitch in side of each row to the top corner. Chain 6, slip stitch in same corner stitch. This is your button loop. 2 slip stitch in next corner, slip stitch to end of row. Tie off. Repeat process in reverse for the right shoe.

Sew buttons on with needle and thread.

July 29

Doggie Doo Baggie Bag

Materials

- Worsted weight yarn
- Crochet hook size 4.25 mm
- Hair elastic
- Button
- Needle and thread

Directions

- Working around elastic loop, crochet a chain of 3 stitches, with first chain loop over the hair elastic.
- Round 1: 20 double crochet around the band. Slip stitch to join at the top of chain 3.
- Round 2: Chain 3, in back loops only, double crochet to end of round. Join with slip stitch.
- Rounds 3-6: Chain 3, double crochet in each stitch to end of round. Join with slip stitch. You can add more rounds if you want a larger bag.
- Last rounds: Single crochet 2 stitches together all the way around until bag is closed. Tie off.

Finishing

- To make the handle, pick up from where you tied off and chain 7. Double crochet across and join at top of bag with a slip stitch.
- Sew button on front with the needle and thread. The space in the double crochet on the handle will act as a button hole.

July 30

Square Chair Pad

Materials

- Worsted weight yarn, 2 colors

- Crochet hook size 5.5 mm

Directions

- Crochet a chain measuring 14".
- Row 1: Skip first chain, double crochet to end of row. Chain 1 and turn.
- Row 2: Skip first stitch, half double crochet to end of row. Chain 2 and turn.
- Row 3: Skip first stitch, double crochet to end of row. Chain 1 and turn.
- Rows 4-end: Repeat rows 2 and 3 until you have a square, ending with a double crochet row.
- Edging row: With second color, join yarn at the edge of one side. Chain 2, 2 double crochet in next stitch. * Chain 2, skip next stitch, 3 double crochet in next stitch. Repeat from * to the corner. In corner stitch, 3 double crochet, chain 1, 3 double crochet. Continue in a shell pattern all the way around. Tie off and leave a long tail.

Ties
- With yarn tail from edging, crochet a chain measuring 8". Tie off.
- Crochet a second chain measuring 8", and attach with a slip stitch to corner opposite first tie. Tie off.

July 31

Lip Balm Holder/Key Ring

Materials

- #3 crochet cotton
- Crochet hook size 3.25 mm
- Key ring

Directions

- Crochet a chain of 13 stitches.'
- Row 1: Skip first chain, single crochet in next chain and in each chain to end of row. Chain 1 and turn.
- Rows 2-25: Single crochet in each stitch to end of row. Chain 1 and turn. At end of last row, tie off and weave ends through work.
- Attach yarn at corner and crochet 2 rows of single crochet down each side of piece.

Tab
- Crochet a chain of 13 stitches.
- Row 1: Skip first chain, single crochet in next chain and in each chain to end of row. Chain 1 and turn.
- Rounds 2-5: Single crochet in each stitch to end of row. Chain 1 and turn. Tie off and weave in ends at end of last row.

Finishing
- Slide tap through key ring, and slip stitch edges together to close.
- Fold holder in half, slip stitch along bottom, and the lower 2" together. Opening at top is where you slide the lip balm in.
- Stitch tab piece to the top of the holder. This will also close the top part of the holder

August

There is still a whole month left of the summer, and you have plenty of time to get into the patterns we have for the month of August. Most of these patterns can be made in an afternoon or evening, and many can be made in an hour or less. Make a cute doll carrier for your little girl, a walker organizer for seniors, and even a yarn barn to keep your yarn in one place while you are working on the patterns in this book.

August 1

Doll Carrier

Materials

- Pink and white worsted weight yarn
- Crochet hook size 5.5 mm

Directions

- Crochet a chain of 10 stitches with pink yarn.
- Round 1: Skip first chain, single crochet in each stitch to end of row. Work around to other side, and single crochet back to start of chain. Place stitch marker and move as you finish each round so you can keep track of your work.
- Round 2: Single crochet in each stitch all the way around.
- Continue in rounds until piece is an oval measuring approximately 15" X 10" (or size to fit doll it will carry). Tie off and weave ends through work.
- Edging row: Attach white yarn with slip stitch, chain 2, 2 double crochet in same stitch. * Chain 1, skip next stitch, 3 double crochet in next stitch. Repeat from * to end of round. Tie off and weave ends through work.

Handles (2)

The handles will go on both of the long sides.
- Row 1: Attach yarn approximately 4.5" from end. 5 single crochet, chain 1 and turn.
- Row 2: Skip first stitch, single crochet to end of row. Chain 1 and turn. Continue until strap measures 12". Measure 6" on main piece, and attach end of strap at this mark. Repeat on other side of doll carrier. Tie off and weave ends through work.

August 2

Fringed Poncho

Materials

- Cotton worsted weight yarn
- Crochet hook size 4.5 mm

Directions

Front
- Crochet a chain of 58 stitches.
- Row 1: With wrong side facing, skip first chain, single crochet in next chain and in each chain to end of row. Turn.
- Row 2: Chain 3. * 3 double crochet, chain 2, skip 2 stitches. Repeat from * 4 times. 2 double crochet. 1 double crochet, chain 3, 1 double crochet in next stitch (this is the V-point of the poncho). 2 double crochet, chain 2, skip 2 stitches. Repeat from * 4 more times to chain 3 space of center V point. 3 double crochet, chain 3, 3 double crochet in chain 3 space. Chain 2. Repeat from * to end of row. End row with 1 double crochet at the top of chain 3. Turn.

- Chain 5. * 3 double crochet in next chain 2 space, chain 2. Repeat from * to chain 3 space of center V point. 3 double crochet, chain 3, 3 double crochet in chain 3 space. Chain 2. Repeat from * to end of row, ending with 1 double crochet in top of chain 3. Turn.
- Row 4: Chain 3. * 3 double crochet in next chain 2 space, chain 2. Repeat from * to chain 3 space of center V point. 3 double crochet, chain 3, 3 double crochet in chain 3 space. Chain 2. Repeat from * to end of row, ending with 1 double crochet in 3rd chain of chain 5. Turn.
- Repeat last 2 rows 8 or more times, depending on how long you want the poncho to be. Tie off.
- Make an identical piece for the back.

Finishing
- Sew front and back pieces together with a slip stitch.
- Crochet a chain measuring 50". Tie off, and weave chain through chain 2 spaces at the neck hole.
- Add a fringe all the way around the bottom of the poncho.

August 3

Laptop Case

Materials
- Worsted weight yarn
- Crochet hook size 5.5 mm
- Old cotton belt (1" wide)
- 1" D-rings

Directions
- Crochet a chain of 41 stitches.
- Row 1: Skip first chain, single crochet in each chain to end of row. Turn.
- Rows 2-80: Chain 1, single crochet in each stitch to end of row. Turn. Tie off and weave ends through work at end of last round.

Finishing
- Lay flat, right side facing you. Fold short end upwards, 10", so there is 6" of overhang for a flap. Sew sides together, and turn piece right side out.
- For top straps, cut two 5" pieces of the belt. Put one end through 2 D-rings, so the fabric folds over the flat part of the rings. Stitch a seam here to close rings. You may want to use a sewing machine for this part. Fold other end of belt piece under for a hem, and stitch in place. Do the same procedure for a second strap.
- Measure 3" from sides of flap, and attach straps to flap.
- For lower straps, cut 2 7.5" pieces of the belt. Create a hem at one edge and stitch to bottom section of bag so they line up with the flap straps.

August 4

Ridged Washcloth

Materials
- Worsted weight cotton yarn
- Crochet hook size 5 mm

Directions

- Crochet a chain of 44 stitches.
- Row 1: Skip first 2 chains, half double crochet in each chain to end of row. Turn.
- Row 2: Chain 2, half double crochet in the back loops of each stitch to end of row. Turn.
- Rows 3-end: Repeat row 2 until piece measures approximately 11". Tie off and weave ends through work.

August 5

Baby Bib

Materials

- Soft baby yarn, 2 balls main color and 1 ball for edging
- Crochet hook size 4 mm
- Button
- Needle and thread

Directions

- With main color, crochet a chain of 20 stitches.
- Row 1: Skip first chain, single crochet in each chain to end of row. Turn.
- Row 2: Chain 1, 2 single crochet in first stitch, single crochet to last stitch, 2 single crochet in last stitch. Chain 1 and turn.
- Row 3: Single crochet to end of row. Turn.
- Rows 4-9: Repeat last 2 rows.
- Rows 10-neck: Work even single crochet until piece measures about 7", ending with right side facing.
- Neck row 1: Chain 1, 6 single crochet. YO and draw up loop in each of next 2 stitches. YO and draw through all 3 loops. Turn. Don't work the rest of the stitches.
- Row 2: Chain 1, single crochet 2 stitches together (decrease). Single crochet to end of row. Turn.
- Row 3: Chain 1, single crochet to last 2 stitches, decrease. Turn.
- Rows 4-13: Work even single crochet to end of each row.
- Next row: (wrong side facing) Chain 1, 2 single crochet in first stitch, 1 single crochet to last 2 stitches, decrease. Turn.
- Next row: Chain 1, decrease, single crochet to last stitch, decrease. Turn.
- Repeat last 2 rows twice. Tie off and weave ends through work.
- With right side facing, skip 11 stitches, join main color with a slip stitch to the next stitch, chain 1. Decrease, single crochet to end of row. Turn.
- Work the same way as you did for the other side, only in reverse.
- Edging round 1: Join second color with slip stitch at top corner of neck edge. Chain 1, single crochet in same space as last slip stitch. Single crochet all the way around, join to first stitch with a slip stitch.
- Round 2 (only on outer edge, not neck hole): Chain 1. * 3 single crochet, chain 3, slip stitch in first chain (picot stitch). Repeat from * to other side. Tie off. Chain 8, and join with a slip stitch to make a button loop.
- Go around the inside part of the neck with single crochet in second color. Tie off and weave ends through work.

Finishing

Sew a button to other neck strap.

August 6

Open Work Summer Infinity Scarf

Materials

- Lightweight cotton yarn
- Crochet hook size 9 mm

Directions

Crochet a chain of 14 stitches.

Row 1: Skip first chain, single crochet to end of row. Chain 1 and turn.

Rows 2-end: Single crochet to end of row, chain 1 and turn. Work this pattern until piece reaches desired length (the longer the better because it looks really cool and you can wrap it around your neck several times). At end of last row, join ends with a slip stitch.

Finishing
- Put a tassel every 4-5 inches all the way around.
- If you want a finished edge, single crochet all the way along each side.

August 7

Shelled Bookmark

Materials

- Cotton crochet thread, variegated and white
- Crochet hook size 2.25 mm

Directions

- Crochet a chain of 8 stitches with variegated thread. Join with slip stitch to create a ring.
- Round 1: Chain 3, 3 double crochet, chain 2, 3 double crochet in ring. Turn.
- Round 2: * Chain 3, 3 double crochet, chain 2, 3 double crochet in center of previous chain 2 space of shell. Double crochet in top of chain 3. Repeat from * until you have 17 rows of shells. Tie off and weave ends through work.

Edging

With white thread, join with slip stitch, chain 1, and single crochet all the way around shell rows. Repeat with a second round of single crochet. Tie off and weave ends through work.

August 8

Kids' Super Hero Cape

Materials

- Red Heart Super Saver yarn
- Crochet hook size 10 mm

Directions

- Crochet a chain of 34 stitches.
- Row 1: Skip first 2 chains, double crochet in next stitch and in each stitch to end of row. Chain 2 and turn.
- Rows 2-7: Double crochet in each stitch. Chain 2 and turn.
- Row 8: Double crochet first 2 stitches together (decrease). Double crochet in each stitch to last 2 stitches, decrease. Chain 2 and turn.
- Rows 9-10: Double crochet in each stitch. Chain 2 and turn.
- Row 11: Decrease, double crochet to last 2 stitches, decrease. Chain 2 and turn.
- Row 12: Double crochet in each stitch. Chain 2 and turn.
- Row 13: Decrease, double crochet to last 2 stitches, decrease. Chain 2 and turn.
- Row 14: Double crochet in each stitch. Chain 2 and turn.
- Row 15: Decrease, double crochet to last 2 stitches, decrease. Chain 2 and turn.
- Row 16: Double crochet in each stitch. Chain 1, don't turn.

Finishing
- Row 1: Single crochet around to opposite side of row 16, with 2 single crochet in each corner.
- Row 2: Chain 31, slip stitch in 2nd chain from hook and each chain, single crochet in same stitch of corner. Single crochet to top of row 16 to opposite corner, with 1 single crochet in that corner. Chain 31, slip stitch in 2nd chain from hook and each chain, single crochet in same stitch of row 16 corner. Join with slip stitch to first single crochet. Tie off and weave ends through work.

August 9

Kids' Super Hero Mask

Materials

- Red Heart Super Saver yarn
- Crochet hook size 10 mm

Directions

- Crochet a chain of 13 stitches.
- Row 1: Skip first chain, single crochet in next chain and in each chain to end of row. Chain 1 and turn.
- Row 2: Single crochet first 2 stitches together (decrease). Chain 5, skip 3 stitches, 2 single crochet, chain 5, skip 3 stiches, decrease, chain 1 and turn.
- Row 3: Single crochet in first stitch, 5 single crochet in chain 5 space, 2 single crochet, 5 single crochet in chain 5 space, 1 single crochet. Chain 1.
- Row 4: Slip stitch up side of mask to row 1. Chain 32 and turn.

- Row 5: Skip first chain, single crochet in next chain and in each stitch to end of chain. Join with slip stitch to mask. Slip stitch across top of row 1 to other corner. Chain 32, skip first chain, single crochet in each chain to end. Slip stitch to back of mask. Tie off and weave ends through work.

August 10

Survival Whistle Bracelet

Materials

- 15 feet of paracord
- Crochet hook size 10 mm
- 3/8" shackle (available at hardware stores)
- Survival whistle

Directions

- Crochet a chain of 11 stitches.
- Row 1: Skip first chain, single crochet in each chain to end of row. Chain 1 and turn.
- Row 2: Skip first stitch, single crochet in each stitch to end of row. Tie off, leave ends.

Finishing
- Tie each end of bracelet to shackle ends.
- Attach survival whistle to shackle. Weave ends or tie in a couple of knots to secure.

August 11

Hippy Headpiece

Materials

- Red Heart Super Saver yarn (2 colors for flowers and band)
- Crochet hook size 3.75 mm
- Buttons (should contrast with flower color)
- Needle and thread

Directions

Headband

With 2 strands of yarn, crochet a chain of 100 stitches, or long enough to wrap around your head twice. Join with a slip stitch to create a ring, being careful not to twist chain. Tie off.

Flowers (make 12)
- Crochet a chain of 4 stitches. Join with slip stitch to create a ring.
- Round 1: Chain 2, 8 single crochet in ring.
- Round 2: Chain 2, triple crochet in same space, double crochet in same space, slip stitch in next space, 1 double crochet, 2 triple crochet, and 1 double crochet in next space, slip stitch in next space. Repeat until you have 5 petals. Tie off.

Finishing

Fasten 1 flower with button using needle and thread to headband. Twist chains, and attach next flower. Continue until all of the flowers are attached.

August 12

Hooded Baby Blanket

Materials

- Soft baby yarn
- Crochet hook size 6 mm

Directions

Special Stitch Pattern

- Row 1: Skip 2 stitches, 2 double crochet in next stitch. * Skip 2 stitches, 1 single crochet and 2 double crochet in next stitch. Repeat from * to end of row, ending on skip 2. Chain 1, single crochet in last stitch. Chain 1 and turn.
- Row 2: 2 double crochet in first stitch. * Skip 2 stitches, 1 single crochet and 2 double crochet in next stitch. Repeat from * to end of row, ending with a single crochet on top of chain. Chain 2 and turn.
- Row 3: Repeat row 2.

Blanket

Crochet a chain of 108 stitches. Work special stitch pattern until piece measures 28". Tie off.

Hood

- Crochet a chain of 4 stitches.
- Row 1: 2 double crochet in 4th chain from hook. Chain 3 and turn.
- Row 2: 2 double crochet in first stitch, 1 double crochet, 3 double crochet in top of t-chain. Chain 3 and turn.
- Row 3: 6 double crochet, 2 double crochet in top of t-chain. Chain 3 and turn.
- Row 4: 2 double crochet in first stitch, double crochet in each stitch to t-chain, 3 double crochet at top of t-chain. Chain 3 and turn.
- Row 5: Double crochet in each stitch to t-chain, 3 double crochet at top of t-chain. Chain 3 and turn. Repeat rows 4-5 until there are 48 double crochet and 1 t-chain. Chain 3 and turn.
- Edging row: 2 double crochet in first stitch. * Skip 2 stitches, 1 single crochet and 2 double crochet in next stitch. Repeat from * to end, ending with 1 single crochet in t-chain. Tie off.

Finishing

Lay right side of hood over a blanket corner, making sure edges match up. Stitch with slip stitch, and work row 2 of pattern all the way around.

August 13

Bolster

Materials

- Worsted weight yarn
- Crochet hook size 5.5 mm
- Fiberfill stuffing

Directions

- Crochet a chain measuring 24". Join with slip stitch to create a ring, being careful not to twist chain.
- Round 1: Skip first chain, double crochet in each chain to end of round.
- Round 2: Chain 2, skip first stitch, double crochet in each stitch to end of round. Repeat round 2 until piece measures 6".
- Next round: Chain 1, skip first stitch, single crochet to end of round.
- Repeat round 2 until piece measures 42 inches.
- Next round: Chain 2, skip first stitch, double crochet in each stitch to end of round. Repeat round until section measures 6".

Finishing
- Crochet 2 chains measuring 24".
- Weave 1 chain through last row of double crochet before single crochet begins. Pull tight and tie in a bow.
- Stuff bolster firmly with fiberfill stuffing.
- Weave second chain through double crochet at other end, pull tight and tie in a bow. Bolster should look like a huge piece of wrapped candy.

August 14

Walker Organizer

Materials

- Red Heart Super Saver yarn
- Crochet hook size 5 mm
- Velcro
- Needle and thread

Directions

- Crochet a chain measuring 18".
- Row 1: Skip first chain, single crochet to end of row. Turn.
- Row 2: Chain 1, skip first stitch, single crochet to end of row. Turn.
- Rows 3-end: Repeat row 2 until piece measures 18".

Pockets (make 3)
- Crochet a chain measuring 5".
- Row 1: Skip first chain, single crochet to end of row. Turn.
- Row 2: Chain 1, skip first stitch, single crochet to end of row. Turn.

- Rows 3-end: Repeat row 2 until piece measures 8".

Finishing
- Mark 6 inches down from top of main piece. Attach Velcro to top edge with needle and thread (or with a sewing machine for a more secure stitch), and attach the other piece of Velcro at the 6" mark. This section folds over and attaches to the front section of the walker.
- Lay main piece flat, and arrange pockets on front. Stitch pockets on using a slip stitch. Tie off all ends and weave through work.

August 15

Yarn Barn

Materials

- Worsted weight yarn
- Crochet hook size 5 mm

Directions

- Crochet a chain of 5 stitches. Join with a slip stitch to create a ring.
- Round 1: 5 double crochet in ring.
- Round 2: Chain 2, 2 double crochet in each stitch to end of round.
- Round 3: Chain 2, double crochet in each stitch to end of round.
- Rounds 4-end of bottom: Continue increasing until piece measures 6" across.
- Side round 1: Chain 2, skip first stitch, double crochet in each stitch to end of round.
- Rounds 2-end: Repeat side round 1 until piece measures 15".
- Edging row: 2 double crochet in each stitch to end of round. Tie off and weave ends through work.

Finishing
- Crochet a chain measuring 18" and tie off.
- Weave chain through double crochet stitches, 3" down from top. This is the drawstring to open and close the yarn barn.

August 16

Rainbow Tie Belt

Materials

- Worsted weight yarn in multiple colors (red, yellow, green, blue, etc.)
- Crochet hook size 5 mm

Directions

- Crochet a chain of 10 stitches with any color
- Row 1: Skip first chain, single crochet in each chain to end of row. Turn.
- Row 2: Chain 1, skip first stitch, single crochet in each stitch to end of row. Turn.

- Row 3: Switch to another color, and repeat row 2 twice. Keep switching colors and repeating row 2 twice until piece measures 48". Tie off and weave ends through work.

Finishing

Add fringes to each short end of belt.

August 17

Stress Squishee

Materials

- Crochet cotton
- Crochet hook size 3.5 mm
- Fiberfill stuffing

Directions

- Crochet a chain of 5 stitches. Join with a slip stitch to create a ring.
- Round 1: 5 single crochet in ring. Chain 1.
- Round 2: 2 single crochet in each stitch to end of round.
- Round 3: Chain 1, 2 single crochet in each stitch to end of round.
- Round 4: Chain 1, 2 single crochet in each stitch to end of round.
- Round 5: Chain 1, single crochet in each stitch to end of round. Repeat this round until piece measures 4".
- Next round: Single crochet 2 stitches together all the way around (decrease).
- Next round: Single crochet in each stitch all the way around.
- Stuff with fiberfill stuffing.
- Next round: Decrease all the way around. Continue decreasing until there are just 2-3 stitches remaining. Pull tight, tie off, and weave ends through work.

August 18

Tube Dress for 11" Fashion Doll

Materials

- Cotton embroidery floss
- Crochet hook size 2 mm
- Tiny snaps or narrow strip of Velcro
- Needle and thread

Directions

- Crochet a chain of 32 stitches.
- Row 1: Skip first 2 chains, single crochet in next chain and in each chain to end of row. Turn.
- Row 2: Chain 2, single crochet in each stitch to end of row. Turn.
- Rows 3-end: Repeat row 2 until piece measures 6-7". Tie off and weave ends through work.

Finishing

Attach tiny snaps all the way along back seam, or attach strips of Velcro.

August 19

Baby Jingle Ring Toy

Materials

- Scraps of worsted weight yarn
- Crochet hook size 4.25 mm
- 3 jingle bells
- Fiberfill stuffing

Directions

Thinner rings (make 2)
- Crochet a chain of 6 stitches. Join with a slip stitch to create a ring.
- Round 1: Single crochet in each stitch around ring. Continue to do this, stuffing every inch or so, until piece measures 6-7". Finish stuffing and stitch ends together to create a large ring. Tie off and weave ends through work.

Jingle Ring
- Crochet a chain of 6 stitches. Join with a slip stitch to create a ring.
- Rounds 1-5: Single crochet around ring, do not join. Place stitch marker to keep track of rounds, moving at the end of each round. Stuff this section.
- Round 6: 1 single crochet, 2 single crochet in next stitch, 1 single crochet, 2 single crochet in next stitch, 1 single crochet.
- Round 7: 1 single crochet, 2 single crochet in next stitch, 3 single crochet, 2 single crochet in next stitch, 2 single crochet.
- Round 8: Single crochet in each stitch to end of round.
- Round 9: Single crochet, single crochet 2 stitches together (decrease), 3 single crochet, decrease, 2 single crochet. Stuff 1 bell into this section.
- Round 10: Single crochet in each stitch to end of round.
- Rounds 11-16: Single crochet in each stitch to end of round. Stuff section.
- Rounds 17-21: Repeat rounds 6-10.
- Rounds 22-27: Repeat rounds 11-16.
- Rounds 28-32: Repeat rounds 6-10.
- Round 33: Single crochet in each stitch to end of round. Finish stuffing section. Slide one end through 2 thinner rings, attach at the end to form the jingle ring. Tie off and weave ends through work.

August 20

Table Runner

Materials

- Red Heart Super Saver yarn, white and variegated
- Crochet hook size 6.5 mm

Directions

- Crochet a chain of 31 stitches with variegated yarn.
- Row 1: Skip first chain, single crochet in each chain to end of row. Chain 1 and turn.

- Row 2: Skip first stitch, single crochet in each stitch to end of row. Chain 1 and turn.
- Row 3: Repeat row 2 until piece measures 8". Switch to white yarn.
- Next row: Skip first stitch, single crochet to end of row. Chain 1 and turn.
- Repeat last row until white section measures 12".
- Next row: Attach variegated yarn, and work in single crochet until section measures 8". Tie off ends and weave through work.

August 21

Computer Mouse Wrist Cushion

Materials

- Sport weight yarn
- Crochet hook size 4 mm
- Scraps of fabric
- Uncooked rice
- Needle and thread

Directions

Make 2
- Crochet a chain measuring 6".
- Row 1: Skip first chain, single crochet in next chain and in each chain to end of row. Turn.
- Row 2: Chain 1, skip first stitch, single crochet in next stitch and in each stitch to end of row. Turn.
- Rows 3-end: Repeat row 2 until piece measures 4'. Tie off ends and weave through work.

Finishing
- Lay both pieces together, and stitch up 3 sides with slip stitch.
- Make a cloth bag that will fit inside the crochet work. Fill bag with rice and stitch shut.
- Insert rice bag into crochet work. Close last side with slip stitch. Tie off ends and weave through work.

August 22

Dresser Scarf

Materials

- #10 bedspread cotton (2 colors)
- Crochet hook size 3.25 mm

Directions

- With one strand of each color, crochet a chain of 46 stitches.
- Row 1: Skip first 3 chains, double crochet in next chain and in each chain to end of row. Turn.
- Row 2: Chain 3. * Skip next stitch, 2 double crochet, 1 double crochet in skipped double crochet. Repeat from * to last stitch, 1 double crochet.
- Rows 3-24: Repeat row 2.
- Row 25: Chain 3, double crochet in each stitch to end of row. Switch to 2 strands of the same color.

Edging

- Row 1: Chain 1, single crochet around post of last double crochet. 2 single crochet around post of last double crochet in each row. Single crochet around post of double crochet at end of last row. Join with a slip stitch at top of same stitch.
- Row 2: Chain 3, double crochet in each stitch around, with 1 double crochet, chain 1, 1 double crochet, chain 1, 1 double crochet in each corner. Join with slip stitch to top of first chain 3.
- Row 3: Slip stitch between next 2 stitches. Chain 3, double crochet in same space. 2 double crochet in space between next 2 stitches, all the way around. Join with slip stitch at top of first chain 3. Tie off and weave ends through work.

August 23

Round Scalloped Dishcloth

Materials

- Worsted weight yarn
- Crochet hook size 5 mm

Directions

- Crochet a chain of 3 stitches.
- Round 1: 10 half double crochet in 3rd chain from hook. Join with slip stitch to first stitch.
- Round 2: Chain 2, 2 half double crochet in each stitch to end of round. Join with slip stitch to first stitch.
- Round 3: Chain 2. * 2 half double crochet in next stitch, 1 half double crochet. Repeat from * to end of round. Join.
- Round 4: Chain 2. * 2 half double crochet in next stitch, 2 half double crochet. Repeat from * to end of round. Join.
- Round 5: Chain 2. * 2 half double crochet in next stitch, 3 half double crochet. Repeat from * to end of round. Join.
- Round 6: Chain 2. * 2 half double crochet in next stitch, 4 half double crochet. Repeat from * to end of round. Join.
- Round 7: Chain 2. * 2 half double crochet in next stitch, 5 half double crochet. Repeat from * to end of round. Join.
- Round 8: Chain 1. * 2 single crochet in next stitch, 6 single crochet. Repeat from * to end of round. Join.
- Round 9: Chain 1. * 2 single crochet in next stitch, 7 single crochet. Repeat from * to end of round. Join.
- Round 10: * Chain 3, 3 double crochet in same space as slip stitch. Skip 2 stitches, slip stitch in next stitch. Repeat from * to end of round. Tie off and weave ends through work.

August 24

Crochet Wire Bracelet

Materials

- 24 gauge silver colored craft wire (or sterling silver wire if you like)
- Crochet hook size 3 mm
- Beads

- Bracelet clasp (available at craft stores in jewelry findings)

Directions

Using wire as yarn, crochet a chain measuring 7.5", adding a bead every ½". Do this by placing all of the beads on the wire before you start working, and slip 1 bead into a chain stitch.

Wrap ends of wire around each end of bracelet clasp several times, twist around bracelet ends, and cut with wire cutters.

August 25

Trinket Basket

Materials

- Worsted weight yarn
- Crochet hook size 5 mm
- Fabric stiffener (equal parts of white glue and water)

Directions

Bottom
- Crochet a chain measuring 6".
- Row 1: Skip first chain, single crochet to end of row. Turn.
- Row 2: Chain 1, skip first stitch, single crochet to end of row. Turn. Repeat this row until piece measures 6". Tie off and weave ends through work.

Sides (make 4)
- Crochet a chain measuring 6.5".
- Row 1: Skip first chain, single crochet to end of row. Turn.
- Row 2: Chain 1, skip first stitch, single crochet to end of row. Turn. Repeat this row until piece measures 4". Tie off and weave ends through work.

Finishing
- Attach the side pieces together using single crochet stitches on outsides of pieces to give an edge.
- Attach sewn side pieces to bottom of box.
- Soak box in fabric stiffener, let dry overnight.

August 26

Bingo Bag

Materials

- Worsted weight yarn
- Crochet hook size 5 mm

Directions

Bag section
- Crochet a chain of 5 stitches. Join with a slip stitch to create a ring.
- Round 1: 12 half double crochet in ring. Do not join. Place a stitch marker and move it after every round to keep track of your work.
- Round 2: 2 half double crochet in each stitch to end of round.
- Round 3: Repeat round 2.
- Rounds 4-5: 1 half double crochet in each stitch to end of round.
- Round 6: * 3 half double crochet, 2 half double crochet in next stitch. Repeat from * to end of round.
- Rounds 7-24: Half double crochet in each stitch around. Slip stitch to join in last stitch.
- Drawstring round: Chain 3, skip 1 stitch. * 1 half double crochet, chain 1. Repeat from * to end.
- Edging round: * Chain 3, 1 double crochet, chain 1, 1 double crochet, chain 1, 1 double crochet, chain 3, slip stitch in next stitch. Repeat from * to end of round. Tie off and weave ends through work.

Pocket
- Crochet a chain of 40 stitches. Join with slip stitch to create a ring, being careful not to twist chain.
- Round 1: Chain 1, 50 half double crochet in loop. Do not join.
- Round 2: Half double crochet in each stitch to end of round.
- Round 3: * 1 half double crochet, 2 half double crochet in next stitch. Repeat from * to end of round.
- Round 4: Repeat round 3.
- Rounds 5-14: Half double crochet in each stitch to end of round. Join with slip stitch at end of last round. Tie off and weave ends through work.

Finishing
- Stitch pocket to bottom of bag with a slip stitch. Every 14 stitches all the way around, stitch a line going up the side of the pocket. This way you will have multiple pockets all the way around bag. Tie off and weave ends through work.
- Crochet a chain measuring 18".
- Weave chain through drawstring section of bag.

August 27

Mile-a-Minute Afghan

Materials

- Worsted weight yarn
- Crochet hook size 5.5 mm

Directions

Make 12 strips. Each strip is a super-long round.
- Crochet a chain of 172 stitches.
- Round 1: Skip first 3 chains, 5 double crochet in next chain. * Skip 3 chains, 1 double crochet, chain 1, 1 double crochet in next chain (V-stitch). Skip 3 chains, 5 double crochet in next chain (shell). Repeat from * to last 8 stitches. Skip 3 chains, V-stitch in next chain, skip 3 chains, 11 double crochet in last chain. Work

around to opposite side of chain, skip 3 chains, V-stitch in chain under V-stitch on other side of chain. **
Skip next chain 3, 1 shell under next shell. Skip 3 stitches, V-stitch in chain under next V-stitch. Repat from
**, ending with skip 3 chain. 1 shell in chain under last shell. Join with slip stitch.

- Round 2: Chain 3, 3 double crochet in next stitch. Skip a stitch, V-stitch. * Skip 3 stitches, 1 shell in chain 1 space of next V-stitch. Skip 3 stitches, V-stitch in next stitch. Repeat from * to end of strip. V-stitch in 3rd double crochet of 11 double crochet at end of strip. Skip 2 stitches. 7 double crochet in next stitch (middle of 11 stitch shell). Skip 2 stitches, V-stitch in next stitch. Repeat from * to end, ending with 3 double crochet in top of chain 3 of first round. Join.
- Round 3: Chain 3, 3 double crochet in same space as last slip stitch. Skip next stitch, V-stitch in next stitch, skip 3 stitches. 1 shell in chain 1 space of next V-stitch. * Skip 3 stitches, V-stitch in next stitch (center of shell). Skip 3 stitches, shell in chain 1 space of next V-stitch. Repeat from * across, ending with skip next 2 stitches. V-stitch in next stitch. Skip next 3 stitches, 3 double crochet in same space as first slip stitch. Slip stitch to the top of beginning chain 3. Tie off and weave ends through work.

Finishing
- With single crochet, stitch each strip together.
- Add a tassel to the point of each strip.

August 28

Baby Rattle

Materials

- Baby yarn
- Crochet hook size 3.75 mm
- 1/8" ribbon
- Film canister
- Uncooked rice
- Craft stick

Directions

- Crochet a chain of 3 stitches.
- Round 1: 7 half double crochet in 3rd chain from hook. Single crochet in the top of first chain 3 to join.
- Round 2: Single crochet in each stitch. Keep working in rounds until piece measures about 4", or long enough to cover craft stick.
- Next round (top section): 2 single crochet in each stitch to end of round.
- Next round: Single crochet in each stitch. Continue working in rounds until piece is long enough to cover film canister. Join with slip stitch.
- Next round: Chain 4, single crochet in each stitch around. Slip stitch in next chain 4 space.
- Next round: Chain 3, 1 double crochet, chain 2, 2 double crochet in next space. 2 double crochet, chain 2, 2 double crochet in each chain 4 space. Join with slip stitch. Tie off.

Finishing
- Weave ribbon through chain 4 spaces on round 2.
- Poke a hole in bottom of film canister and insert a craft stick.
- Fill film canister half way with uncooked rice. Place lid on top and tape to hold it shut.
- Slide craft stick into crochet piece.

- Wrap top of crochet piece around film canister.
- Pull ribbon tight, tie a tight knot, make a bow, and tie the bow in a double knot to secure. Tie off all ends and weave through work.

August 29

Oval Placemat

Materials

- Worsted weight yarn, variegated
- Crochet hook size 5 mm

Directions

- Crochet a chain of 10 stitches.
- Round 1: Skip first chain, single crochet to end of row. Turn and work single crochet along other side of chain. Place stitch marker and move it after each round to keep track of your work.
- Round 2: Double crochet in each stitch to end of round.
- Round 3: Single crochet in each stitch to end of round.
- Rounds 4-end: Repeat rows 2 and 3 until piece reaches desired size, ending with single crochet round. Tie off and weave ends through work.

August 30

Striped Scarf for American Girl Dolls

Materials

- Worsted weight yarn (3 colors)
- Crochet hook size 5.5 mm

Directions

- Crochet a chain measuring 6".
- Row 1: Skip first chain, double crochet in each chain to end of row. Turn.
- Row 2: Chain 2, skip first stitch, double crochet in each stitch to end of row. Turn.
- Rows 3-4: Switch to second color, repeat row 2.
- Rows 5-6: Switch to third color, repeat row 2.
- Repeat stripe pattern until piece reaches desired length (about 24")

Finishing
- Add fringes to each end of the scarf.
- Tie a knot at each end of the scarf.

August 31

Chair Blanket

Materials

- Worsted weight yarn (2 colors)
- Crochet hook size 5 mm

Directions

- Crochet a chain measuring 18".
- Row 1: Skip first chain, single crochet in each stitch to end of row. Turn.
- Row 2: Chain 2, skip first stitch, double crochet in each stitch to end of row. Turn.
- Row 3: Chain 1, skip first stitch, single crochet in each stitch to end of row. Turn.
- Rows 4-end: Repeat rows 2 and 3 until piece measures 36". Tie off and weave ends through work.

Edging

Attach second color of yarn to 1 corner of the chair blanket. * Chain 2, skip a stitch, 3 double crochet in next stitch. Repeat from * to end of edge. For each corner, 3 double crochet, chain 1, 3 double crochet in corner stitch. Continue this pattern all the way around chair blanket. Tie off and weave ends through work.

September

Summer is over, and the kids are back at school. That means you have even more time to enjoy some fun crochet projects that you can easily do in a few hours. This month, you will find some fun back to school patterns, including a pencil case and a backpack, as well as loads of other great patterns such as scarves, hats, and even a beanbag chair.

September 1

Pencil Case

Materials

- Worsted weight yarn
- Crochet hook size 5 mm
- Button
- Needle and thread

Directions

- Crochet a chain measuring 3".
- Row 1: Skip first chain, single crochet in each chain to end of row. Turn.
- Row 2: Skip first stitch, single crochet in each stitch to end of row. Turn.
- Rows 3-end: Repeat row 2 until piece measures 18".

Finishing
- Measure 8", and fold at this spot. You will have 2" of overhang.
- Stitch up sides of case using a slip stitch.
- Crochet a chain measuring 2 inches.
- Stitch chain to edge of overhang at the center to form a button loop.
- With needle and thread, sew the button onto the front of the pencil case.

September 2

Jewelry Hanger/Organizer

Materials

- Worsted weight yarn
- Crochet hook size 5.5 mm
- 12"X14" piece of felt
- Needle and thread
- 14" dowel rod and ball ends (available at hardware stores and craft stores)

Directions

- Crochet 5 chains measuring 10".
- Row 1: Skip first chain, single crochet in each stitch to end of chain. Tie off and weave ends through work.

Finishing
- Lay felt flat, and wrap one end around dowel rod (from 14" side). Sew in place with the needle and thread.
- With the needle and thread, attach each chain to the felt so they go across, with a 1" border on either side. Hang earrings, necklaces, and bracelets from the chains.

September 3

Kids' Overstuffed Beanbag-Style Chair

Materials

- 5-6 Skeins Red Heart Super Saver Yarn
- Crochet hook size 5 mm
- Fiberfill stuffing

Directions

- Crochet a chain of 5 stitches. Join with a slip stitch to create a ring.
- Round 1: 15 single crochet in ring. Place stitch marker here, and move at the end of each round to keep track of your work.
- Round 2: Chain 1, 2 single crochet in each stitch to end of round. Join with a slip stitch.
- Round 3: Chain 1. * 2 single crochet in next stitch, 1 single crochet. Repeat from * to end of round.
- Rounds 4-end: Repeat round 3 until piece is as big around as you want it.
- Next round: Chain 1, single crochet in each stitch to end of round.
- Next rounds: Repeat last round until piece is the height that you want.
- Next round: Count the stitches in the round, and place markers where the increases will go (there should be 16 increases in each round). Single crochet to the marker, 2 single crochet in next stitch. Continue in this manner until the end of the round. Repeat this round until there is an opening at the top of the beanbag chair that is about 6".

Finishing
- Stuff chair with fiberfill stuffing.
- Continue decrease rounds until chair is closed. Tie off and weave ends through work.

September 4

Coupon Wallet

Materials

- Worsted weight yarn
- Crochet hook size 5 mm
- Velcro
- Needle and thread

Directions

- Crochet a chain measuring 7".
- Row 1: Skip first chain, single crochet in each chain to end of row. Turn.
- Row 2: Chain 1, skip first stitch, single crochet in each stitch to end of row. Turn.
- Rows 3-end: Repeat row 2 until piece measures 8". Tie off and weave ends through work.

Finishing
- Fold piece so that there is a 2" overhang.
- Stitch up sides using a slip stitch.
- Attach Velcro with needle and thread to front of wallet and to underside of flap.

September 5

Tissue Box Cover

Materials

- Worsted weight yarn
- Crochet hook size 4.5 mm

Directions

Sides (done in 1 piece)
- Crochet a chain of 19 stitches.
- Row 1: Skip first chain, single crochet in each stitch to end of row. Turn.
- Rows 2-17: Chain 1, single crochet in each stitch to end of row. Turn.
- Row 18: Single crochet in the back loops only in each stitch to end of row.
- Rows 19-35: Chain 1, single crochet in each stitch to end of row. Turn.
- Row 36: Repeat row 18.
- Rows 37-52: Repeat row 19.
- Row 53: Repeat row 18.
- Rows 54-68: Repeat row 19.
- Row 69: Slip stitch sides together to create an open-ended box.

Top
- Crochet a chain of 18 stitches.
- Row 1: Skip first chain, single crochet in each chain to end of row. Turn.
- Rows 2-8: Chain 1, single crochet in each stitch to end of row. Turn.
- Row 9: Chain 1, 6 single crochet, 5 slip stitches, 6 single crochet. Turn.
- Row 10: Chain 1, 6 single crochet, chain 5, 6 single crochet. Turn.
- Rows 11-18: Chain 1, single crochet in each stitch to end of row.

Finishing

Using a slip stitch, sew the top to the sides.

September 6

Slouchy Beret

Materials

- Red Heart Soft Yarn
- Crochet hook size 6 mm

Directions

- Crochet a chain of 4 stitches.
- Round 1: 15 double crochet in fourth chain from hook. Slip stitch to join.

- Round 2: Chain 3, 1 double crochet in same stitch as chain 2. Double crochet in each stitch to end of round. Join.
- Round 3: Chain 3. * 1 double crochet, 2 double crochet in next stitch. Repeat from * to end of round. Join.
- Round 4: Chain 3. * 2 double crochet, 2 double crochet in next stitch. Repeat from * to end of round. Join.
- Round 5: Chain 3: * 3 double crochet, 2 double crochet in next stitch. Repeat from * to end of round. Join.
- Rounds 6-13: Chain 3, double crochet in each stitch to end of round. Join.
- Round 14: Chain 3. * 3 double crochet, double crochet 2 stitches together (decrease). Repeat from * to end of round. Join.
- Round 15: Chain 2, 1 single crochet, single crochet 2 stitches together (decrease). * 2 single crochet, decrease. Repeat from * to end of round. Join.
- Rounds 16-17: Chain 2, single crochet in each stitch. Join. Tie off and weave ends through work.

September 7

Toddler Scarf

Materials

- Red Heart Soft Yarn
- Crochet hook size 6 mm

Directions

- Crochet a chain measuring 6".
- Row 1: Skip first chain, double crochet in each stitch to end of row. Turn.
- Row 2: Chain 2, skip first stitch, double crochet in each stitch to end of row. Turn.
- Row 3: Chain 1, skip first stitch, single crochet in each stitch to end of row. Turn.
- Row 4: Repeat row 3.
- Row 5: Repeat row 2.
- Row 6: Repeat row 2.
- Rows 7-end: Continue working patterns in 2 rows of row 2 and 2 rows of row 3 until piece measures 36". Tie off and weave ends through work.

Finishing
- Put a fringe along each edge of scarf.
- Tie each end of scarf in a knot.

September 8

Tube and Chain Necklace

Materials

- Crochet thread, various colors
- Crochet hook size 3 mm
- Necklace clasp (available at craft stores in jewelry findings)

Directions

- Crochet a chain of 4 stitches. Join with slip stitch to create a ring. Make sure these stitches are loose, so you can gather them up to tighten the end later.
- Round 1: 4 single crochet in ring. Work in rounds, do not join. Place stitch marker and move after each round to keep track of your work.
- Round 2: 2 single crochet in each stitch to end of round.
- Next rounds: Single crochet in each stitch to end of round. Continue in this manner until piece measures 1".
- Next round: Single crochet 2 stitches together all the way around. Pull tight to close, chain 5, switch colors. Chain 4, join with slip stitch at beginning of chain.
- Repeat pattern for this color, and for each subsequent color until necklace reaches desired length. Tie off, do not weave ends through work.

Finishing

Tie thread tails to each end of the necklace clasp.

September 9

Lunch Money Pouch

Materials

- Worsted weight yarn
- Crochet hook size 5 mm

Directions

- Crochet a chain of 4 stitches. Join with a slip stitch to create a ring.
- Round 1: 5 single crochet in loop. Place stitch marker to mark end of round, move after each round to keep track of your work.
- Round 2: 2 single crochet in each stitch to end of round.
- Round 3: * 2 single crochet in next stitch, 1 single crochet. Repeat from * to end of round.
- Round 4: Repeat round 3. Continue working increase round until piece measures 4" across.
- Next round: Single crochet in each stitch to end of round. Continue working in single crochet until piece measures 6".
- Next round: Double crochet in each stitch to end of round.
- Last round: 2 single crochet in each stitch to end of round. Tie off and weave ends through work.

Finishing
- Crochet a chain measuring 12". Do not tie off.
- Weave chain through double crochet round of bag.
- Join chain with a slip stitch. This is the drawstring and handle for the lunch money pouch. Tie off.

September 10

Doggie Treat Ball

Materials

- Cotton worsted weight yarn
- Crochet hook size 4.5 mm

Directions

- Round 1: Chain 2. 6 single crochet in second chain from hook.
- Round 2: 2 single crochet in each stitch.
- Round 3: * 1 single crochet, 2 single crochet in next stitch. Repeat from * to end of round.
- Round 4: * 2 single crochet, 2 single crochet in next stitch. Repeat from * to end of round.
- Round 5: * 3 single crochet, 2 single crochet in next stitch. Repeat from * to end of round.
- Rounds 6-10: Single crochet in each stitch to end of round.
- Round 11: * 3 single crochet, single crochet 2 stitches together (decrease). Repeat from * to end of round.
- Round 12: * 2 single crochet, decrease. Repeat from * to end of round.
- Round 13: * 1 single crochet, decrease. Repeat from * to end of round.
- Round 14: Decrease to end of round. Tie off and weave ends through work. Fill ball with your dog's favorite treats.

September 11

Pencil Holder Lanyard

Materials

- Worsted weight yarn
- Crochet hook size 5 mm

Directions

- Crochet a chain of 5 stitches. Join with a slip stitch to create a ring.
- Round 1: 5 double crochet in ring. Place stitch marker and move after each round to keep track of your work.
- Round 2: 2 double crochet in each stitch.
- Rounds 3-end: Double crochet in each stitch to end of round. Repeat until piece measures 7".

Lanyard Strap
- Row 1: At top of pencil holder, 3 double crochet. Turn.
- Rows 2-end: Chain 2, skip first stitch, 2 double crochet. Turn. Continue working this row until piece measures 36".

Finishing

Slip stitch end of strap to pencil holder. Tie off and weave ends through work.

September 12

Super-Simple Shrug

Materials

- Red Heart Super Saver yarn
- Crochet hook size 6 mm

Directions

- Crochet a chain of 101 stitches.
- Row 1: Skip first chain, single crochet in each chain to end of row. Turn.
- Row 2: Chain 1, single crochet in each stitch to end of row. Turn.
- Row 3: Chain 2, double crochet in each stitch to end of row. Turn.
- Row 4: Chain 3, triple crochet in each stitch to end of row. Turn.
- Rows 5-25: Repeat rows 2-4 7 times, or until piece fits nicely around your upper arms.
- Next row: Chain 1, single crochet in each stitch to end of row. Turn.
- Last row: Chain 1, single crochet in each stitch to end of row. Tie off and weave ends through work.

Finishing

Fold piece in half lengthwise, right sides together. At one end, slip stitch edges together for 20". Repeat on other side to make second sleeve.

September 13

Scrap Yarn Area Rug

Materials

- Scraps of worsted weight yarn
- Crochet hook size 6 mm

Directions

Working with scrap yarn, join a new color whenever a color runs out.
- Crochet a chain of 3 stitches. Join with a slip stitch to create a ring.
- Round 1: 8 single crochet in ring. Place stitch marker and move after each round to keep track of your work.
- Round 2: * 1 single crochet, 2 single crochet in next stitch. Repeat from * 3 times.
- Round 3: * 1 single crochet, 2 single crochet in next stitch. Repeat from * 5 times.
- Round 4: * 2 single crochet in next stitch, 2 single crochet. Repeat from * 5 times.
- Round 5: * 2 single crochet in next stitch, 3 single crochet. Repeat from * 5 times.
- Round 6: * 2 single crochet in next stitch, 4 single crochet. Repeat from * 5 times.
- Continue working in rounds, adding 1 single crochet to each set of stitches, until piece reaches desired size. Tie off and weave ends through work.

September 14

Lacy Belt

Materials

- Cotton crochet yarn
- Crochet hook size 5 mm
- Belt rings

Directions

Squares (make 14)
- Crochet a chain of 4 stitches. Join with a slip stitch to create a ring.
- Round 1: Chain 3, 11 double crochet in ring. Slip stitch in 3rd stitch of beginning chain to join.
- Round 2: Chain 3. * 2 double crochet and 1 triple crochet in next stitch, 1 triple crochet and 2 double crochet in next stitch (corner. Double crochet in next stitch. Repeat from * to end of round. Join.
- Round 3: Chain 1, 3 single crochet. * 2 single crochet in each of the next 2 stitches, 5 single crochet. Repeat from * twice, 2 single crochet in each of the next 2 stitches, 2 single crochet. Join, tie off and weave ends through work.

Finishing
- Stitch each square together with slip stitches. Tie off and weave ends through work.
- Attach belt rings to one end with slip stitches. Tie off and weave ends through work.

September 15

Baby Washcloth

Materials

- Cotton yarn, 2 colors
- Crochet hook size 3.75 mm

Directions

- Crochet a chain of 28 stitches.
- Row 1: Single crochet in each stitch to end of row. Turn.
- Row 2: Chain 1, 2 double crochet in first stitch. * Skip 2 stitches, 1 single crochet and 2 double crochet in next stitch. Repeat from * to last 3 stitches, skip 2 stitches, 1 single crochet. Turn.
- Row 3: Chain 1, 2 double crochet in first stitch. * Skip 3 stitches, 1 single crochet and 2 double crochet in next stitch. Repeat from * to last 3 stitches, skip 3 stitches, 1 single crochet. Turn. Repeat this row until piece measures 4".
- Last row: Single crochet to end of row. Tie off and weave ends through work.

Edging
- Row 1: Join second color with a slip stitch in first stitch of last row. Chain 1, 1 single crochet in same stitch. Single crochet in each stitch to last stitch, 3 single crochet in last stitch. Single crochet to next corner, 3 single crochet in corner. Continue in this manner all the way around. Turn.

- Row 2: Chain 2, half double crochet in each stitch to corner. 1 half double crochet in corner stitch, chain 9, 2 half double crochet in same corner stitch. Half double crochet in each stitch, with 3 half double crochet in each corner stitch. Tie off and weave ends through work.

September 16

Ear Warmer Headband

Materials

- Worsted weight yarn
- Crochet hook size 6 mm

Directions

- Crochet a chain of 11 stitches.
- Row 1: Skip first 2 chains, single crochet in 3rd chain. * Chain 1, skip next chain, single crochet. Repeat from * to end of row. Chain 1 and turn.
- Row 2: Single crochet in next chain 1 space, chain 1. Repeat to end of row. Chain 1 and turn.
- Rows 3-end: Repeat row 2 until piece is long enough to fit around your head.

Finishing

Slip stitch ends together. Decorate with crochet appliques found throughout this pattern book.

September 17

Back to School Backpack

Materials

- Worsted weight cotton yarn
- Crochet hook size 5 mm

Directions

- Crochet a chain of 4 stitches. Join with a slip stitch to create a ring.
- Round 1: Chain 1, 6 single crochet in ring. Join with slip stitch.
- Round 2: 2 single crochet in each stitch to end of round.
- Round 3: * 1 single crochet, 2 single crochet in next stitch. Repeat from * to end of round.
- Round 4: * 2 single crochet, 2 single crochet in next stitch. Repeat from * to end of round.
- Round 5: * 3 single crochet, 2 single crochet in next stitch. Repeat from * to end of round.
- Rounds 6-end: Single crochet to end of round. Continue until piece measures 15".
- Next round: 1 double crochet, chain 1, skip next stitch, 1 double crochet. Repeat to end of round.
- Next 3 rounds: Single crochet in each stitch and chain space to end of round. Tie off and weave ends through work.

Drawstring

Crochet a chain measuring 18-24". Weave through double crochet round in bag.

Straps (make 2)
- Crochet a chain measuring 2".
- Row 1: Skip first chain, single crochet to end of row. Turn.
- Row 2: Chain 1, skip first stitch, single crochet to end of row. Turn.
- Rows 3-end: Repeat row 2 until strap measures 14". Tie off and weave ends through work.

Finishing

Slip stitch straps to bag at top and bottom to create shoulder backpack straps.

September 18

Baby Cocoon

Materials

- Chunky or bulky yarn
- Crochet hook size 6 mm

Directions

- Crochet a chain of 5 stitches. Join with a slip stitch to create a ring.
- Round 1: 10 double crochet in ring. Join with a slip stitch.
- Round 2: Chain 2, double crochet in same stitch. 2 double crochet in each stitch to end of round.
- Rounds 3-4: Double crochet in same stitch and in each stitch to end of round.
- Round 5: 3 double crochet, 2 double crochet in next stitch. Repeat pattern to end of round.
- Round 6: 2 double crochet, 2 double crochet in next stitch. Repeat pattern to end of round.
- Rounds 7-10: Double crochet in each stitch to end of round.
- Round 11: 10 double crochet, 2 double crochet in next stitch. Repeat pattern to end of round.
- Round 12-34: Double crochet in each stitch to end of round. Add more rows if you need the cocoon to be longer.
- Round 35: 2 single crochet in each stitch to end of round. Tie off and weave ends through work.

September 19

Recipe Folder

Materials

- Worsted weight yarn
- Crochet hook size 5 mm
- Button
- Needle and thread

Directions

- Crochet a chain measuring 8".
- Row 1: Skip first chain, single crochet in each chain to end of row. Turn.
- Row 2: Chain 1, skip first stitch, single crochet in each stitch to end of row. Turn.
- Rows 3-end: Repeat row 2 until piece measures 8".
- Next row: Single crochet 2 stitches together to end of row. Turn.
- Next row: Single crochet each stitch to end of row. Turn.

- Next row: Single crochet 2 stitches together to end of row. Turn.
- Next row: Single crochet each stitch to end of row. Continue in decrease pattern until piece comes to a point. Chain 10, join with slip stitch (button loop). Tie off and weave ends through work.

Finishing
- Mark the first decrease row with a stitch marker. Fold piece so bottom edge meets this row.
- Stitch sides using a slip stitch.
- With needle and thread, sew button to front of folder so it meets up with the button loop on the flap.

September 20

Boys' Bow Ties

Materials

- Red Heart Super Saver yarn
- Crochet hook size 3.75 mm
- Button
- Needle and thread

Directions

Main section
- Crochet a chain of 37 stitches.
- Row 1: (back loops only) Skip first chain, single crochet in each stitch to end of row. Turn.
- Row 2: (working both loops now) Chain 1, single crochet in each stitch to end of row. Turn.
- Rows 3-7: Repeat row 2. Tie off and leave tail for stitching.

Center band
- Crochet a chain of 11 stitches.
- Row 1: (back loops only) Skip first chain, single crochet in each stitch to end of row. Turn.
- Row 2: Chain 1, single crochet in each stitch to end of row. Tie off and leave tail for stitching.

Collar
- Crochet a chain of 60 stitches.
- Row 1: Skip first chain, single crochet in each chain to end of row. Turn.
- Row 2: Chain 1, skip first stitch, single crochet in each stitch to end of row. Tie off and weave ends through work.

Finishing
- Wrap center band around middle part of main section, stitch in place with a slip stitch.
- Attach bow section to center of collar.
- With the needle and thread, sew button to one end of the collar. Spread apart a stitch on the other end to use as a buttonhole.

September 21

Checkerboard Dish Cloth

Materials

- Worsted weight cotton yarn, 2 colors
- Crochet hook size 5 mm (or size needed for a gauge of 5 single crochet per inch)

Directions

- Crochet a chain of 50 stiches.
- Row 1: 10 single crochet, switch to next color, 10 single crochet. Repeat pattern to end of row. Turn.
- Row 2: Chain 1, 9 single crochet in same color, switch to next color, 10 single crochet. Switch to next color, 10 single crochet. Switch colors as needed to end of row.
- Rows 3-end: Repeat row 2 until piece measures 10".

Edging

2 single crochet in each stitch all the way around piece.

September 22

Finger Puppet

Materials

- Scraps of worsted weight yarn, 2 colors
- Crochet hook size 5 mm
- Tiny googly eyes
- Small black bead
- Glue gun and glue

Directions

- Crochet a chain of 11 stitches. Join with a slip stitch to create a ring.
- Round 1: Single crochet in each chain around. Work in rounds and do not join.
- Rounds 2-4: Single crochet in each stitch to end of round.
- Round 5: Switch to second color on last stitch of last round. Single crochet in each stitch to end of round.
- Rounds 6-9: Repeat round 2.
- Round 10: Single crochet 2 stitches together, 5 times. Pull top closed, tie off and weave ends through work.

Finishing
- At top section, glue on eyes.
- With contrasting yarn, stitch on a mouth.
- Attach bead with glue for nose.

September 23

Sleepy Time Night Mask

Materials

- Worsted weight yarn, 2 colors
- Crochet hook size 5 mm
- ¼" elastic
- Needle and thread

Directions

- Crochet a chain of 39 stiches.
- Rows 1-10: Skip first stitch, chain 1, single crochet in each stitch to end of row. Tie off and weave ends through work.
- First eye: Join yarn at 8th stitch from end, 7 single crochet in 9th stitch to make a fan. Single crochet all the way around the fan, anchoring each side to the main section. Repeat as many rounds as needed for the size you want. Repeat on other side for other eye.

Finishing
- With contrasting yarn, single crochet all the way around mask.
- Cut a piece of elastic to fit comfortably around your head.
- Stitch elastic to mask with needle and thread.

September 24

Chunky Cowl

Materials

- Super chunky yarn
- Crochet hook size 10 mm

Directions

- Crochet a chain of 40 stitches. Join with slip stitch to create a ring, being careful not to twist the chain.
- Round 1: Chain 1, skip first chain, single crochet in next chain and in each stitch to end of round. Place stitch marker and move after every row to keep track of your work.
- Round 2: Chain 1, single crochet in each stitch to end of round.
- Rounds 3-end: Repeat round 2 until piece is the desired width. Tie off and weave ends through work.

September 25

Bulky Throw

Materials

- Red Heart Super Saver yarn, 3 colors
- Crochet hook size 16 mm

Directions

- With 1 strand of each color held together, crochet a chain of 67 stitches.
- Row 1: Skip first 4 chains, 1 double crochet in next chain. Chain 1, double crochet in same chain (V-stitch). * Skip 2 chains, 1 double crochet, chain 1, 1 double crochet in next chain (V-stitch). Repeat from * to last 2 chain, skip 1 chain, 1 double crochet.
- Rows 2-39: Chain 3, turn. 1 double crochet, chain 1, 1 double crochet in each chain 1 space. 1 double crochet in 3rd chain of turning chain. Tie off and weave ends through work.

Finishing

Add a fringe all the way around using 1 or more of the colors.

September 26

Ribbon Hair Bow

Materials

- Worsted weight yarn
- Crochet hook size 4.25 mm
- 5/8" ribbon
- Sewing machine
- Glue gun and glue
- Hair Clip

Directions

- Crochet a chain of 25 stitches.
- Row 1: Skip first chain, single crochet in next chain and in each chain to end of row. Turn.
- Row 2: Chain 1, single crochet in each stitch to end of row.
- Rows 3-5: Repeat row 2. Tie off, leaving 1 end for stitching.

Finishing
- Cut a piece of ribbon that is ½" shorter than the crocheted piece.
- Pin ribbon on top of crocheted piece, making sure that there are crocheted edged all the way around.
- Stitch ribbon in place with sewing machine.
- Fold piece in half, and stitch together with tail end of yarn.
- Pinch middle, and wrap tail end of yarn around section several times. Tie off and weave ends through work.
- Attach hair pin to back of bow with glue gun.

September 27

Earmuff Headband

Materials

- Bulky yarn
- Crochet hook size 5.5 mm

Directions

Earmuffs (make 2)
- Crochet a chain of 3 stitches. Join with a slip stitch to create a ring.
- Round 1: 10 double crochet in ring.
- Round 2: 2 double crochet in each stitch.
- Round 3: * 2 double crochet in first stitch, 1 double crochet. Repeat from * to end of round.
- Round 4: * 2 double crochet in first stitch, 2 double crochet. Repeat from * to end of round.
- Round 5: * 2 double crochet, 1 double crochet over next 2 stitches. Repeat from * to end of round. Tie off and weave ends through work.

Headband
- Crochet a chain of 36 stitches (or length needed to go from ear to ear).
- Row 1: Double crochet in each stitch to end of row, working around row and double crochet along other side of chain.
- Rounds 2-3: Double crochet in each stitch all the way around. Tie off and weave ends through work.

Finishing

Stitch earmuffs to headband with a slip stitch. You can be done here, or crochet a chain to add to either earmuff for ties.

September 28

Ribbed Toque

Materials

- Worsted weight yarn
- Crochet hook size 5 mm
- Yarn needle

Directions

- Crochet a chain of 45 stitches.
- Row 1: (back loops only) Single crochet to last 5 chains. Skip last 5 stitches in this row, and in every 4th row. Chain 1 and turn. The skipped stitches will become the tapered part of the hat at the top.
- Row 2: (back loops only) Single crochet in each stitch to end of row. Chain 1 and turn.
- Row 3: (back loops only) Single crochet in each stitch to end of row, including previously skipped 5 chains. Chain 1 and turn.
- Row 4: (back loops only) Single crochet in each stitch to end of row. Chain 1 and turn.
- Rows 5-end: Repeat rows 1-4 until piece reaches desired length (about 17-20" for an adult hat).

Finishing

With yarn needle, sew seam closed at the start of the wider end. Thread needle through top opening and draw closed. Tie off and weave ends through work.

September 29

Triangle Shawl

Materials

- 4 170-gram skeins soft yarn
- Crochet hook size 5 mm

Directions

- Crochet a chain of 246 stitches.
- Row 1: Skip first 5 stitches, double crochet in 6th chain (mesh stitch). * Chain 1, skip 1 chain, 1 double crochet. Repeat from * to end of row. (121 mesh stitches)
- Row 2: Slip stitch in first chain 1 space and in next double crochet. Chain 4. * 1 double crochet, chain 1. Repeat from * to last mesh stitch. Turn, leaving rest of stitches unworked, turn (2 mesh stitches decreased).
- Rows 3-end: Repeat row 2 until there is 1 stitch remaining. Tie off and weave ends through work.

Finishing

Add a fringe to the 2 shorter sides of shawl.

September 30

Wrap-Around Book Marker

Materials

- Scraps of worsted weight yarn
- Crochet hook size 5.5 mm

Directions

- Crochet a chain of 15 stitches.
- Row 1: Skip first chain, single crochet in next stitch and in each stitch to end of row. Turn.
- Row 2: Chain 1, skip first stitch, single crochet in next stitch and in each stitch to end of row. Turn.
- Rows 3-end: Repeat row 2 until piece measures long enough to wrap around book from top to bottom. Tie off and leave ends for stitching.

Finishing

Slip stitch ends together so you have a loop. This will wrap around the book to mark your place.

October

Boo! Halloween is just around the corner, so this month, we have all kinds of fun and creepy patterns. Enjoy making a spider web table cloth, ghost ornaments, costumes, and more. October is also Breast Cancer Awareness Month, so we have some pink ribbon patterns, and even a pattern for a breast prosthesis.

October 1

Chemo Cap

Materials

- Worsted weight yarn (2 colors)
- Crochet hook size 6 mm

Directions

Work with 2 strands of yarn
- Crochet a chain of 6 stitches. Join with a slip stitch to create a ring.
- Round 1: Chain 3, 15 double crochet in ring. Join with a slip stitch to beginning chain.
- Round 2: Chain 3, 1 double crochet in same space. Working in back loops only, 2 double crochet in each stitch to end of round (BLDC). Join.
- Round 3: Chain 3, 1 BLDC in same space. * 3 BLDC, 2 BLDC in next stitch. Repeat from * to end of round. Join.
- Rounds 4-7: Chain 3, BLDC in each stitch to end of round. Join. If you need more length, repeat these rounds.
- Round 8: Chain 1. Working in back loops only, 1 single crochet in each stitch to end of round (BLSC). Join.
- Round 9: Chain 3, 1 BLDC in same space. * 3 BLDC, 2 BLDC in next stitch. Repeat from * to end of round. Join.
- Round 10: Chain 3, 1 BLDC in same stitch. * 4 BLDC, 2 BLDC in next stitch. Repeat from * to end of round. Join.
- Round 11: Chain 1, BLSC in each stitch to end of round. Join. Repeat row twice if you want a larger brim.
- Round 12: Slip stitch in each stitch to end of round. Tie off and weave ends through work.

October 2

Pumpkin Treat Bag

Materials

- Worsted weight yarn (orange, black, and green)
- Crochet hook size 3.75 mm

Directions

Front and back
- Crochet a chain of 17 stitches with orange yarn.
- Row 1: Single crochet in each stitch to end of row. Chain 1 and turn.
- Rows 2-13: Working in back loops only, 15 single crochet. Chain 1 and turn. Tie off and weave ends through work at end of last round.
- Repeat for other side of treat bag.

Finishing
- Stitch 3 sides of the bag together using slip stitches.

- Attach green yarn to top, and crochet 2 rounds of single crochet.
- Use the black yarn to stitch on facial features. Or, you can use felt, googly eyes, and other fun craft supplies to create the face.

October 3

Skull Scarf

Materials

- Black and white worsted weight yarn
- Crochet hook size 5.5 mm

Directions

All stitches are half double crochet unless otherwise specified.
- Crochet a chain of 28 stitches with black yarn.
- Row 1: Skip first 2 chains, 1 stitch in next chain and in each chain to end of row. Turn.
- Rows 2-4: Chain 2, 1 stitch in each stitch to end of row. Turn.
- Rows 5-6: Chain 2, 8 black stitches. Switch to white yarn, 10 stitches, then finish row with black yarn. Turn.
- Row 7: Chain 2, 5 black. 16 white, 5 half black. Turn.
- Row 8: Chain 2, 4 black, 18 white, 4 black. Turn.
- Row 9: Chain 2, 3 black, 8 white, 4 black, 8 white, 3 black. Turn.
- Row 10: Chain 2, 3 black, 9 white, 2 black, 9 white, 3 black. Turn.
- Row 11: Chain 2, 3 black, 20 white, 3 black. Turn.
- Row 12: Chain 2, 3 black, 3 white, 4 black, 6 white, 4 black, 3 white, 3 black. Turn.
- Rows 13-14: Chain 2, 3 black, 2 white, 6 black, 4 white, 6 black, 2 white, 3 black. Turn.
- Row 15: Repeat row 12. Turn.
- Row 16: Chain 2, 3 black, 20 white, 3 black. Turn.
- Row 17: Chain 2, 4 black, 18 white, 4 black. Turn.
- Row 18: Chain 2, 5 black, 16 white, 5 black. Turn.
- Row 19: Chain 2, 6 black, 14 white, 6 black. Turn.
- Row 20: Chain 2, 8 black, 10 white, 8 black. Turn.
- Rows 21-end: Continue working in black until piece reaches desired length. Repeat skull pattern backwards at this end. Tie off and weave ends through work.

Finishing

Add a white fringe to each end of the scarf.

October 4

Creepy Eyeballs

Materials

- Scraps of worsted weight yarn (black, blue, and white)
- Crochet hook size 4 mm

- Fiberfill stuffing
- Red Sharpie marker

Directions

- Crochet a chain of 2 stitches with black yarn.
- Round 1: 6 single crochet in second chain from hook. Tie off and place stitch marker. Move marker after every round to keep track of your work.
- Round 2: Attach blue yarn, 2 single crochet in each stitch to end of round. Join and tie off.
- Round 3: Attach white yarn. * 2 single crochet in next stitch, 1 single crochet. Repeat from * to end of round.
- Rounds 4-6: Single crochet to end of round.
- Round 7: * 2 single crochet, single crochet 2 stitches together (decrease). Repeat from * to end of round. Start stuffing the eyeball at this point.
- Round 8: Single crochet to end of round.
- Round 9: Decrease to end of round. Finish stuffing, tie off, and weave ends through work. You can also leave tails dangling so you can hang the eyeballs.

Finishing

Use the Sharpie marker to draw "veins" on the white part of the eyeball.

October 5

Spider Web Brooch

Materials

- White worsted weight yarn
- Crochet hook size 4 mm
- Fabric Stiffener (equal amounts of white glue and water)
- Pin backing (available at craft stores in jewelry findings)
- Glue gun and glue

Directions

- Crochet a chain of 1 stitch.
- Row 1: Chain 6. 1 double triple crochet, chain 2 in center chain. Turn.
- Row 2: Chain 9. 1 double triple crochet in next stitch, chain 4, 1 double triple crochet, chain 5, 1 triple crochet in 4th chain of turning chain 6. Turn.
- Row 3: Chain 12. 1 double triple crochet, chain 7, 1 double triple crochet, chain 8, 1 triple crochet in 4th chain of turning chain 9. Turn.
- Row 4: Chain 15. 1 double triple crochet, chain 10, 1 double triple crochet, chain 11, 1 triple crochet in 4th chain of turning chain 12. Turn.
- Row 5: Chain 18. 1 double triple crochet, chain 10, 1 double triple crochet, chain 11, 1 triple crochet in 4th chain of turning chain 15. Do not turn.
- Round 6: Chain 4, slip stitch in second chain from hook, slip stitch in next 2 chains. Working around and going over the ends of each row, single crochet at the top of the last triple crochet. 4 single crochet over the side of the same stitch. * 5 single crochet over side of end stitch of next row. Repeat from * 4 times. 1 single crochet, 1 double crochet, 1 single crochet in last loop of center chain. Repeat from * once. 4 single crochet in turning chain 18 space. ** Chain 4, slip stitch in second chain from hook, slip stitch in next 2 chains **. 14 single crochet in same turning chain 18 space, 1 single crochet. Repeat from ** to **. 13 single crochet in next

space, 1 single crochet. Repeat from ** to **. 14 single crochet in next space. Join. Tie off and weave ends through work.

Finishing
- Soak piece in fabric stiffener and let dry overnight.
- Attach pin backing with glue.

October 6

Spider for Spider Web Brooch

Materials

- Black worsted weight yarn
- Crochet hook size 4 mm
- Glue gun and glue

Directions

- Crochet a chain of 3 stitches. Join with a slip stitch to create a ring.
- Round 1: 6 single crochet in ring.
- Round 2: 2 single crochet in each stitch to end of round. Join with a slip stitch.
- Round 3: Chain 2, 3 double crochet in same stitch, slip stitch in same stitch (head). Slip stitch in next stitch, chain 5, slip stitch in second chain from hook, 3 slip stitches, 1 slip stitch in body section. First leg completed. Repeat process until there are 4 legs on one side of the body, then 2 slip stitches. Chain 2, slip stitch in second chain from hook, 2 slip stitches in body, make 4 more legs, chain 2, 2 slip stitches in second chain from hook. Tie off and weave ends through work.

Finishing

Glue spider to spider web brooch.

October 7

Halloween Eye Mask

Materials

- Worsted weight yarn
- Crochet hook size 5 mm
- ¼" elastic
- Needle and thread

Directions

- Crochet a chain of 21 stitches. Slip stitch in first chain to create a loop. Chain 21, slip stitch to make a second loop (you will have a figure-8).
- Round 1: Chain 1, 1 single crochet in each of the next 2 chains. 30 single crochet in loop, moving them around so they are even all the way around. Single crochet in the back of the center 2 chains, 30 single crochet in next loop. Do not join.

- Round 2: Single crochet 2 center stitches together. * 5 half double crochet, 4 double crochet, 5 half double crochet, 2 double crochet. Repeat from * to end of round. Slip stitch in first stitch. Tie off and weave ends through work.

Finishing
- Measure elastic so it and the mask fit comfortably.
- With needle and thread, attach elastic to mask.

October 8

Toddler's Witch/Wizard Hat

Materials

- Black and yellow worsted weight yarn
- Crochet hook size 5 mm

Directions

- Crochet a chain of 6 stitches with black yarn.
- Round 1: 6 single crochet in second chain from hook. Place a stitch marker and move after each round to keep track of your work.
- Round 2: Single crochet in each stitch to end of round.
- Round 3: * 3 single crochet, 2 single crochet in next stitch (increase). Repeat form * to end of round.
- Round 4: * 3 single crochet, increase. Repeat from * to end.
- Round 5: * 4 single crochet, increase. Repeat from * to end.
- Round 6: Repeat round 2.
- Round 7: * 3 single crochet, increase. Repeat from * to end.
- Rounds 8-9: Repeat round 2.
- Round 10: * 4 single crochet, increase. Repeat from * to end.
- Rounds 11-12: Repeat round 2.
- Round 13: * 5 single crochet, increase. Repeat from * to end.
- Rounds 14-15: Repeat round 2.
- Round 16: * 6 single crochet, increase. Repeat from * to end.
- Rounds 17-18: Repeat round 2.
- Round 19: * 3 single crochet, increase. Repeat from * to end.
- Round 20: Repeat round 2.
- Round 21: * 4 single crochet, increase. Repeat from * to end.
- Round 22: Repeat round 2.
- Round 23: * 5 single crochet, increase. Repeat from * to end.
- Round 24: Repeat round 2.
- Round 25: * 6 single crochet, increase. Repeat from * to end.
- Round 26: Repeat round 2.
- Round 27: * 7 single crochet, increase. Repeat from * to end.
- Round 28: Repeat round 2.
- Round 29: * 8 single crochet, increase. Repeat from * to end.
- Round 30: Repeat round 2.
- Round 31: * 9 single crochet, increase. Repeat from * to end.
- Rounds 32-39: Repeat round 2. Tie off and attach yellow yarn.

- Rounds 40-43: Repeat round 2.
- Round 44: Join black yarn, repeat round 2.
- Round 45: Working in front loops only, slip stitch in first stitch, chain 3, double crochet in same stitch as joining, 2 double crochet in each stitch to end of round. Join with a slip stitch.
- Round 46: Chain 3, double crochet in each stitch to end of round. Tie off and weave ends through work.

October 9

Ballerina Tutu

Materials

- Worsted weight yarn
- Crochet hook size 5 mm
- 1 yard tulle
- ½" elastic
- Needle and thread

Directions

Pattern written for 15" waist. Sizes for 20 and 30" waists in ( ).
- Crochet a chain of 50 stitches (60, 90). Join with a slip stitch to create a ring, being careful not to twist the chain.
- Round 1: Chain 2, double crochet in each stitch to end of round. Join with a slip stitch.
- Round 2: Chain 2, half double crochet in each stitch to end of round. Join.
- Round 3: Repeat round 2.
- Round 4: Repeat round 1. Tie off and leave tail for stitching.

Finishing
- Cut elastic to length of crochet piece.
- With needle and thread, attach elastic so it stays in place.
- Fold crocheted piece in half lengthwise and stitch all the way around. Tie off and weave ends through work.
- Cut tulle into strips that are 6" wide.
- Attach tulle strips in the same manner as for making tassels.

October 10

Grim Reaper Chains

Materials

- Grey worsted weight yarn
- Crochet hook size 5.5 mm

Directions

- Crochet a chain of 20 stiches. Join with a slip stitch to create a ring, being careful not to twist chain.
- Round 1: Single crochet in each stitch to end of round. Join with a slip stitch.
- Round 2: Single crochet in each stitch to end of round. Tie off and weave ends through work.

- Repeat pattern for as many links as you want. After crocheting the chain, loop it through a link before joining and then continue stitching.

October 11

Kitty Ears

Materials

Make 2
- Worsted weight yarn
- Eyelash yarn
- Crochet hook size 5.5 mm

- Plastic hairband
- Glue gun and glue
- Pipe cleaners

Directions

- With worsted weight yarn, crochet a chain of 13 stitches.
- Row 1: Skip first chain, single crochet in next chain and in each chain to end of row. Chain 1 and turn.
- Rows 2-3: Repeat row 1.
- Row 4: 1 single crochet, single crochet 2 stitches together (decrease), 9 single crochet. Chain 1 and turn.
- Row 5: 1 single crochet, decrease, 8 single crochet. Chain 1 and turn.
- Row 6: 1 single crochet, decrease, 7 single crochet. Chain 1 and turn.
- Row 7: 1 single crochet, decrease, 6 single crochet. Chain 1 and turn.
- Row 8: 1 single crochet, decrease, 5 single crochet. Chain 1 and turn.
- Row 9: 1 single crochet, decrease, 4 single crochet. Chain 1 and turn.
- Row 10: 1 single crochet, decrease, 3 single crochet. Chain 1 and turn.
- Row 11: 1 single crochet, decrease, 2 single crochet. Chain 1 and turn.
- Row 12: 1 single crochet, decrease, 1 single crochet. Chain 1 and turn.
- Row 13: 1 single crochet, decrease. Tie off and weave ends through work.

Finishing
- Wrap pipe cleaner around each ear. Using eyelash yarn, single crochet all the way around ear, looping stitches around pipe cleaner.
- Glue ears to the top of the plastic hair band.

October 12

Kitty Tail

Materials

- Bulky weight yarn
- Crochet hook size 5 mm

Directions

- Crochet a chain of 2 stitches.
- Round 1: 6 single crochet in first chain.
- Round 2: Chain 1, double crochet in each stitch to end of round.

- Rounds 3-end: Double crochet in each stitch to end of round. Repeat round until tail is the desired length.
- Next 6 rows: 4 single crochet. Tie off and weave ends through work. This last piece is a tab you can use to attach the tail to clothing with a safety pin.

October 13

Pink Ribbon Afghan Square

Materials

- Pink and white worsted weight yarn
- Crochet hook size 5 mm

Directions

All stitches are single crochet unless otherwise specified.
- With white yarn, crochet a chain of 29 stitches.
- Row 1: Skip first chain, single crochet in next chain and in each chain to end of row. Turn.
- Row 2: Chain 1, 5 white, 4 pink, 10 white, 4 pink, 5 white. Turn.
- Row 3: Chain 1, 6 white, 4 pink, 8 white, 4 pink, 6 white. Turn.
- Row 4: Repeat row 3. Turn.
- Row 5: Chain 1, 7 white, 4 pink, 6 white, 4 pink, 7 white. Turn.
- Row 6: Repeat row 5. Turn.
- Row 7: Chain 1, 8 white, 4 pink, 4 white, 4 pink, 8 white. Turn.
- Row 8: Repeat row 7. Turn.
- Row 9: Chain 1, 9 white, 4 pink, 2 white, 4 pink, 9 white. Turn.
- Row 10: Repeat row 9.
- Row 11: Chain 1, 10 white, 8 pink, 10 white. Turn.
- Row 12: Repeat row 11. Turn.
- Row 13: Chain 1, 11 white, 6 pink, 11 white. Turn.
- Row 14: Repeat row 13.
- Row 15: Chain 1, 10 white, 8 pink, 10 white. Turn.
- Row 16: Chain 1, 9 white, 4 pink, 2 white, 4 pink, 9 white. Turn.
- Row 17: Repeat row 16.
- Row 18: Chain 1, 9 white, 3 pink, 4 white, 3 pink, 9 white. Turn.
- Row 19: Chain 1, 8 white, 4 pink, 4 white, 4 pink, 8 white. Turn.
- Row 20: Chain 1, 8 white, 3 pink, 6 white, 3 pink, 8 white. Turn.
- Rows 21-22: Repeat row 20.
- Row 23: Chain 1, 8 white, 4 pink, 4 white, 4 pink, 8 white. Turn.
- Row 24: Chain 1, 9 white, 3 pink, 4 white, 3 pink, 9 white. Turn.
- Row 25: Chain 1, 9 white, 4 pink, 2 white, 4 pink, 9 white. Turn.
- Row 26: Chain 1, 10 white, 8 pink, 10 white. Turn.
- Row 27: Chain 1, 12 white, 4 pink, 12 white. Turn.
- Row 28: Chain 1, 28 white.
- Edging row: With white yarn, single crochet all the way around square, with 3 single crochet in each corner stitch. Tie off and weave ends through work.

October 14

Devil Horn Hair Clips

Materials

- Red #10 crochet thread
- Crochet hook size 4.5 mm
- 2 hair clips or bobby pins
- Glue gun and glue

Directions

- Make 2
- Crochet a chain of 3 stitches. Join with a slip stitch to create a ring.
- Round 1: Chain 1, 12 half double crochet in ring. Join with a slip stitch at the top of beginning half double crochet. Chain 1 and turn.
- Rounds 2-3: 2 half double crochet in next stitch, 1 half double crochet. Repeat to end of round. Join. Chain 1 and turn.
- Round 4: Working in back loops only, half double crochet in each stitch to end of round. Join. Chain 1 and turn.
- Round 5: Half double crochet in each stitch to end of round. Join. Chain 1 and turn.
- Round 6: 2 half double crochet, half double crochet 2 stitches together (decrease), 3 half double crochet. Repeat pattern to end of round. Join. Chain 1 and turn.
- Round 7: 1 half double crochet, 1 decrease, 5 half double crochet. Repeat pattern to end of round. Join. Chain 1 and turn.
- Round 8: 1 half double crochet, 1 decrease, 4 half double crochet. Repeat pattern to end of round. Join. Chain 1 and turn.
- Rounds 9-10: 1 decrease, 2 half double crochet. Repeat pattern to end of round. Join. Chain 1 and turn.
- Round 11: 1 decrease, 1 half double crochet. Repeat pattern to end of round. Join. Chain 1 and turn.
- Round 12: Decrease all the way around. Tie off and weave ends through work.

Finishing

Glue devil horns to hair clips or bobby pins.

October 15

Pirate Eye Patch

Materials

- Black worsted weight yarn
- Crochet hook size 5 mm

Directions

- Crochet a chain measuring 3".
- Row 1: Skip first chain, single crochet in each chain to end of row. Turn.
- Row 2: Chain 1, skip first stitch, single crochet in each stitch to end of row. Turn.
- Rows 3-4: Repeat row 2.
- Row 5: Single crochet 2 stitches together (decrease), single crochet to last 2 stitches, decrease. Turn.

- Row 6: Decrease, single crochet to last 2 stitches, decrease. Turn.
- Row 7: Decrease, single crochet to last 2 stitches, decrease. Tie off and weave ends through work.

Finishing
- At the top of one side of the eye patch, join yarn and crochet a chain measuring 15".
- Repeat on other side of eye patch. This is the tie.

October 16

Hippie Headband

Materials

- Worsted weight yarn (4 colors)
- Crochet hook size 3.75 mm
- Buttons, beads, sequins, and other decorations
- Glue gun and glue

Directions

Work 4 rows of each color in this order: A, B, A, C, A, D. Repeat color pattern throughout your work.
- Crochet a chain of 7 stitches with A.
- Row 1: Skip first chain, single crochet in next chain and in each chain to end of row. Turn.
- Row 2: Chain 1, single crochet in each stitch to end of row. Work 2 more rows in color A. Start color pattern and work until piece is long enough to wrap around your head.
- End point row 1: Chain 1, single crochet 2 stitches together (decrease), 2 single crochet, decrease. Turn.
- End point row 2: Chain 1, 2 decreases. Tie off.
- Beginning end point row 1: With right side facing, join A, chain 1, 1 decrease, 2 single crochet, 1 decrease. Turn.
- Beginning end point row 2: Chain 1, 2 decreases. Tie off and weave ends through work.

Finishing
- Make the tie by joining color B with a slip stitch at one of the end points. Chain 1, single crochet in same stitch. Crochet a chain measuring 10". Tie off.
- Repeat on other end for tie chain. Tie off.

October 17

Witch's Cauldron

Materials

- Black or dark grey worsted weight yarn
- Crochet hook size 5 mm

Directions

- Crochet a chain of 5 stitches. Join with a slip stitch to create a ring.

- Round 1: Chain 1, 6 single crochet in ring. Join.
- Round 2: Chain 2, 2 single crochet in each stitch (increase) to end of round. Join.
- Round 3: Chain 1, 2 single crochet in same stitch as join, 1 single crochet. * Increase, 1 single crochet. Repeat from * to end of round. Join.
- Round 4: Chain 1, 2 single crochet in same stitch as join, 2 single crochet. * Increase, 2 single crochet. Repeat from * to end of round. Join.
- Round 5: Chain 1, 2 single crochet in same stitch as join, 3 single crochet. * Increase, 3 single crochet. Repeat from * to end of round. Join.
- Round 6: Chain 1, in back loops only, single crochet in each stitch to end of round. Join.
- Round 7: Chain 1, 2 single crochet in same stitch as join, 4 single crochet. * Increase, 4 single crochet. Repeat from * to end of round. Join.
- Round 8: Chain 1, single crochet in each stitch to end of round. Join.
- Round 9: Chain 1, 2 single crochet in same stitch as join, 5 single crochet. * Increase, 5 single crochet. Repeat from * to end of round. Join.
- Rounds 10-11: Repeat round 8.
- Round 12: Chain 1. * Single crochet 2 stitches together (decrease), 5 single crochet. Repeat from * to end of round. Join.
- Round 13: Repeat round 8.
- Round 14: Chain 1. * Decrease, 4 single crochet. Repeat from * to end of round. Join.
- Round 15: Repeat round 8.
- Round 16: Chain 1, reverse single crochet in each stitch to end of round. Tie off and weave ends through work.

October 18

Prosthetic Breast

Materials

- Worsted weight yarn (flesh and pink colors)
- Crochet hook size 5 mm
- Fiberfill stuffing

Directions

- Crochet a chain of 4 stitches with pink yarn. This will be the nipple. Join with a slip stitch to create a ring.
- Round 1: 4 single crochet in ring.
- Round 2: Working in back loops only, single crochet in each stitch. Join.
- Round 3: Working in front loops only, 2 single crochet in each stitch. Join.
- Round 4: * 1 single crochet, 2 single crochet in next stitch. Repeat from * to end. Join.
- Round 5: Repeat round 4. Tie off.
- Round 6: Attach flesh colored yarn. Working in back loops only, * 2 single crochet, 2 single crochet in next stitch. Repeat from * to end. Join.
- Round 7: * 2 single crochet, 2 single crochet in next stitch. Repeat from * to end. Join.
- Round 8: Repeat round 7.
- Round 9: * 3 single crochet, 2 single crochet in next stitch. Repeat from * to end. Join.
- Rounds 10-13: Single crochet in each stitch to end. Join.
- Round 14: * 3 single crochet, single crochet 2 stitches together (decrease). Repeat from * to end. Join.
- Round 15: * 2 single crochet, decrease. Repeat from * to end. Join.

- Round 16: Repeat round 15.
- Round 17: * 1 single crochet, decrease. Repeat from * to end. Join. Begin stuffing now.
- Round 18: Repeat round 17.
- Round 19: Decrease. Join. Tie off and weave ends through work.

October 19

Ghost Ornaments

Materials

- White worsted weight yarn
- Crochet hook size 4.25 mm
- 1 ½" Styrofoam balls
- Black felt
- Glue gun and glue

Directions

- Crochet a chain of 2 stitches. Join with a slip stitch.
- Round 1: Chain 1, 6 single crochet in ring. Join.
- Round 2: Chain 1, single crochet in base of same stitch as chain, 2 single crochet in each stitch to end of round. Join.
- Round 3: Repeat round 2.
- Round 4: Chain 1, single crochet in each stitch to end of round. Join.
- Rounds 5-8: Repeat round 4. Put Styrofoam ball in now to create the head.
- Round 9: Chain 1. * Single crochet 2 stitches together (decrease). Repeat from * to end. Join.
- Round 10: Repeat round 4.
- Rounds 11-12: Repeat round 2.
- Rounds 13-16: Repeat round 4.
- Round 17: * Chain 1, skip 2 stitches, slip stitch, chain 1, skip 4 stitches, slip stitch, chain 12, slip stitch. Repeat form * to end of round. Tie off and weave ends through work.

Finishing

Cut out eyes and a mouth from the felt and glue to the head.

October 20

Baby Pumpkin Beanie

Materials

- Green and orange worsted weight yarn
- Crochet hook size 5.5 mm

Directions

- With orange yarn, crochet a chain of 25 stitches.
- Row 1: Work in back loops only. Skip 2 chains, 1 half double crochet in next chain and in each chain to end of row. Chain 2 and turn.
- Rows 2-23: Working in back loops only, half double crochet in each stitch to end. Chain 2 and turn.

- Row 24: Working in back loops only, half double crochet in each stitch to end. Chain 1 and turn.

Finishing
- Join ends and stitch down length of hat. Tie off and weave ends through work.
- Attach green yarn with a single crochet at the top of the hat. Single crochet all the way around, do not join. Then, single crochet all the way around until there are 4-5 stitches left. Single crochet in each stitch around for 6 rounds to create the stem. Tie off and weave ends through work.

October 21

Tombstone

Materials
- Grey worsted weight yarn
- Scraps of black worsted weight yarn
- Crochet hook size 4 mm
- Fiberfill stuffing

Directions
- Crochet a chain of 2 stitches.
- Round 1: 8 single crochet in first chain. Place stitch marker, and move after each round to keep track of your work.
- Round 2: 2 single crochet in next stitch, 2 single crochet. 2 single crochet in each of next 2 stitches, 2 single crochet in next stitch, 2 single crochet in last stitch.
- Round 3: 2 single crochet in next stitch, 4 single crochet. 2 single crochet in each of next 2 stitches, 4 single crochet, 2 single crochet in last stitch.
- Round 4: 2 single crochet in next stitch, 6 single crochet. 2 single crochet in each of next 2 stitches, 6 single crochet, 2 single crochet in last stitch.
- Rounds 5-16: Single crochet in each stitch to end. Tie off and weave ends through work. Stuff tombstone.

Base
- Crochet a chain of 9 stitches.
- Row 1: Skip first chain, single crochet in next chain and in each chain to end of row.
- Rows 2-3: Chain 1, turn, single crochet in each stitch to end. Tie off and stitch base to bottom of stuffed tombstone.

Finishing

Use scraps of black yarn to stitch RIP on the tombstone.

October 22

Hanging Skull Ornament

Materials
- White worsted weight yarn
- Crochet hook size 4 mm
- Fiberfill stuffing

- Black felt tipped marker

Directions

- Crochet a chain of 2 stitches.
- Round 1: 6 single crochet in first chain. Place stitch marker and move after each round to keep track of your work.
- Round 2: 2 single crochet in each stitch to end of round.
- Round 3: * 2 single crochet in next stitch, 1 single crochet. Repeat from * to end.
- Round 4: * 2 single crochet in next stitch, 2 single crochet. Repeat from * to end.
- Round 5: * 2 single crochet in next stitch, 3 single crochet. Repeat from * to end.
- Rounds 6-11: Single crochet in each stitch to end of round.
- Round 12: Single crochet 2 stitches together (decrease) 6 times.
- Rounds 13-15: Single crochet in each stitch to end of round. Start stuffing skull now and stuff as you work more rounds.
- Round 16: * Decrease, 2 single crochet. Repeat from * to end of round.
- Round 17: * Decrease, 1 single crochet. Repeat from * to end of round.
- Round 18: * Decrease 6 times. Tie off and weave ends through work.

Finishing

- Join yarn at top of skull, and crochet a chain to hang it from.
- Use the black marker to draw on a face.

October 23

Spider Fridge Magnet

Materials

- Black worsted weight yarn
- Crochet hook size 4 mm
- Small googly eyes
- Glue gun and glue
- Magnet

Directions

- Crochet a chain of 2 stitches.
- Round 1: 6 single crochet in first chain. Place stitch marker and move after each round to keep track of your work.
- Round 2: 2 single crochet in each stitch to end of round.
- Round 3: * 2 single crochet in next stitch, 1 single crochet. Repeat from * to end of round.
- Round 4: * 2 single crochet in next stitch, 2 single crochet. Repeat from * to end of round.

Legs

Attach yarn at 4 spots on each side of the body, and crochet a chain of 9 stitches at each spot (8 legs). Tie off and weave ends through work.

Finishing

- Glue eyes to the spider.
- Glue magnet to back of spider.

October 24

Witch's Hat Ornament

Materials

- Black worsted weight yarn
- Crochet hook size 4 mm
- Fiberfill stuffing
- Yellow felt
- Glue gun and glue

Directions

- Crochet a chain of 2 stitches. Leave long tail for hanging up the ornament later.
- Round 1: 4 single crochet in first chain. Place stitch marker and move after each round to keep track of your work.
- Round 2: * 2 single crochet in next stitch, 1 single crochet. Repeat from * to end of round.
- Rounds 3-14: Repeat round 2, adding 1 stitch each time (ie 2 single crochet in next stitch, 2 single crochet) until you end with doing 2 single crochet in 1 stitch and 13 single crochet.
- Round 15: Single crochet in each stitch to end of round.
- Round 16: * 2 single crochet in next stitch, 4 single crochet. Repeat from * to end of round.
- Round 17: * 2 single crochet in next stitch, 5 single crochet. Repeat from * to end of round. Tie off and weave ends through work.

Finishing

Cut out a narrow strip of felt to use as the hat band and glue to the hat.

October 25

Child's Ragdoll Wig

Materials

- Red Heart Super Saver Yarn
- Crochet hook size 6 mm

Directions

- Crochet a chain of 4 stitches. Join with a slip stitch to create a ring.
- Round 1: Chain 3, 1 half double crochet. * Chain 1, 1 half double crochet. Repeat from * to end of round. Join.
- Round 2: Chain 3, half double crochet in same space, chain 1, 1 half double crochet in next chain space. * Chain 1, 1 half double crochet in next chain space, chain 1, 1 half double crochet in same space, chain 1, 1 half double crochet in next space. Repeat from * to end of round. Join.
- Round 3: Repeat round 2.
- Round 4: Chain 3, 1 half double crochet in same space. Chain 1, 1 half double crochet in next space (twice). * Chain 1, 1 half double crochet in next space, chain 1, 1 half double crochet in same space, (chain 1, 1 half double crochet in next space – twice). Repeat from * to end of round. Join.
- Round 5: Chain 3. * Chain 1, 1 half double crochet in next space. Repeat from * to end of round. Join.
- Rounds 6-7: Repeat rounds 4 and 5. Tie off and weave ends through work.

Finishing

Cut many lengths of yarn (8"). At top of hat, start attaching yarn in the same way you would add fringes to an afghan.

October 26

Breast Cancer Pink Ribbon

Materials

- Worsted weight yarn
- Crochet hook size 5.5 mm
- Safety pin

Directions

- Crochet a chain of 37 stitches.
- Row 1: Work in back ridge only. Skip first 2 chains, double crochet in next chain and in each chain to end of row. Tie off and weave ends through work.

Finishing
- Fold piece to create the ribbon, slip stitch in center to join.
- Attach to clothing with the safety pin.

October 27

Pumpkin Basket

Materials

- Orange and black worsted weight yarn
- Crochet hook size 5 mm
- Black felt
- Glue gun and glue
- Gallon size bleach bottle (empty and completely cleaned out)
- Orange spray paint

Directions

- Crochet a chain of 5 stitches with orange yarn. Join with a slip stitch to create a ring.
- Round 1: Chain 3, 15 double crochet in ring. Join.
- Round 2: Chain 4. * 1 double crochet, chain 1. Repeat from * to end of round. Join.
- Round 3: Slip stitch in next space, chain 5, 1 double crochet in same space. * 1 double crochet, chain 2, 1 double crochet all in next space. Repeat from * to end of round. Join.
- Rounds 4-10: Slip stitch in next space, chain 6, 1 double crochet in same space. * 1 double crochet, chain 3, 1 double crochet all in the next space. Repeat from * to end of round. Tie off and weave ends through work.
- Round 11: Join black yarn. * Insert hook between double crochet stitches and make a slip stitch. Chain 1, 3 double crochet in next chain space, chain 1. Repeat from * to end of round. Tie off and weave ends through work.

Finishing
- Cut bleach bottle so the top is about 1/2" shorter than the crochet basket.
- Cut out felt pieces for the face and glue them to the front of the basket.

October 28

Pumpkin Coaster

Materials

- Orange and green worsted weight yarn
- Crochet hook size 5.5 mm

Directions

- Crochet a chain of 4 stitches. Join with a slip stitch to create a ring.
- Round 1: 2 single crochet in each stitch to end of round. Do not join. Work in rounds until piece is desired size.
- Rounds 2-end: Single crochet in each stitch to end of round. Tie off and weave ends through work.

Finishing
- Attach green yarn at top of pumpkin.
- Row 1: 4 single crochet. Turn.
- Row 2: Chain 1, skip first stitch, 3 single crochet. Tie off and weave ends through work.

October 29

Ghost Hand Puppet

Materials

- White worsted weight yarn
- Crochet hook size 5.5 mm
- Black felt tipped marker

Directions

Make 2
- Crochet a chain measuring 4".
- Row 1: Skip first chain, single crochet in each chain to end of row. Turn.
- Row 2: Chain 1, skip first chain, single crochet in each stitch to end of row. Turn.
- Rows 3-arms: Repeat row 2 until piece measures 5". Do not turn at end of last row.
- Next row: Chain 10, turn, skip first chain, single crochet in each chain, and in each stitch to end of row. Chain 10.
- Next row: Skip first chain, single crochet in rest of chains and until end of row.
- Next 4 rows: Chain 1, skip first stitch, single crochet to end of row. Turn.
- Next row: Slip stitch first 10 stitches, single crochet to last 10 stitches. Turn.
- Next row-end: Chain 1, skip first stitch, single crochet to end of row. Turn. Repeat this row until section measures about 3". Tie off and weave ends through work.

Finishing
- Stitch both pieces together along sides, leaving bottom open.
- Use the felt tipped marker to draw on a face.

October 30

Black and Orange Halloween Dishcloth

Materials

- Black and orange worsted weight yarn
- Crochet hook size 5 mm

Directions

- Crochet a chain measuring 9".
- Row 1: Skip first chain, single crochet in next chain and in each chain to end of row. Turn.
- Row 2: Chain 1, skip first stitch, double crochet in next stitch and in each stitch to end of row. Turn.
- Row 3: Chain 1, skip first stitch, single crochet in next stitch and in each stitch to end of row. Turn.
- Row 4: Chain 2, skip first stitch, double crochet in next stitch and in each stitch to end of row. Turn.
- Rows 5-8: Join second color and repeat rows 1-4.
- Repeat orange and black stripe pattern until piece is close to being square. Tie off and weave ends through work.

October 31

Black Witch's Shawl

Materials

- Red Heart Super Saver yarn
- Crochet hook size 16 mm

Directions

- Crochet a chain measuring 70".
- Row 1: Skip first chain, single crochet in next chain and in each chain to end of row. Turn.
- Rows 2-end: Skip first stitch, single crochet 2 stitches together. Single crochet in each stitch until last 2 stitches. Single crochet last 2 stitches together. Repeat this row until there are no stitches left and you have a triangle.

Finishing

Add a fringe on the 2 shorter sides of shawl.

November

This month, we give thanks for our families, our homes, and everything good in our lives. We also pay respect to our members, both alive and dead, by wearing poppies for Remembrance Day. We have some poppy patterns for you, along with some fun Thanksgiving Day patterns, hats, cowls, and much more.

November 1

Preemie Beanie

Materials

- Red Heart Soft yarn
- Crochet hook size 6 mm

Directions

- Crochet a chain of 5 stitches. Join with a slip stitch to create a ring.
- Round 1: Chain 3, 11 double crochet in ring. Join.
- Round 2: Chain 3, 2 double crochet in same stitch, 2 double crochet in each stitch to end of round. Join.
- Round 3: Chain 3, 2 double crochet in first stitch, 1 double crochet in each stitch to end of round. Join.
- Round 4: Chain 3. * 2 double crochet in next stitch, 2 double crochet. Repeat form * to end of round. Join.
- Round 5: Chain 3, double crochet in each stitch to end of round. Join. Continue this round for 6 rows.
- Last round: Chain 1, single crochet in each stitch to end of round. Join. Tie off and weave ends through work.

November 2

Stuffed Candy Corn

Materials

- Worsted weight yarn in white, yellow, and orange
- Crochet hook size 4 mm
- Fiberfill stuffing

Directions

- Crochet a chain of 2 stitches with white yarn.
- Round 1: 4 single crochet in first chain. Place marker and move after each round to keep track of your work.
- Round 2: 2 single crochet in each stitch to end of round.
- Round 3: 1 single crochet in each stitch to end of round.
- Round 4: * 2 single crochet in next stitch, 1 single crochet. Repeat from * to end of round.
- Round 5: 1 single crochet in each stitch to end of round.
- Round 6: * 2 single crochet in next stitch, 2 single crochet. Repeat from * to end of round. Switch to orange yarn,
- Round 7: 1 single crochet in each stitch to end of round.
- Round 8: * 2 single crochet in next stitch, 3 single crochet. Repeat from * to end of round.
- Round 9: 1 single crochet in each stitch to end of round.
- Round 10: * 2 single crochet in next stitch, 4 single crochet. Repeat from * to end of round.
- Round 11: 1 single crochet in each stitch to end of round. Switch to yellow yarn.
- Rounds 12-16: 1 single crochet in each stitch to end of round. Tie off, leave tail for stitching.

Finishing
- Stuff with fiberfill.
- Slip stitch the bottom closed. Tie off and weave ends through work.

November 3

Double-Thick Pumpkin Pot Holder

Materials

- Orange worsted weight yarn
- Scraps of green worsted weight yarn
- Crochet hook size 4 mm
- Black felt
- Needle and black thread or sewing machine

Directions

Make 2
- Crochet a chain of 4 stitches with orange yarn,
- Round 1: Skip first 3 chains, 11 double crochet in 4th chain. Join with a slip stitch at the top of beginning chain.
- Round 2: Chain 3, double crochet in same stitch, 2 double crochet in each stitch to end of round. Join.
- Round 3: Chain 3, 2 double crochet in next stitch. * 1 double crochet, 2 double crochet in next stitch. Repeat from * to end of round. Join.
- Round 4: Chain 3, 1 double crochet, 2 double crochet in next stitch. * 2 double crochet, 2 double crochet in next stitch. Repeat from * to end of round. Join.
- Round 5: Chain 3, 2 double crochet, 2 double crochet in next stitch. * 3 double crochet, 2 double crochet in next stitch. Repeat from * to end of round. Join.
- Round 6: Chain 1, single crochet in same stitch, slip stitch in next stitch. 1 single crochet, 1 double crochet, 2 double crochet in next stitch. * 4 double crochet, 2 double crochet in next stitch. Repeat from * to end of round. Join. Tie off and weave ends through work.

Finishing
- Cut pumpkin face pieces out of the black felt.
- Sew face onto one side of the pumpkin.
- With wrong sides facing, slip stitch pumpkin together to create the double thickness.
- Join green yarn at top of pumpkin. Chain 20, skip first 3 chains, double crochet in next chain and in each to end of row. Stitch end to pumpkin to create a loop for hanging. Tie off and weave ends through work.

November 4

Music Notes

Materials

- Scraps of worsted weight Yarn
- Crochet hook size 3.75 mm

Directions

- Crochet a chain of 3 stitches. Join with a slip stitch to create a ring.
- Round 1: 6 single crochet in ring. Join.
- Round 2: Chain 1, 2 single crochet in each stitch to end of round. Join.

- Round 3: Slip stitch in first 4 stitches. Chain 15. Turn, slip stitch in 3rd chain from hook. Slip stitch in next 3 chains. Skip 3 chains, slip stitch in 4th chain from hook, 5 slip stitches. Slip stitch all the way around the circle section. Tie off and weave ends through work.

November 5

Music Note Scarf

Materials

- Black and white worsted weight yarn
- Crochet hooks sizes 3.75 mm and 5.5 mm

Directions

- With crochet hook size 5.5 mm, crochet a chain measuring 10" with black yarn.
- Row 1: Skip first chain, half double crochet in each chain to end of row. Turn.
- Row 2: Chain 2, skip first stitch, half double crochet in next stitch and each stitch to end of row. Turn.
- Rows 3-end: Repeat row 2 until piece reaches desired length. Tie off and weave ends through work.

Finishing
- Make several music notes according to the Music Note pattern from November 4.
- Attach music notes with slip stitches in random places on the scarf. The layout is completely up to you.
- Add a fringe, alternating black and white fringes to mimic the appearance of a piano keyboard.

November 6

Cute Stuffed Pumpkin

Materials

- Orange worsted weight yarn
- Scraps of brown and green worsted weight yarn
- Black beads
- Black embroidery thread
- Crochet hook size 4 mm
- Fiberfill stuffing

Directions

- With orange yarn, crochet a chain of 2 stitches.
- Round 1: 6 single crochet in first chain. Place marker and move after each round to keep track of your work.
- Round 2: 2 single crochet in each stitch to end of round.
- Round 3: * 2 single crochet in next stitch, 1 single crochet. Repeat from * to end of round.
- Round 4: * 1 single crochet, 3 half double crochet in each of the next 2 stitches. Repeat from * to end of round.
- Rounds 5-13: * 1 single crochet, 6 half double crochet. Repeat from * to end of round.
- Round 14: * 1 single crochet, single crochet 3 stitches together (twice). Repeat from * to end of round.
- Round 15: * Single crochet 2 stitches together, 1 single crochet. Repeat from * to end of round.

- Round 16: * Single crochet 2 stitches together. Repeat from * to end of round. Tie off and stuff pumpkin with fiberfill stuffing.

Stem

- Attach brown yarn at top of pumpkin. Chain 2.
- Round 1: 6 single crochet in first chain. Place marker.
- Round 2: 2 single crochet in each stitch to end of round.
- Round 3: Working in back loops only, single crochet in each stitch to end of round.
- Round 4: Single crochet in each stitch to end of round. Tie off.

Leaf

Attach green yarn, chain 4. Skip first chain, 2 double crochet in next chain, 1 half double crochet in next chain, 3 single crochet in last chain. Work your way around to the other side. Chain 1, 1 half double crochet in next chain, 2 double crochet in last chain. Tie off and weave ends through work.

November 7

Fingerless Gloves

Materials

- Worsted weight yarn
- Crochet hook size 4.5 mm
- ½" ribbon

Directions

- Crochet a chain of 30 stitches. Join with a slip stitch to create a ring, being careful not to twist chain.
- Round 1: Chain 2, half double crochet in each chain to end of round. Join with slip stitch.
- Rounds 2-6: Chain 2, half double crochet in each stitch to end of round. Join. You can work more rounds for longer gloves.
- Round 7: Chain 2, 9 half double crochet. Chain 4, skip 4 stitches, half double crochet to end of round. You have made the thumb hole. Join.
- Rounds 8-15: Chain 2, half double crochet in each stitch to end of round.
- Last round: With wrong side facing, chain 3, double crochet in first stitch. Slip stitch next stitch. Yarn over, insert hook through next stitch, yarn over, and pull through stitch. You should have 3 loops on the hook. Yarn over again, pull through 2 loops. Yarn over, insert hook into same stitch, yarn over, pull loop back through stitch. Yarn over and pull through all 4 loops on hook. Continue this pattern all the way around. Tie off and weave ends through work.

Finishing

Weave ribbon through the bottom of each glove, and tie in a bow. Instead of ribbon, you can also use a crochet chain.

November 8

Chunky Wrist Warmers

Materials

- Chunky, 14-ply yarn
- Crochet hook size 15.75 mm

Directions

- Crochet a chain of 8 stitches. Join with a slip stitch to create a ring.
- Round 1: 1 single crochet in second chain from hook, and in each stitch to end of round. Join with a slip stitch at top of first single crochet.
- Rounds 2-6: Chain 1, single crochet in each stitch to end of round. Join.
- Round 7: Chain 2, skip first 2 stitches, 6 single crochet. Join at top of first chain.
- Round 8: Chain 1, 2 single crochet in chain 2 space, 6 single crochet. Join with slip stitch. Tie off and weave ends through work.

November 9

Poppy Pin

Materials

- Scraps of red and green worsted weight yarn
- Crochet hook size 5 mm
- Pin back (available at craft stores in jewelry findings)
- Glue gun and glue

Directions

- Crochet a chain of 3 stitches with green yarn. Join with a slip stitch to create a ring.
- Round 1: Chain 1, 16 single crochet in ring. Attach red yarn.
- Round 2: * Chain 2, 1 double crochet in same stitch as chain. 2 triple crochet in each of the next 2 stitches. 1 double crochet, slip stitch in same space, 1 slip stitch in next stitch. Repeat from * to end of round. You will have the 4 petals. Tie off and weave ends through work.

Finishing

Glue pin backing to back of crochet poppy.

November 10

Poppy Necklace

Materials

- Scraps of green and red worsted weight yarn
- Crochet hook size 5 mm

- Necklace clasp (available at craft stores in jewelry findings)

Directions

- Crochet a chain measuring 16-18".
- Attach necklace clasp to each end of the chain by tying the ends.
- Make as many of the poppies from the Poppy Pin pattern for November 9, and attach to chain with slip stitches.

November 11

Poppy Headband

Materials

- Scraps of red, green, and black worsted weight yarn
- Crochet hook size 5 mm

Directions

- With black yarn, rochet a chain long enough to fit comfortably around your head. Join with a slip stitch to create a ring, being careful not to twist chain.
- Round 1: Single crochet in each stitch to end of round. Join.
- Round 2: Chain 2, double crochet in each stitch to end of round. Join.
- Round 3: Chain 1, single crochet in each stitch to end of round. Tie off and weave ends through work.

Finishing

Make 3 poppies from the Poppy Pin pattern. Attach them to 1 side of the headband. If you want to add poppies all the way around, it's totally up to you.

November 12

Shopping Bag

Materials

- Worsted weight yarn
- Crochet hook size 5.5 mm

Directions

- Crochet a chain of 3 stitches.
- Round 1: 12 double crochet in first chain. Join at top of first double crochet with a slip stitch.
- Round 2: Chain 2, 2 double crochet in each stitch to end of round. Join.
- Round 3: Chain 2. * 1 double crochet, 2 double crochet in next stitch. Repeat from * to end of round. Join.
- Round 4: Chain 2. * 2 double crochet, 2 double crochet in next stitch. Repeat from * to end of round. Join.
- Round 5: Chain 3. * 1 double crochet, chain 1. Repeat from * to end of round. Do not slip stitch to join. Insert hook in first chain 1 space of this round and go right in to the next round.
- Rounds 6-23: 1 double crochet and chain 1 in each chain 1 space. Repeat to end of round.

- Round 24: Chain 2. Double crochet in each chain 1 space.
- Round 25: Chain 2. Double crochet between each double crochet stitch of last round.

Handles
- Row 1: Picking up where you left off with the bag part, chain 2, 9 double crochet.
- Row 2: Chain 2, turn. Double crochet next 2 stitches together (decrease). 5 double crochet, 1 decrease.
- Row 3: Chain 2, turn. Decrease, 3 double crochet, decrease.
- Rows 4-15: Chain 2, turn. 5 double crochet. If you want longer straps, add more of this row.
- Fold bag in half so you know where to start the next handle. Attach yarn, and repeat process. Slip stitch both sides of the handle together. Tie off and weave ends through work.

November 13

Comfy Slippers

Materials
- Worsted weight yarn
- Crochet hook size 6.5 mm

Directions
- Pattern for smaller size. Larger sizes are in ( )
- Crochet a chain of 19 (21-23) stitches.
- Row 1: With right side facing, skip first chain, single crochet in next chain and in each chain to end of row. Turn.
- Row 2: Chain 1, single crochet in each stitch to end of row. Turn.
- Row 3: Chain 1, 2 single crochet in first stitch, 1 single crochet in each stitch to last 2 stitches. 2 single crochet in last stitch. Turn.
- Row 4: Repeat row 2.
- Row 5: Repeat row 3.
- Row 6: Single crochet in each stitch to end of row for 4 (5-6) rows. Tie off and place stitch marker at end of last row.
- With right side facing, skip 3 stitches. Join with slip stitch in next stitch. Chain 1, 16 (18-20) single crochet. Turn without working rest of stitches in row.
- Last rows: Single crochet in each stitch to end of row. With wrong sides facing together. Fold last row in half and sew together to create the heel seam.

Finishing

With wrong sides together, fold slipper in half and stitch instep seam. Fold toe flat and sew toe seam. Tie off and weave ends through work.

November 14

Thanksgiving Wreath

Materials

- Red, orange, and brown worsted weight yarn
- Crochet hook size 4 mm
- Yellow ribbon bow
- Glue gun and glue

Directions

Make 3 tubes, 1 in each color
- Crochet a chain of 2 stitches
- Round 1: 5 single crochet in second chain from hook. Insert marker and move after each round to keep track of your work.
- Rounds 2-56: Single crochet in each stitch to end of round. Slip stitch to join. Tie of and leave tails.

Finishing
- Braid the 3 tubes together.
- Join with the ends that haven't been cut off. Weave ends through work.
- Glue bow to the front of the wreath.

November 15

Acorn Table Ornaments

Materials

- Scraps of worsted weight yarn (brown and beige)
- Crochet hook size 5 mm
- Fiberfill stuffing

Directions

- With beige yarn, crochet a chain of 2 stitches.
- Round 1: 5 single crochet in second chain from hook.
- Round 2: 2 single crochet in each stitch to end of round.
- Round 3: * 1 single crochet, 2 single crochet in nest stitch. Repeat from * to end of round.
- Rounds 4-6: Single crochet in each stitch to end of round.
- Round 7: * 3 single crochet, single crochet 2 stitches together. Repeat from * to end of round. Stuff with fiberfill stuffing.

Acorn Cap
- With brown yarn, crochet a chain of 2 stitches.
- Round 1: 5 single crochet in second chain from hook.
- Round 2: 2 single crochet in each stitch to end of round.
- Round 3: * 1 single crochet, 2 single crochet in next stitch. Repeat from * to end of round.
- Round 4: * 2 single crochet, 2 single crochet in next stitch. Repeat from * to end of round.

- Round 5: * 2 single crochet, single crochet 2 stitches together. Repeat from * 4 times. Tie off and leave tail for stitching.

Finishing
- With original tail at center of acorn cap, crochet a chain of 5 stitches.
- Row 1: Skip first chain, single crochet in next 4 chains. Tie off and weave ends through work.
- With outer tail, slip stitch cap to acorn bottom. Tie off and weave ends through work.

November 16

Scented Pumpkin Pie Ornament

Materials

- Scraps of grey, orange, and beige worsted weight yarn
- Crochet hook size 5 mm
- Fiberfill stuffing
- Cardboard or plastic canvas
- Pumpkin pie spice
- Sachet bag
- 1" white pompom
- Glue gun and glue

Directions

Pie pan
- With grey yarn, crochet a chain of 5 stitches. Join with a slip stitch to create a ring.
- Round 1: 6 single crochet in ring.
- Round 2: 2 single crochet in each stitch to end of round.
- Round 3: * 2 single crochet in next stitch, 1 single crochet. Repeat from * to end of round.
- Round 4: * 2 single crochet in next stitch, 2 single crochet. Repeat from * to end of round.
- Round 5: * 2 single crochet in next stitch, 3 single crochet. Repeat from * to end of round.
- Round 6: In back loops only, * 2 single crochet in next stitch, 9 single crochet. Repeat from * to end of round.
- Round 7: Working in both loops, single crochet in each stitch to last stitch, 2 single crochet in last stitch (increase).
- Rounds 8-9: Single crochet in each stitch to last stitch, 1 increase. Tie off but leave tail for stitching.

Pie
- With orange yarn, crochet a chain of 5 stitches. Join with a slip stitch to create a ring.
- Round 1: 6 single crochet in ring.
- Round 2: 2 single crochet in each stitch to end of round.
- Round 3: * 2 single crochet in next stitch, 1 single crochet. Repeat from * to end of round.
- Round 4: * 2 single crochet in next stitch, 2 single crochet. Repeat from * to end of round.
- Round 5: * 2 single crochet in next stitch, 3 single crochet. Repeat from * to end of round.
- Round 6: * 2 single crochet in next stitch, 4 single crochet. Repeat from * to end of round.
- Round 7: Switch to beige yarn. Working in front loops only, single crochet in each stitch to end of round.
- Round 8: Working in both loops, 6 half double crochet in next stitch, 2 slip stitches. Repeat to end of round. Tie off and leave tail for stitching.

Finishing

- Cut out cardboard or plastic canvas into a circle that will fit inside the pie pan to use as a base.
- Fill sachet bag with pumpkin spice, place in pie pan.
- Slip stitch top of pie to top of pan. Tie of and weave ends through work.
- Glue pompom to top of pie to look like whipped cream.

November 17

Pumpkin Applique

Materials

- Scraps of orange and green worsted weight yarn
- Crochet hook size 5 mm
- Pin back (available at craft stores in jewelry findings)
- Glue gun and glue

Directions

- With orange yarn, crochet a chain of 3 stitches.
- Row 1: Skip first chain, single crochet in next chain, 2 single crochet in next chain.
- Row 2: 2 single crochet in first stitch, 2 single crochet, 2 single crochet in last stitch.
- Rows 3-5: Single crochet in each stitch to end of row.
- Row 6: Single crochet 2 stitches together (decrease). Chain 1, slip stitch, chain 1 decrease.
- Row 7: Chain 1, slip stitch in end of each row around outer edge. Once you are at the top of the opposite side at row 6, chain 1, slip stitch, slip stitch in center slip stitch, slip stitch in next stitch, slip stitch in beginning slip stitch. Tie off and weave ends through work.

Finishing
- Attach green yarn at top of pumpkin. Crochet a chain of 5 stitches.
- Row 1: Skip first chain, single crochet in each stitch to end of chain. Tie off and weave ends through work.

November 18

Hood

Materials

- Worsted weight yarn
- Crochet hook size 8 mm

Directions

- Crochet a chain of 75 stitches.
- Row 1: Skip first chain, double crochet in next chain and in each chain to end of row. Turn.
- Row 2: Chain 2, double crochet in same stitch and in each stitch to end of row. Turn.
- Rows 3-4: Repeat row 2.
- Row 5: Chain 1, double single crochet in each stitch to end of row. Tie off and weave ends through work.

Finishing
- Make 2 braids using 9 strands of yarn.
- Attach braids to either side of hood for ties.

November 19

Ruffled Mittens

Materials

- Worsted weight yarn
- Crochet hook size 3.5 mm

Directions

- Crochet a chain of 4 stitches. Join with a slip stitch to create a ring.
- Round 1: 12 single crochet in ring.
- Rounds 2-3: 2 single crochet in next stitch (increase), single crochet to last 2 stitches, increase. Place a stitch marker.
- Round 4: Single crochet in each stitch to end of round.
- Round 5: Repeat row 2. Repeat rounds 4-5 until there are 36 stitches. Work in straight single crochet until piece measures 6". Draw yarn through loop that is 2 stitches before the marker.

Make thumb

- Crochet a chain of 4 stitches. Join with a slip stitch to create a ring.
- Round 1: 6 single crochet in ring.
- Round 2: 2 single crochet in each stitch.
- Next rounds: Single crochet in each stitch to end of round. Continue working in rounds until piece measures 1.5".
- Next round: Increase, single crochet to last stitch, increase.

Finishing

Place thumb and main pieces together, right sides facing, so there are 5 stitches between the increase stitches of the thumb and 5 stitches of the main section. Use 5 single crochet to attach both pieces. Work in single crochet going around the entire area. In the corner where the hand and thumb meet, decrease 2 stitches every 2nd round, 5 times, and then 9 rounds of straight single crochet. In the last 3 rounds, 2 single crochet in each stitch.

November 20

Pinecones

Materials

- Brown crochet cotton #10
- Crochet hook size 4.5 mm

Directions

- Crochet a chain of 6 stitches. Join with a slip stitch to create a ring.
- Round 1: 1 single crochet, chain 3, 1 double crochet, 1 triple crochet, chain 1, slip stitch in top of triple crochet, double crochet, chain 3 single crochet. Repeat 5 more times, and you have 6 petals.
- Round 2: Chain 3, single crochet between each petal to end of round. Join.

- Round 3: In each chain space all the way around, 1 single crochet, chain 3, 1 double crochet, 1 triple crochet, chain 1, slip stitch in top of triple crochet, 1 double crochet, chain 3, 1 single crochet, chain 3, 1 triple crochet, chain 1, slip stitch in top of triple crochet, 1 double crochet, chain 3, 1 single crochet. Join.
- Round 4: * Chain 3, skip 2 petals, single crochet between single crochet stitches. Repeat from * to end of round. Join.
- Round 5: Repeat round 3.
- Round 6: Repeat round 2.
- Round 7: Repeat round 3.
- Round 8: Repeat round 2.
- Round 9: Repeat round 3.
- Round 10: Repeat round 2.
- Round 11: Repeat round 3.
- Round 12: Repeat round 2.
- Round 13: In each chain 3 space all the way around, 1 single crochet, chain 3, 1 double crochet, 1 triple crochet, chain 1, slip stitch in top of triple crochet, 1 double crochet, chain 3, 1 single crochet. Join.
- Round 14: * Chain 2, skip 1 petal, single crochet between single crochet stitches. Repeat from * to end of round.
- Round 15: Create 2 petals spaced across from one another. Tie off and weave ends through work.

November 21

Bubble Cowl

Materials

- Red Heart Super Saver yarn
- Crochet hook size 5.5 mm

Directions

Bubble stitch: Yarn over hook, insert hook in required stitch, yarn over, draw up a loop, yarn over and pull through 2 loops on hook. * Yarn over, insert hook in same stitch, yarn over, draw up a loop, yarn over, pull through 2 loops on hook. Repeat from * 5 times. Now there are 7 loops on hook. Yarn over and pull through all loops.

- Crochet a chain of 78 stitches. Join with a slip stitch to create a ring, being careful not to twist chain.
- Round 1: Chain 1, single crochet in each chain to end of round. Join with a slip stitch.
- Round 2: Chain 3, double crochet in each stitch to end of round. Join.
- Round 3: Chain 1, single crochet in each stitch to end of round. Join.
- Round 4: Chain 1, 1 bubble. * Chain 1, skip next stitch, 1 bubble. Repeat from * to end of round. Chain 1 and join.
- Round 5: Chain 1, single crochet in each stitch and in each chain 1 space to end of round. Join.
- Rounds 6-9: Repeat rounds 2 and 5.
- Rounds 10-11: Repeat rounds 2 and 3. Tie off and weave ends through work.

November 22

Pumpkin Pie Slices

Materials

- Orange and beige worsted weight yarn
- Crochet hook size 4.5 mm

Directions

- Crochet a chain of 13 stitches with orange yarn.
- Row 2: Skip first chain, single crochet in next chain and in each chain to end of row. Chain 1 and turn.
- Row 2: Single crochet in each stitch to end of row. Chain 1 and turn.
- Row 3: Single crochet 2 stitches together (decrease), 8 single crochet, decrease. Chain 1 and turn.
- Row 4: Repeat row 2.
- Row 5: Decrease, 6 single crochet, decrease. Chain 1 and turn.
- Row 6: Repeat row 2.
- Row 7: Decrease, 4 single crochet, decrease. Chain 1 and turn.
- Row 8: Repeat row 2.
- Row 9: Decrease, 2 single crochet, decrease. Chain 1 and turn.
- Row 10: Repeat row 2.
- Row 11: 2 decrease. Chain 1 and turn.
- Row 12: Repeat row 2.
- Row 13: Decrease, chain 1, single crochet around all edges of pie slice. Tie off and weave ends through work.

Finishing

Attach beige yarn at top corner of triangle. 4 double crochet in next stitch, slip stitch, 4 double crochet in next stitch, slip stitch. Repeat to end of row to create the "pie crust".

November 23

Pumpkin Pie Slice Bunting

Materials

- Orange and beige worsted weight yarn
- Crochet hook size 4.5 mm

Directions

- Make 10 or more Pumpkin Pie Slices from November 22 pattern. Set aside.
- Crochet a chain measuring 10 or more feet.
- Row 1: Skip first chain, single crochet in each chain to end of row. Turn.
- Row 2: Chain 1, skip first stitch, single crochet in each stitch to end of row. Tie off and leave tails for tying up the bunting.

Finishing

Every foot or so along the chain, attach the pumpkin pie slices with slip stitches. Tie off and weave ends through work.

November 24

Frosted Cookies

Materials

- Pink and beige worsted weight yarn
- Crochet hook size 5 mm
- Large pieces of glitter or sequins
- Glue gun and glue

Directions

Cookies
- Crochet a chain of 4 stitches with beige yarn. Join with a slip stitch to create a ring.
- Round 1: 10 double crochet in ring. Join.
- Round 2: 2 double crochet in each stitch to end of round. Tie off and weave ends through work.

Frosting
- Crochet a chain of 4 stitches with pink yarn. Join with a slip stitch to create a ring.
- Round 1: 10 half double crochet in ring. Join.
- Round 2: 2 half double crochet in each stitch to end of round. Tie off, leave tail for stitching.

Finishing
- Slip stitch frosting on top of cookie pieces.
- Make several dots of glue on the frost, and stick sequins or glitter on to mimic sprinkles.

November 25

Pumpkin Hot Pad

Materials

- Orange worsted weight yarn
- Scraps of green worsted weight yarn
- Crochet hook size 5 mm

Directions

Make 2
- Crochet a chain of 4 stitches. Join with a slip stitch to create a ring.
- Round 1: Chain 3, 13 double crochet in ring. Join.
- Round 2: Chain 3, 2 double crochet in each stitch to end of round. Join.

- Round 3: Chain 3, 1 double crochet in same stitch. * 1 double crochet, 2 double crochet in next stitch. Repeat from * to end of round. Join. Tie off and weave ends through work.

Finishing
- Slip stitch both pieces together all the way around.
- Join green yarn at top of pumpkin, and crochet a chain of 8 stitches to start the stem.
- Row 1: Skip first chain, 7 single crochet to end of chain. Tie off and weave ends through work.

November 26

Pumpkin Pie Coasters

Materials

- Orange and beige worsted weight yarn
- Crochet hook size 5 mm

Directions

Special stitch for crust: Attach beige yarn to any stitch. Chain 1. * Insert hook in first stitch to the right of the hook. Yarn over, pull through, yarn over, pull through both loops. Repeat from * to end of round. Tie off and weave ends through work.
- Crochet a chain of 4 stitches with orange yarn. Join with a slip stitch to create a ring.
- Round 1: Chain 3, 11 double crochet in ring. Join.
- Round 2: Chain 3, 2 double crochet in each stitch to end of round. Join.
- Round 3: Round 3: Chain 3, 1 double crochet in same stitch. * 1 double crochet, 2 double crochet in next stitch. Repeat from * to end of round. Tie off and weave ends through work.
- Crust round: Use special stitch.

November 27

Hat/Cowl with Pony Tail Hole

Materials

- Worsted weight yarn
- Crochet hook size 5 mm

Directions

- Crochet a chain of 64 stitches. Join with slip stitch to create a ring, being careful not to twist chain.
- Round 1: Chain 2, double crochet in each stitch to end of round. Join.
- Round 2: Chain 2, front post double crochet (FPDC) below same stitch. Back post double crochet (BPDC) around next double crochet. * FPDC around next double crochet, BPDC around next double crochet. Repeat from * to end of round. Join.
- Round 3: Chain 2, FPDC around FPDC, BPDC around next BPDC. * FPDC around next FPDC, BPDC around next BPDC. Repeat from * to end of round. Join.
- Round 4: Chain 2. Working in back loops only, double crochet in each stitch to end of round. Join.

- Round 5: Chain 2, double crochet in each stitch to end of round. Join.
- Rounds 6-15: Repeat round 5.
- Round 16: Repeat round 4.
- Round 17: Chain 2, FPDC around double crochet, BPDC around next double crochet. * FPDC around next double crochet, BPDC around next double crochet. Repeat from * to end of round. Join.
- Round 18: Chain 2, FPDC around double crochet, BPDC around next double crochet. * FPDC around next double crochet, BPDC around next double crochet. Repeat from * to end of round. Tie off and weave ends through work.

Finishing
- Crochet a chain of 90 stitches or longer. Tie off.
- Weave chain through last row of FPDC stitches. This will be the drawstring for the pony tail hole.

November 28

Double Ruffled Baby Blanket

Materials
- Red Heart Baby yarn (2 colors)
- Crochet hook size 5.5 mm

Directions
- Crochet a chain of 66 stitches.
- Row 1: Skip first 2 chains, double crochet in next chain and in each chain to end of row. Turn.
- Row 2: Chain 2, double crochet in each stitch to end of row. Turn.
- Rows 3-end: Repeat row 2 until piece reaches desired size. Tie off and switch to second color.

First Ruffle
- Round 1: Chain 1, single crochet in each stitch all the way around blanket, with 3 single crochet in each corner. Join.
- Round 2: Working in front loops only, chain 2, 2 double crochet in each stitch all the way around blanket. Tie of and weave ends through work.

Second Ruffle
- Round 1: Attach other color of yarn to base row. Chain 2, double crochet in the back loops of the base row all the way around blanket, with 3 double crochet in each corner.
- Round 2: Chain 2, 2 double crochet in each stitch to end of round. Join.
- Round 3: Chain 2. * 1 double crochet, 2 double crochet in next stitch. Repeat from * to end of round. Join. Tie off and weave ends through work.

November 29

Bejeweled Neck Warmer

Materials

- Worsted weight yarn
- Crochet hook size 5.5 mm
- Jeweled clasp (available at craft stores in findings, or take from an old piece of jewelry)
- Needle and thread

Directions

- Crochet a chain measuring 14".
- Row 1: Skip first 3 chains, double crochet in next chain and in each chain to end of row. Turn.
- Row 2: Chain 3, skip first stitch, double crochet in each stitch to end of row. Continue repeating this round until piece measures about 6". Tie off and weave ends through work.

Finishing
- Weave a piece of yarn through each end, and pull tight to gather ends. Tie off and weave ends through work.
- With needle and thread, attach jeweled clasp parts to either end of the neck warmer.

November 30

Receiving Blanket

Materials

- 2 10-ounce skeins baby yarn
- Crochet hook size 5.5 mm

Directions

- Crochet a chain of 121 stitches. Place a marker in the first chain from hook.
- Row 1: Skip first 2 chains, single crochet in next chain. * Chain 1, skip next chain, 1 single crochet. Repeat from * to end of row. Chain 1 and turn.
- Row 2: * 1 single crochet in next chain 1 space, chain 1. Repeat from * to end of row. At end of row, single crochet in same stitch as marker. Move marker after each row to keep track of your work. Chain 1 and turn.
- Rows 3-end: Repeat row 2 until pieces reaches desired size. Tie off and weave ends through work.

December

The holidays are almost upon us, and this is a great time to make gifts for loved ones. After all, a hand-crafted gift is always more appreciated than something that comes from the store, because it comes from the heart. This month, you will find all kinds of fun holiday patterns, including a Christmas tree skirt, holiday ornaments, hats, scarves, and many other patterns that are ideal for just about anyone on your holiday gift list.

December 1

Christmas Tree Skirt

Materials

- Variegated worsted weight yarn
- White worsted weight yarn
- Crochet hook size 5 mm

Directions

- Crochet a chain of 6 stitches. Join with a slip stitch to create a ring.
- Row 1: Chain 3, 16 double crochet in ring. Turn, 17 double crochet. Turn.
- Row 2: Chain 3, 2 double crochet in each stitch to end of row. Turn.
- Row 3: Chain 3, 1 double crochet in each stitch to end of row. Turn.
- Row 4: Chain 3. * 1 double crochet, 2 double crochet in next stitch. Repeat from * to end of row. Turn.
- Row 5: Repeat row 3.
- Row 6: Chain 3. * 2 double crochet, 2 double crochet in next stitch. Repeat from * to end of row. Turn.
- Row 7: Repeat row 3.
- Row 8: Chain 3. * 3 double crochet, 2 double crochet in next stitch. Repeat from * to end of row. Turn.
- Row 9: Repeat row 3.
- Row 10: Chain 3. * 4 double crochet, 2 double crochet in next stitch. Repeat form * to end of row. Turn.
- Row 11: Repeat row 3.
- Row 12: Chain 3. * 5 double crochet, 2 double crochet in next stitch. Repeat from * to end of row. Turn.
- Row 13: Repeat row 3.
- Row 14: Chain 3. * 5 double crochet, 2 double crochet in next stitch. Repeat from * to end of row. Turn.
- Repeat rows 3 and 14 until piece measures 36" in diameter. Tie off and switch to white yarn.
- Last round: Chain 3, 2 double crochet in next stitch. 3 double crochet in each stitch to end of row. Tie off and weave ends through work.

December 2

Holiday Tree

Materials

- Green worsted weight yarn
- Crochet hook size 4 mm
- Fiberfill stuffing
- Beads, pompoms, etc. for ornaments
- Green felt
- Cardboard
- Glue gun and glue

Directions

- Crochet a chain of 2 stitches.
- Round 1: 6 single crochet in second chain from hook. Join with a slip stitch.
- Round 2: Working in back loops only, 2 single crochet in each stitch to end of round. Join.
- Rounds 3-4: Chain 1, single crochet in each stitch to end of round. Join.
- Round 5: Chain 1. * 1 single crochet, 2 single crochet in next stitch. Repeat from * to end of round. Join.
- Rounds 6 and 7: Repeat rounds 3 and 4.
- Round 8: Chain 1. * 2 single crochet, 2 single crochet in next stitch. Repeat from * to end of round. Join.

- Rounds 9-10: Repeat rounds 3 and 4.
- Round 11: Chain 1. * 3 single crochet, 2 single crochet in next stitch. Repeat from * to end of round. Join.
- Rounds 12-13: Repeat rounds 3 and 4.
- Round 14: Chain 1. * 4 single crochet, 2 single crochet in next stitch. Repeat from * to end of round. Join.
- Rounds 15-16: Repeat rounds 3 and 4.
- Continue in this pattern, adding 1 single crochet to the pattern in every third round until you have 66 stitches.
- Last 2 rounds: Chain 1, single crochet in each stitch to end of round. Tie off and weave ends through work.

Finishing
- Stuff tree.
- Cut out felt and cardboard circles the same size as the bottom of the tree.
- Glue circles to bottom of tree.
- Glue ornaments to tree.

December 3

Pinwheel Garland

Materials

- Red, white, and green worsted weight yarn
- Crochet hook size 4 mm

Directions

Make red and white, and green and white pinwheels
- Crochet a chain of 4 stitches. Join with a slip stitch to create a ring. Chain 1, 1 single crochet, 4 half double crochet in ring. Pick up second color, 1 single crochet, 4 half double crochet in ring.
- Round 1: With first color, 2 half double crochet in each of the second color stitches. Pick up second color, and 2 half double crochet in each of the first color stitches.
- Round 2: With first color, 2 double crochet in each of the next 10 stitches, 1 half double crochet. * 1 half double crochet, 1 single crochet, slip stitch, chain 5. * Tie off first color and pick up second color. 2 half double crochet in next stitch. Repeat pattern in second color from * to * across next 3 stitches. Tie off, and leave long tails.

Finishing

Tie pinwheels together with the tails, making bows.

December 4

Snowman Table Ornament

Materials

- White worsted weight yarn
- Crochet hook size 3.75 mm
- Black and orange beads for eyes and nose
- Fiberfill stuffing
- Red felt

Directions

- Crochet a chain of 2 stitches.
- Round 1: 6 single crochet in second chain from hook. Join with a slip stitch.
- Round 2: Chain 1, 2 single crochet in each stitch to end of round. Join.
- Round 3: Chain 1. * 1 single crochet, 2 single crochet in next stitch. Repeat from * to end of round. Join.
- Round 4: Chain 1. * 2 single crochet, 2 single crochet in next stitch. Repeat from * to end of round. Join.
- Rounds 5-6: Repeat pattern until there are 36 stitches.
- Next round: Chain 1, single crochet in each stitch to end of round. Join.
- Repeat last round until piece measures 5".
- Next round: Chain 1. * 4 single crochet. Yarn over, draw up a loop in each of the next 2 stitches. Yarn over, draw through all loops. Repeat from * to end of round. Join.
- Next round: Chain 1. 3 single crochet, single crochet 2 stitches together (decrease). Repeat from * to end of round. Join and stuff snowman body.
- Next round: Chain 1. * 2 single crochet, decrease. Repeat from * to end of round. Join.
- Next round: Chain 1. * 1 single crochet, decrease. Repeat from * to end of round. Join.
- Next round: Chain 1. Decrease to end of round. Tie off, leaving tail for stitching.

Finishing
- Stuff snowman head, slip stitch closed.
- Glue eye and nose beads on face.
- Cut a scarf from the felt and tie it around snowman's neck.

December 5

Holiday Lightbulb Ornaments

Materials

- Green and grey worsted weight yarn
- Crochet hook size 4.5 mm
- Fiberfill stuffing
- ¼" silver ribbon
- Glue gun and glue

Directions

- Crochet a chain of 2 stitches with green yarn.
- Round 1: 6 single crochet in second chain from hook.
- Round 2: * 1 single crochet, 2 single crochet in next stitch. Repeat from * to end of round.
- Round 3: Single crochet in each stitch to end of round.
- Round 4: * 2 single crochet, 2 single crochet in next stitch. Repeat from * to end of round.
- Round 5: Repeat round 3.
- Round 6: * 3 single crochet, 2 single crochet in next stitch. Repeat from * to end of round.
- Round 7: * 4 single crochet, 2 single crochet in next stitch. Repeat from * to end of round.
- Rounds 8-11: Repeat round 3.
- Round 12: * 1 single crochet, single crochet 2 stitches together (decrease). Repeat from * to end of round. Start stuffing now and continue stuffing as you work.
- Round 13: * 2 single crochet, decrease. Repeat from * to end of round.
- Round 14-15: Repeat round 3. Tie off and weave ends through work.

- Round 16: Attach grey yarn. Chain 2, 9 single crochet in second chain from hook. Join with a slip stitch in first stitch. Tie off and weave ends through work. Slip stitch socket closed.

Finishing

Glue ribbon to ornament, and tie in a bow at the front.

December 6

Pinwheel Coasters

Materials

- White, red, and green worsted weight yarn
- Crochet hook size 5 mm

Directions

- With white yarn, crochet a chain of 4 stitches. Join with a slip stitch to create a ring. Chain 1, 1 single crochet, 1 half double crochet, 3 double crochet in ring. Pick up green yarn, 1 single crochet, 1 half double crochet, 3 double crochet in ring.
- Round 1: With white yarn, 2 double crochet in each green stitch. Pick up green yarn, 2 double crochet in each white stitch.
- Round 2: With white yarn, 2 double crochet in each of the next 10 stitches. * 1 half double crochet, 1 single crochet, slip stitch in next stitch. Tie off white and pick up green yarn. Repeat from * across next 3 stitches. Tie off and weave ends through work.

Finishing

With right side facing you, join red yarn, chain 1. * 1 single crochet, chain 2, 1 single crochet in same stitch. Repeat all the way around. Join. Tie off and weave ends through work.

December 7

Pinwheel Placemat

Materials

- White, red, and green worsted weight yarn
- Crochet hook size 5 mm

Directions

- With white yarn, crochet a chain of 4 stitches. Join with a slip stitch to create a ring. Chain 1, 1 single crochet, 1 half double crochet, 3 double crochet in ring. Pick up green yarn, 1 single crochet, 1 half double crochet, 3 double crochet in ring.
- Round 1: With white yarn, 2 double crochet in each green stitch. Pick up green yarn, 2 double crochet in each white stitch.
- Round 2: With white yarn, * 1 double crochet, 2 double crochet in next stitch. Repeat from * for 45 stitches. Pick up green yarn and repeat pattern to last stitch, 1 double crochet in last stitch.

- Round 3: With white yarn, * 3 double crochet, 2 double crochet in next stitch. Repeat from * for 83 stitches. Pick up green yarn, ** 6 double crochet, 2 double crochet in next stitch. Repeat from ** 11 times, 6 double crochet.
- Round 4: With white yarn, * 10 double crochet, 2 double crochet in next stitch. Repeat from * 8 times, 6 double crochet. Pick up green yarn, ** 6 double crochet, 2 double crochet in next stitch. Repeat from ** 14 times, 4 double crochet.
- Round 5: With white yarn, * 10 double crochet, 2 double crochet in next stitch. Repeat from * 10 times, 6 double crochet. Pick up green yarn, ** 10 double crochet, 2 double crochet in next stitch. Repeat from ** 11 times, 5 double crochet.
- Round 6: With white yarn, * 14 double crochet, 2 double crochet in next stitch. Repeat from * 9 times, 2 double crochet. Pick up green yarn, ** 18 double crochet, 2 double crochet in next stitch. Repeat from ** 7 times, 13 double crochet. Place a marker in the 77th stitch from hook.
- Round 7: With white yarn, * 18 double crochet, 2 double crochet in next stitch. Repeat from * to marker. ** 2 half double crochet, 1 single crochet, 1 slip stitch. Tie off white and pick up green yarn. Repeat form ** across next 4 stitches. Tie off and weave ends through work.'
- Finishing
- With right side facing you, join red yarn, chain 1. * 1 single crochet, chain 2, 1 single crochet in same stitch. Repeat all the way around. Join. Tie off and weave ends through work.

December 8

Holiday Stocking

Materials

- Red Heart Super Saver yarn, red
- Scraps of white yarn
- Crochet hook size 5.5 mm

Directions

Leg
- Crochet a chain of 47 stitches with white yarn.
- Row 1: Skip first chain, single crochet in next chain and in each chain to end of row. Turn.
- Row 2: Chain 1, single crochet in each stitch to end of row. Tie off, attach red yarn and turn.
- Row 3: Repeat row 2 until piece measures 12 ". Tie off.

Heel
- Next row: With right side facing, skip 35 stitches. Join white yarn, 11 single crochet. Move around to other side of leg, 11 single crochet. Turn.
- Next row: Chain 1, single crochet 2 stitches together (decrease), single crochet to last 2 stitches, decrease. Turn.
- Next row: Repeat last row until there are 4 stitches left. Start increasing at the start of each row (2 single crochet in 1 stitch) until there are 22 stitches. Tie off.

Foot
- Next row: With right side facing, skip 11 stitches of heel. Join red yarn, 11 single crochet. 2 decrease, 16 single crochet. 2 decrease, 11 single crochet. Turn. Work in even single crochet rows until foot measures 6". Tie off.

Toe
- Next row: Attach white yarn, chain 1, single crochet in each stitch to end of row. Turn.

- Next row: Chain 1, decrease, 17 single crochet, decrease. Turn.
- Next row: ** Decrease 1 stitch at each end of row until there are 3 stitches left. Tie off.
- With wrong side facing, Join white in next stitch of last long row. Repeat from ** to end of row. Tie off and weave ends through work.

Finishing
- Sew all seams.
- Attach red yarn at top edge of stocking. Chain 10, attach to make loop for hanging stocking.

December 9

Holiday Wreath Ornament

Materials

- Green worsted weight yarn
- Scraps of red yarn
- Crochet hook size 4.25 mm
- 2" ring

irections

- Round 1: Join yarn with a slip stitch around ring. Chain 1, 36 single crochet around ring. Join with a slip stitch to beginning stitch.
- Round 2: Chain 1, 1 single crochet in same stitch, chain 2. * Skip next stitch, 1 single crochet, chain 2. Repeat from * to end of round. Join.
- Round 3: 5 double crochet in first chain 2 space, skip next stitch. * 1 slip stitch, skip next stitch, 5 double crochet in next chain 2 space, skip next stitch. Repeat from * to end of round, ending with a slip stitch. Tie off and weave ends through work.

Finishing
- Cut a bit of red yarn and weave around the wreath.
- Cut another piece of red yarn and tie to the top to hang the ornament.

December 10

Snowflake Ornament

Materials

- White worsted weight yarn
- Scraps of green or red yarn
- Crochet hook size 4 mm

Directions

- Crochet a chain of 3 stitches. Join with a slip stitch to create a ring.
- Round 1: Chain 1, 5 double crochet in ring. Join.
- Round 2: Chain 5, 3 triple crochet and chain 2 in each of the next 5 stitches. 2 triple crochet in last stitch. Join.

- Round 3: Chain 2, 2 triple crochet, chain 3, 3 triple crochet in first chain space. 3 triple crochet, chain 3, 3 triple crochet in each chain space to end of round. Join. Tie off and weave ends through work.
- Round 4: Attach red yarn, chain 2, 1 double crochet in each stitch to end of round. Chain 10, join to create a hanging loop. Tie off and weave ends through work.

December 11

Holiday Bell Ornament

Materials

- White cotton fingering weight yarn
- Scraps of red fingering weight yarn
- Crochet hook size 2.5 mm

Directions

- Crochet a chain of 5 stitches. Join with a slip stitch to create a ring.
- Round 1: 10 single crochet in ring. Join.
- Round 2: 2 single crochet in each stitch to end of round. Join.
- Rounds 3-10: Single crochet in each stitch to end of round, working in spirals. Use a stitch marker to keep track of your work.
- Round 11: 2 single crochet in first stitch, 2 single crochet. Repeat pattern 5 times, 2 single crochet in next stitch, 1 single crochet.
- Round 12: Single crochet in each stitch to end of round.
- Round 13: Switch to red yarn, single crochet in each stitch to end of round. Tie off and weave ends through work.

Finishing

Cut a strand of red yarn and tie at top to create a loop for hanging ornament.

December 12

Handbag

Materials

- Red Heart Super Saver yarn
- Crochet hook size 5 mm
- 1" button
- Needle and thread

Directions

Main section
- Crochet a chain of 29 stitches.
- Row 1: Skip first chain, single crochet in next chain and in each chain to end of row. Turn.
- Rows 2-14: Chain 1, single crochet in each stitch to end of row. Turn.
- Row 15: Chain 1. Working in back loops only, single crochet in each stitch to end of row. Turn.
- Rows 16-23: Repeat row 2.

- Row 24: Repeat row 15.
- Rows 25-43: Repeat row 2.
- Row 44: Chain 1, single crochet 2 stitches together (decrease) twice. 20 single crochet, 2 decrease. Turn.
- Row 45: Chain 1, decrease twice, 16 single crochet, decrease twice. Turn.
- Row 46: Chain 1, decrease twice, 12 single crochet, decrease twice. Turn.
- Row 47: Chain 1, decrease twice, 8 single crochet, decrease twice. Turn.
- Row 48: Chain 1, decrease twice, 4 single crochet, decrease twice. Turn.
- Row 49: Repeat row 2. Do not turn. Chain 1, 50 single crochet up side, single crochet across back of foundation chain, 50 single crochet up side. 3 slip stitches, chain 8, skip 2 single stitches, join with slip stitch in next stitch to create button hole. Tie off and weave ends through work.

Sides (make 2)
- Crochet a chain of 5 stitches.
- Row 1: Skip first chain, single crochet in next 4 chains. Turn.
- Row 2: Chain 1, 2 single crochet in first stitch, 2 single crochet, 2 single crochet in last stitch. Turn.
- Row 3: Chain 1, single crochet in each stitch to end of row. Turn.
- Row 4: Chain 1, 2 single crochet in first stitch (increase), 4 single crochet, increase. Turn.
- Row 5: Repeat row 3.
- Row 6: Chain 1, increase, 6 single crochet, increase. Turn.
- Row 7: Repeat row 3.
- Row 8: Chain 1, increase, 8 single crochet, increase. Turn.
- Rows 9-12: Repeat row 3.
- Row 13: Chain 1, single crochet 2 stitches together (decrease) twice, 4 single crochet, 2 decrease. Turn.
- Row 14: Repeat row 3.
- Row 15: Chain 1, single crochet in each stitch. Do not turn. Chain 1, 14 single crochet up side, 4 single crochet across top, 14 single crochet down other side. Tie off and weave ends through work.

Strap
- Row 1: At one side of purse, single crochet 4 stitches. Turn.
- Rows 2-20: Single crochet in each stitch. Attach to other side of purse with slip stitches. Tie off and weave ends through work.

Finishing
- Stitch sides to main section of bag.
- With needle and thread, stitch button to front of purse.

December 13

Traditional Tree Ornaments

Materials

- Worsted weight yarn
- Scraps of silver yarn
- Crochet hook size 3.5 mm
- Fiberfill stuffing

Directions

- Crochet a chain of 2 stitches.
- Round 1: 6 single crochet in second chain from hook. Join with a slip stitch.

- Round 2: 2 single crochet in each stitch to end of round. Join.
- Round 3: * 1 single crochet, 2 single crochet in next stitch (increase). Repeat from * to end of round. Join.
- Round 4: * 2 single crochet, increase. Repeat from * to end of round. Join.
- Round 5: * 3 single crochet, increase. Repeat from * to end of round. Join.
- Round 6: * 4 single crochet, increase. Repeat from * to end of round. Join.
- Rounds 7-11: Single crochet in each stitch to end of round. Join.
- Round 12: * 5 single crochet, skip next stitch. Repeat form * to end of round. Join.
- Round 13: * 4 single crochet, skip next stitch. Repeat from * to end of round. Join.
- Round 14: * 3 single crochet, skip next stitch. Repeat from * to end of round. Join.
- Round 15: * 2 single crochet, skip next stitch. Repeat from * to end of round. Join and stuff ball firmly.
- Round 16: Repeat round 15.
- Round 18: 1 single crochet in every second stitch to end of round. Join. Tie off and weave ends through work.

Cap
- With silver yarn, crochet a chain of 2 stitches.
- Round 1: 6 single crochet in second chain from hook. Join.
- Round 2: 2 single crochet in each stitch to end of round. Join.
- Rounds 3-4: Single crochet in each stitch to end of round. Tie off and leave long tail for stitching.

Finishing

Slip stitch cap to top of ornament. Leave long loop for hanging.

December 14

Baby Santa Hat

Materials

- Soft yarn, red and white
- Crochet hook size 5 mm

Directions

- Crochet a chain of 2 stitches with red yarn.
- Round 1: 5 single crochet in second chain from hook. Join with a slip stitch.
- Round 2: Chain 1, 2 single crochet in first stitch (increase), single crochet to last stitch, increase. Join.
- Round 3: Chain 1, 2 single crochet in each stitch to end of round. Join.
- Rounds 4-7: Chain 1, 1 single crochet in each stitch to end of round. Join.
- Round 8: Chain 1, increase. * 1 single crochet, increase. Repeat from * to end of round. Join.
- Round 9: Chain 1, 1 single crochet in each stitch to end of round. Join.
- Round 10: Chain 1, increase. * 2 single crochet, increase. Repeat from * to end of round. Join.
- Rounds 11-13: Repeat round 4.
- Round 14: Chain 1, increase. * 3 single crochet, increase. Repeat from * to end of round. Join.
- Rounds 15-17: Repeat round 4.
- Round 18: Chain 1, increase. * 4 single crochet, increase. Repeat form * to end of round. Join.
- Rounds 19-27: Repeat round 4. Tie off and weave ends through work.

Trim
- With wrong side facing, attach white yarn where you put your last stitch.
- Row 1: Increase. * 8 single crochet, increase. Repeat from * to end of round, ending with 5 single crochet. Join.
- Rows 2-8: Chain 1, turn. Working in back loops only, single crochet in each stitch to end of row. Tie off and weave ends through work.

Finishing
- Turn trim up.
- Make a white pompom and attach it to the top of the hat with slip stitches.

December 15

Elf Ornament

Materials

- Green, white, and red worsted weight yarn
- Crochet hook size 4.5 mm
- Felt
- Glue gun and glue
- Beads for eyes

Directions

Elf hat
- Crochet a chain of 5 stitches. Join with a slip stitch to create a ring.
- Round 1: 4 single crochet in ring.
- Round 2: 2 single crochet in first stitch (increase), 1 single crochet. Repeat pattern to end of round.
- Rounds 3-6: Single crochet in each stitch to end of round.
- Round 7: Increase, 2 single crochet. Repeat to end of round.
- Round 8: Repeat round 3.
- Round 9: Increase, 3 single crochet. Repeat to end of round.
- Round 10: Repeat round 3.
- Round 11: Increase, 4 single crochet. Repeat to end of round.
- Round 12: Increase, 5 single crochet. Repeat to end of round.
- Round 13: Increase, 6 single crochet. Repeat to end of round.
- Round 14: Increase, 7 single crochet. Repeat to end of round. Tie off and switch to red yarn.
- Round 15: Repeat round 3.
- Round 16: 1 single crochet, chain 3, slip stitch in last chain, 1 single crochet. Repeat to end of round. Tie off and weave ends through work.

Finishing
- Create an 8" ball of green yarn, and a 5" ball of white yarn.
- Glue the white ball on top of the green ball. You have the head and body.
- Cut out arms, legs, and ears from felt and glue them in place.
- Glue beads to face for eyes, and a piece of felt for the nose.
- Glue elf hat to the top of the head.

December 16

Fascinator Hat

Materials

- Red Heart Shimmer yarn, black and silver
- Crochet hook size 5 mm
- Needle and thread
- Feather
- Hair clip
- Pendant or other bling
- Glue gun and glue

Directions

- Crochet a chain of 5 stitches with black yarn. Join with a slip stitch to create a ring.
- Round 1: Chain 2, 7 double crochet in ring.
- Round 2: 2 front post double crochet (FPDC) in each stitch to end of round.
- Round 3: 1 FPDC in first stitch, then FPTR (front post triple crochet) in same stitch. 2 FPTR in each stitch to end of round.
- Round 4: FPHDC in next stitch, FPSC in next stitch, slip stitch in top of next stitch. Tie off and weave ends through work.
- Round 5: Turn piece over, and attach silver yarn to the middle of the swirl. Single crochet in each stitch in swirl. Tie off and weave ends through work.

Finishing
- Glue feather to top of fascinator, and add pendant or other bling.
- Glue hair clip to bottom of fascinator.
- If you like, you can cut out pieces of tulle or lace and glue a veil to the fascinator.

December 16

Soft Scarf

Materials

- Red Heart Super Saver yarn
- Crochet hook size 5.5 mm

Directions

- Crochet a chain of 54 stitches.
- Row 1: Skip first 3 chains, 1 triple crochet, chain 1, 2 triple crochet in next chain. Skip 4 chains. 2 triple crochet, chain 1, 2 triple crochet in next stitch (shell), skip 4 chains. Repeat from * to last chain, 2 triple crochet, chain 1, 1 triple crochet in last chain. Chain 3 and turn.
- Row 2: 1 triple crochet, chain 1, 2 triple crochet in first chain space. Shell in each chain space to end, 2 triple crochet, chain 1, 1 triple crochet in last chain space. Chain 3 and turn. Repeat this row until piece reaches desired length. Tie off and weave ends through work

Finishing

Add fringes to each end of the scarf.

December 17

Holiday Candle

Materials

- White, red, and green worsted weight yarn
- Crochet hook size 5 mm
- Empty toilet paper roll

Directions

Candle
- Crochet a chain of 4 stitches with white yarn.
- Round 1: 11 double crochet in fourth chain from hook. Join with a slip stitch at the top of beginning chain 4. Turn.
- Round 2: Single crochet in same stitch as chain 1. * 2 single crochet in next stitch, 1 single crochet. Repeat from * to end of round, ending with 2 single crochet in last stitch. Join.
- Round 3: Working in back loops only, single crochet in each stitch to end of round. Join.
- Rounds 4-17: Working in both loops, repeat round 3. Tie off and weave ends through work.
- Rounds 18-22: Switch to green yarn, repeat round 4.
- Round 23: Working in back loops only, 2 single crochet in each stitch to end of round. Join.
- Round 24: 1 double crochet in same stitch as chain 4. 1 double crochet, chain 1, 1 double crochet in next stitch and in each stitch to end of round. Tie off and weave ends through work.

Base
- With green yarn, chain 15, half double crochet in third chain from hook and in each chain to end of row.
- Attach one end to first green row of candle, and the other end to row 22 (row before working in back loops only). Tie off and weave ends through work.

Flame

With red yarn, crochet a chain of 8 stitches. Slip stitch in second chain from hook. 1 single crochet, 2 half double crochet, 1 single crochet, slip stitch in last stitch. Tie off and attach to the top of candle.

December 18

Party Poncho

Materials

- Bulky or chunky yarn
- Crochet hook size 5.5 mm

Directions

- Crochet a chain of 76 stitches. Join with a slip stitch to create a ring, being careful not to twist chain.
- Round 1: Chain 2, 2 double crochet. * Chain 2, skip 2 stitches, 3 double crochet. Repeat twice. Chain 2, skip 2 stitches, 3 double crochet, chain 2, 3 double crochet in same stitch (front point). Repeat from * 7 times.

Chain 2, skip 2 stitches, 3 double crochet, chain 2, 3 double crochet in same stitch (back point). Repeat from * 3 times, chain 2, slip stitch to join.

- Round 2: Chain 5, 3 double crochet in next space. * Chain 2, 3 double crochet in space of preceding round. Repeat from * to front point. Chain 2, 3 double crochet, chain 2, 3 double crochet in center of point. Repeat from * to back point. Chain 2, 3 double crochet, chain 2, 3 double crochet in center of point. Repeat from * to end, 2 double crochet in last space. Join.
- Round 3: Chain 2, 2 double crochet in space. * Chain 2, 3 double crochet in next space. Repeat from * to end of round. Chain 2, slip stitch.
- Continue working rounds 2 and 3 until piece measures 26" at front and back points. Tie off and weave ends through work.
- Neck edge round: Insert hook in center space at back. Chain 3, 4 double crochet in same space, 4 single crochet in next space. * 5 double crochet in center of 3 double crochet of preceding round, 1 single crochet in next space. Repeat from * to end of round. Join. Tie off and weave ends through work.

Finishing
- Crochet a chain as long as you need for a cord to go through the neck hole.
- Weave chain through stitches at neck hole.
- Add a fringe all the way around bottom of poncho.

December 19

Fringed Party Purse

Materials

- Red Heart worsted weight yarn with metallic threads
- Crochet hook size 5 mm
- Velcro
- Needle and thread

Directions

- Crochet a chain measuring 6".
- Row 1: Skip first chain, single crochet in each chain to end of row. Turn.
- Row 2: Chain 1, skip first stitch, single crochet in each stitch to end of row. Turn.
- Rows 3-end: Repeat row 2 until piece measures 20". Tie off and weave ends through work.

Finishing
- Fold purse so there is a 4" overhang.
- Stitch up sides.
- Stitch Velcro to flap and front of purse for a closure.
- Attach yarn at one side, crochet a chain as long as you want for a strap, attach to other side. Tie off and weave ends through work.
- Add a fringe to the bottom of the purse.

December 20

Holiday Cat Collar

Materials

- Variegated and white worsted weight yarn
- Crochet hook size 5 mm
- Jingle bell
- Small buckle

Directions

- With variegated yarn, rochet a chain long enough to go around your cat's neck, with a couple of extra inches for buckling.
- Row 1: Skip first chain, single crochet in next chain and in each chain to end of row. Turn.
- Row 2: Switch to white yarn. Chain 2, skip first stitch, half double crochet in each stitch to end of row. Turn.
- Row 3: Switch back to variegated yarn. Chain 1, skip first stitch, single crochet in each stitch to end of row. Tie off and weave ends through work.

Finishing

- Attach buckle pieces to either end of collar.
- Attach jingle bell to center of collar.

December 21

Candy Cane Holders

Materials

- Red and white worsted weight yarn
- Crochet hook size 5 mm

Directions

- With white yarn, crochet a chain of 5 stitches. Join with a slip stitch to create a ring.
- Round 1: 10 single crochet in ring. Join, chain 1.
- Round 2: 2 single crochet in each stitch to end of round. Join. Attach red yarn and chain 1.
- Round 3: 2 half double crochet in first stitch, 1 half double crochet. Repeat to end of round. Join.
- Round 4: Double crochet in each stitch to end of round. Join. Attach white yarn, chain 1.
- Round 5: 2 single crochet in first stitch, 1 single crochet. Repeat until you have made 12 single crochet. Chain 1 and turn.
- Round 6: Single crochet in each stitch to end of round. Join. Attach red yarn, chain 15, attach to make loop for hanging. Tie off and weave ends through work.

Finishing
- Attach red yarn to 2 spots on bottom of circle.
- Crochet a chain of 5 stitches for each spot, and attach at back side. These are the loops for holding onto the candy cane. Tie off and weave ends through work.

December 22

Holiday Gift Bag

Materials

- Worsted weight yarn with metallic threads
- Crochet hook size 5 mm
- Bow
- Glue gun and glue

Directions

- Crochet a chain that measures the length you want the bottom of the gift bag to be.
- Row 1: Skip first chain, single crochet in next chain and in each chain to end of row. Turn.
- Row 2: Chain 2, skip first stitch, half double crochet in each stitch to end of row. Turn.
- Row 3: Chain 1, skip first stitch, single crochet in each stitch to end of row. Turn.
- Rows 4-end: Repeat rows 2 and 3 until piece measures the height you want the bags to be. Remember, there will be a drawstring, so the finished bags will be a bit shorter. Tie off and weave ends through work.

Finishing
- Crochet a chain long enough to use as a drawstring.
- Weave drawstring through top of bag.
- Glue bow to front of bag.

December 23

Holiday Scarf

Materials

- Red Heart Super Saver yarn in red, white, and green
- Crochet hook size 5.5 mm

Directions

- With red yarn, crochet a chain measuring 8".
- Row 1: Skip first chain, double crochet in next chain and in each chain to end of row. Turn.
- Row 2: Chain 2, skip first stitch, double crochet in next stitch and in each stitch to end of row. Turn.
- Rows 3-4: Switch to green yarn, repeat row 2.
- Rows 5-6: Switch to white yarn, repeat row 2.
- Continue in striping pattern until piece reaches desired length.

Finishing

Add a fringe with all 3 colors at each end of the scarf.

December 24

Party Shawl

Materials

- Worsted weight yarn with metallic threads
- Crochet hook size 6.5 mm

Directions

- Crochet a chain of 4 stitches. Join with a slip stitch to create a ring.
- Round 1: Chain 4, 2 double crochet, 1 triple crochet in ring. Turn.
- Round 2: Chain 4. * 1 double crochet in space between stitches, chain 1. Repeat from * twice. ** 1 double crochet, chain 1, 1 triple crochet in turning chain. Turn.
- Round 3: Chain 4. 1 double crochet, chain 1, 1 double crochet in first chain 1 space. Chain 1. * 1 double crochet in next chain 1 space, chain 1. Repeat from * to turning chain, 1 double crochet, chain 1, 1 triple crochet in turning chain. Turn. Repeat this row until piece reaches desired size.
- Edging round: Chain 1, 1 single crochet in first chain 1 space. * 3 double crochet in next chain 1 space, 1 single crochet in next chain 1 space. Repeat from * to turning chain, 1 single crochet in turning chain. Tie off and weave ends through work.

Finishing

Add a fringe along the 2 shorter sides.

December 25

Fleece Blanket with Crochet Edging

Materials

- Worsted weight yarn
- Crochet hook size 5.5 mm
- Fleece (43" by 54")
- Needle and thread

Directions

- Crochet a chain of 4 stitches.
- Row 1: Wrong side facing. Skip first 3 chains, 6 double crochet, chain 3, slip stitch in 4th chain from hook. Turn.
- Row 2: Chain 3, 6 double crochet, chain 3, slip stitch over last chain 3 of previous row. Turn.
- Row 3: Repeat row 2 until edging is big enough to go all the way around the fleece. Tie off and weave ends through work.

Finishing
- Round the corners of the fleece.
- With needle and thread, stitch crochet piece to fleece.

December 26

Wreath Ornament

Materials

- Red and green crochet thread, #10
- Crochet hook size 3 mm
- 1/4" ribbon, red
- Glue gun and glue

Directions

- Crochet a chain of 30 stitches. Join with a slip stitch to create a ring, being careful not to twist chain. Chain 1 and turn.
- Round 1: 60 single crochet in ring. Join. Chain 1 and turn.
- Round 2: 4 single crochet in each stitch to end of round. Join. Chain 2 and turn.
- Round 3: 1 double crochet in each stitch to end of round. Join. Tie off and weave ends through work.

Finishing
- Tie a piece of ribbon into a bow and glue to front of ornament.
- Tie a piece of ribbon to the top to use as a hanger.

December 27

Kid's Holiday Hat

Materials

- Red and white soft worsted weight yarn
- Crochet hook size 5 mm

Directions

- With red yarn, crochet a chain of 11 stitches.
- Row 1: Skip first chain, 1 single crochet in next chain and in each chain to end of row. Chain 1 and turn.
- Row 2: Skip first stitch. Working in back loops only, single crochet in each stitch to end of row. Switch to white yarn at last stitch. Chain 2 and turn work.
- Row 3: Skip first stitch. Working in back loops only, single crochet in each stitch to end of row. Chain 1 and turn.
- Row 4: Skip first stitch. Working in back loops only, single crochet in each stitch to end of row. At last stitch, switch to red yarn. Chain 1 and turn work. Repeat stripe pattern until there are 56 rows. You can make this part smaller or larger, depending on the size of the intended wearer's head.
- Turn piece so stripes are vertical. Work along the edge of the striped band. With red yarn, chain 1, single crochet in same space. Mark stitch. 1 single crochet in each stitch along the rows so you have a total of 56 stitches.
- Next 4 rounds: Work in spirals, move marker to keep track of your work. Single crochet in each stitch to end of round, working in both loops.
- Next round: Single crochet 2 stitches together (decrease). Mark stitch. 3 single crochet. * Decrease, 3 single crochet. Repeat from * to end of round.
- Next 5 rounds: Single crochet in each stitch to end of round.
- Next round: Decrease, 3 single crochet, decrease, 3 single crochet. Repeat pattern to end of round.

- Next 10 rounds: Single crochet in each stitch to end of round. Tie off and weave ends through work.

Finishing

Make a white pompom and attach it to the top of the hat.

December 28

Candy Cane Ornament

Materials

- Red and white worsted weight yarn
- Crochet hook size 5 mm
- Pipe cleaner

Directions

- Crochet a chain of 5 stitches with red yarn.
- Row 1: Skip first chain, single crochet in next 4 chains. Turn.
- Row 2: Single crochet in each stitch to end of row. Switch to white yarn, chain 1 and turn.
- Row 3: Single crochet in each stitch to end of row. Chain 1 and turn.
- Row 4: Repeat row 3, attach red yarn, chain 1 and turn. Repeat striping pattern until you have 24 rows. Tie off and leave long tail for stitching.

Finishing

- Cut pipe cleaner to length of crochet piece, plus ½". Bend ¼" at each end to get rid of the pointy ends.
- Wrap crochet piece around pipe cleaner, stitch all the way up the side and top and bottom edges. Tie off and weave ends through work.
- Curve piece into a candy cane shape.

December 29

Holiday Wreath

Materials

- Red, white, and green worsted weight yarn
- Crochet hook size 5.5 mm
- Fiberfill stuffing
- Jingle bells
- Large red bow
- Needle and thread

Directions

- Crochet a chain of 20 stitches with red yarn. Join with a slip stitch to create a ring, being careful not to twist chain.
- Round 1: Skip first chain, single crochet in next chain and in each chain to end of round. Join.
- Rounds 2-4: Chain 1, skip first stitch, single crochet in each stitch to end of round. Join. Switch to white yarn.

- Rounds 5-8: Repeat round 2. Continue with 4 rounds of each color until piece measures 20", making sure that there are different colors at each end. Tie off and leave tail for stitching.

Finishing
- Stuff tube.
- Make tube into a ring, slip stitch ends together.
- Sew jingle bells to various spots around wreath.
- Sew bow to front of wreath.

December 30

Stocking Ornament

Materials

- Cotton crochet thread, red
- Crochet hook size 5 mm

Directions

- Crochet a chain of 34 stitches.
- Row 1: Skip first 2 chains, half double crochet in next chain and in each chain to end of row. Chain 2 and turn.
- Row 2: 15 half double crochet, 2 half double crochet in next stitch (increase) twice for heel. 15 half double crochet, chain 2, turn.
- Row 3: Decrease twice for toe (1 half double crochet over 2 stitches), 13 half double crochet, increase, 13 half double crochet, decrease twice. Chain 2 and turn.
- Row 4: Decrease twice, 24 half double crochet, decrease twice, chain 1 and turn.
- Row 5: 5 slip stitches, 18 half double crochet, leave last 5 stitches unworked. Chain 2 and turn.
- Rows 6-15: Half double crochet in each stitch to end of row. Chain 1 and turn.
- Row 16: Single crochet in first stitch, chain 3, single crochet in same stitch. * Skip next stitch, 1 single crochet, chain 3, 1 single crochet in same stich. Repeat from * 3 times. Skip 1 stitch, single crochet in next stitch, chain 10 (hanging loop), single crochet in same stitch. ** Skip next stitch, 1 single crochet, chain 3, 1 single crochet in same stitch. Repeat from ** 3 times. Single crochet in last stitch.
- Edging round: Single crochet all the way around stocking ornament. Fold in half and slip stitch seams together.

December 31

Toboggan Ornament

Materials

- Beige worsted weight yarn
- Scraps of red worsted weight yarn
- Crochet hook size 5.5 mm
- Fabric stiffener (equal parts of white glue and water)

Directions

- Crochet a chain of 10 stitches with beige yarn.
- Row 1: Skip first chain, single crochet in next chain and in each chain to end of row. Turn.
- Row 2: Chain 1, skip first stitch, single crochet in next stitch and in each stitch to end of row. Continue working this row until piece measures 10". Tie off and weave ends through work.

Finishing
- Attach red yarn to one corner, and chain 6. Repeat on other corner.
- Curl end that has red chains so it looks like the front of a toboggan, and attach chains to base part so curled end stays curled.
- At other end of toboggan, attach red yarn at middle, crochet a chain of 10 stitches, attach to make hanging loop.
- Soak piece in fabric stiffener. Let dry overnight.

Crochet Hook Conversion Chart

Metric	USA	UK
2.00 mm	NA	14
2.25 mm	1 / B	13
2.50 mm	NA	12
2.75 mm	C	11
3.00 mm	NA	11
3.25 mm	D	10
3.50 mm	4 / E	9
3.75 mm	F	NA
4.00 mm	6	8
4.25 mm	G	NA
4.50 mm	7	7
5.00 mm	8 / H	6
5.50 mm	9 / I	5
6.00 mm	10 / J	4
6.50 mm	10 1/2 / K	3
7.00 mm	NA	2
8.00 mm	NA	0
9.00 mm	15 / N	00
10.00 mm	P	000
15.75 mm or 16mm	Q	NA

Tips and Tricks

How to Make Fringes

- Cut as many strands as you want for your fringes. Remember, there will be double the amount of strands when you are done.
- Fold strands in half.
- Slip folded end through crochet piece.
- Bring loose ends under and through the loop, draw down through loop.
- Pull tight.

How to Make Tassels

- Cut as many strands as you want for each tassel. Remember, there will be double the amount of stands when you are done.
- Fold strands in half.
- Bring up one strand, and loop it around the group of strands (about 1" from the top) 3-4 times. Tie tightly to secure.
- To hang (method 1): Loop a strand of yarn through top of tassel and tie to work. (method 2)   Crochet a chain, loop through top of tassel, and stitch to work.

How to Make Pompoms

- Cut a piece of heavy cardboard as wide as you want the pompom to be.
- Wrap yarn around the cardboard until it is fat like a ball. Cut end, leaving a tail.
- Slide yarn ball off cardboard, being careful to not let it unravel.
- Tightly wrap yarn tail around the center of the yarn ball 5-6 times. Tie off and cut end to same length as pompom end.
- Snip yarn loops to create pompom.
- Trim the ends with scissors to make pompom neat and perfectly round.

Conclusion

A year has passed. Were you able to complete all of the patterns? Don't worry if you couldn't. After all, we all have days when there is no time to sit around crafting. But, if you didn't finish them all, you still have some projects to take you into next year. Have fun and keep on crocheting.

Pattern Pictures (For Reference Only)

January

1) http://r.search.yahoo.com/_ylt=A0LEV2q2R_RV6UAA87jrFAx.;_ ylu=X3oDMTEyYmFvNGxqBGNvbG8DYmYxBHBvcwMxBHZ0aWQDQjA5NTlfMQRzZWMDc2M-/RV=2/RE=1442101303/RO=10/RU=http%3a%2f%2fwww.pinterest.com%2fpin%2f347269821236921060%2f/RK=0/RS=wgAR67qX8l_CjUZpvIfAJ.Q9EH8-
2) http://gretchkalsloomknitting.files.wordpress.com/2009/09/dscf0270.jpg
3) http://r.search.yahoo.com/_ylt=A0LEV2IZSPRVSqoArwnrFAx.;_ ylu=X3oDMTEyMmo1azFzBGNvbG8DYmYxBHBvcwMyBHZ0aWQDQjA5NTlfMQRzZWMDc2M-/RV=2/RE=1442101402/RO=10/RU=http%3a%2f%2fbaby-born-haakpatronen.clubs.nl%2ffoto%2fdetail%2f10759694_053-gehaakte-ponchojpg/RK=0/RS=rnAqHET1VcQMFSSHe1xT6ycz4yc-
4) http://media-cache-ak0.pinimg.com/736x/75/ae/90/75ae90b6a7e856b6be7d255e52fac8af.jpg
5) https://sp.yimg.com/ib/th?id=JN.hPgYYcWcL90hFBmmSflUlw&pid=15.1&P=0&w=300&h=300
6) http://img0.etsystatic.com/035/1/6084355/il_fullxfull.519322924_cbn3.jpg
7) http://cf2.primecp.com/master_images/AllFreeCrochet/crochet-clutch.jpg
8) http://4.bp.blogspot.com/-QLK_zVNH3Mk/T3pTLNZQaJI/AAAAAAAABt0/jZz05XSEfSQ/s1600/DSC_0522.JPG
9) http://4.bp.blogspot.com/_tlkclNHd8gk/S78Rhi-4jBI/AAAAAAAAFac/RiEF99OiFtQ/s1600/Vic%27s+red+shawl+and+black+jacket+002.JPG
10) S
11) http://3.bp.blogspot.com/-jj4SYcs5m1s/UZTD51z0yiI/AAAAAAAAPfw/ru5etkscgCE/s1600/DSC04669.JPG
12) http://ny-image3.etsy.com/il_fullxfull.121790747.jpg
13) http://djiqd110ru30i.cloudfront.net/upload/115420/pattern/43614/full_1313_43614_ReallyEasySlouchyBeanie_1.jpg
14) http://4.bp.blogspot.com/_Nuy3C-4CzOc/S76p7ZdOksI/AAAAAAAAAQ0/0sYQqBeZNYE/s1600/soap+saver+001.jpg
15) http://www.crochetspot.com/wp-content/uploads/2009/11/lanyard.jpg
16) http://2.bp.blogspot.com/-1sApiRM2Xig/Uai92VCotEI/AAAAAAAAArc/6jM_fKNnf1o/s1600/2013-05-31+15.11.00.jpg
17) http://cdnpix.com/show/1103382595591740874_VYc6ToDm_c.jpg
18) https://img0.etsystatic.com/013/0/6382433/il_214x170.427552872_pi1t.jpg
19) https://sp.yimg.com/ib/th?id=JN.FiQRIkfGp1FAblZSpsT4HQ&pid=15.1&P=0&w=300&h=300
20) http://3.bp.blogspot.com/-jL5z5Mfi7cM/T1eQeg0PCZI/AAAAAAAAcGQ/OEu1bwnXr_U/s400/Crochet-frames-212%2B060.jpg
21) http://s4.thisnext.com/media/largest_dimension/77A81DE1.jpg
22) http://cf.primecp.com/master_images/AllFreeCrochet/easy-child-apron.jpg (without top piece)
23) http://3.bp.blogspot.com/-cBdUF-PVnLc/URV0H8qweBI/AAAAAAAAArI/jL-sQsjU0GQ/s1600/IMG_5539.JPG
24) http://www.artfire.com/uploads/product/2/662/59662/5559662/5559662/large/blue_ombre_key_ring_change_purse_crocheted_d111671d.jpg
25) http://4.bp.blogspot.com/-ljSira3ZssM/T9Zt0z9JvWI/AAAAAAAAHa0/ZspPihwu5tI/s320/P1430342.JPG
26) http://www.how-to-crochet-instructions.com/images/crochetsamples11.jpg
27) http://www.mooglyblog.com/wp-content/uploads/2013/03/Cotton-Bib.jpg
28) http://www.craftsunleashed.com/wp-content/uploads/2013/11/crochet-bow-9.jpg
29) https://sp.yimg.com/ib/th?id=JN.w0MEYcA2Ik6hSdmrRe4PYg&pid=15.1&P=0&w=300&h=300
30) http://www.clipwithpurpose.com/wp-content/uploads/2011/05/IMG_00562-300x196.jpg
31) http://www.lomets.com/wp-content/uploads/2014/06/remote-control-holder-crochet1.jpg

February

1) https://sp.yimg.com/ib/th?id=JN.PBlHoe8L62SqzNP1iFRWQw&pid=15.1&P=0&w=300&h=300

2) http://s2.hubimg.com/u/9490821_f260.jpg
3) https://farm2.staticflickr.com/1413/1479583618_252558ba95.jpg
4) https://sp.yimg.com/ib/th?id=JN.gyzQlz2cyg8lWg60GnajBA&pid=15.1&P=0&w=300&h=300
5) http://media-cache-ak0.pinimg.com/736x/9d/ee/58/9dee5851b186cee19618744ba0037e97.jpg
6) http://3.bp.blogspot.com/_pZ4M75ciE44/TULTdBYqGAI/AAAAAAAACH4/FJe9SD1wB_o/s1600/
CrochetHeartEarrings%2Bset2.jpg
7) http://www.everythingetsy.com/wp-content/uploads/2015/02/Crochet-Kiss-Pattern.jpg
8) http://media-cache-ak0.pinimg.com/736x/aa/57/e3/aa57e37a8d1b94da631e399c0e19486d.jpg
9) http://img1.etsystatic.com/000/0/5204261/il_570xN.195588581.jpg
10) https://sp.yimg.com/ib/th?id=JN.jlx5vTKcP5GO9vN1xhvTWQ&pid=15.1&P=0&w=300&h=300
11) http://www.bestfreecrochet.com/wp-content/uploads/2011/01/FD022-Country-Hearts-Dishcloth_800-
300x289.jpg
12) http://www.cre8tioncrochet.com/wp-content/uploads/2013/01/super-easy-free-crochet-heart-pattern1.jpg
13) S
14) S
15) http://gretchkalsloomknitting.files.wordpress.com/2009/09/dscf0276.jpg
16) http://djiqd110ru30i.cloudfront.net/upload/1489482/pattern/59728/full_9628_59728_
BalletSlippersCrochetbabyGirlShoes_1.jpg
17) S
18) http://www.lionbrand.com/origpics/80933ada.jpg
19) http://www.1dogwoof.com/wp-content/uploads/2013/04/crochet_bracelet-2.jpg
20) S
21) http://cobblerscabin.files.wordpress.com/2010/02/ag-scrapghan.jpg
22) https://img1.etsystatic.com/045/0/6077528/il_340x270.679442817_cwli.jpg (style reference only)
23) https://sp.yimg.com/ib/th?id=JN.ZKkdptKi3kxF459tlLw%2fgw&pid=15.1&P=0&w=300&h=300
24) http://cdn.craftsy.com/upload/497610/project/42447/full_6543_42447_CrochetHookCase_2.jpg
25) http://www.guidepatterns.com/wp-content/uploads/2015/05/Free-Crochet-Bracelet-Patterns.jpg
26) http://images4-d.ravelrycache.com/uploads/Sara1234/52366978/vc_draft_small_best_fit.jpg
27) http://www.crochetnmore.com/fashiondollsleepingbagpix.jpg
28) http://4.bp.blogspot.com/-_29rknk7Eqk/TxGPK-ITxmI/AAAAAAAAIPc/LQO-YdcPYeU/s1600/
May+2010+022.JPG (style reference only)
29) http://www.mooglyblog.com/wp-content/uploads/2012/10/bun-cover-front.jpg

March

1) https://s3.amazonaws.com/suite101.com.prod/article_images/large/9a2ec9c3-cb0e-42af-a476-13587d86ff80.jpg
2) http://media-cache-ak0.pinimg.com/736x/d4/bd/9d/d4bd9d3b89f5ab7626e8636a8760cb73.jpg (design for
reference only)
3) https://sp.yimg.com/ib/th?id=JN.%2ftI4fAqBb19byoZXvYv4Aw&pid=15.1&P=0&w=300&h=300
4) http://media-cache-ak0.pinimg.com/736x/4d/57/36/4d57365a635ea9dbac4fd220d02bd257.jpg
5) S
6) http://1.bp.blogspot.com/-0tkzwOnr490/US9eup60xCI/AAAAAAAAAYc/6I4y2KASfRY/s1600/clover-1d.jpg
7) http://1.bp.blogspot.com/-0tkzwOnr490/US9eup60xCI/AAAAAAAAAYc/6I4y2KASfRY/s1600/clover-1d.jpg
8) http://2.bp.blogspot.com/-XIBL8LjKU6g/UwQBe0EsKVI/AAAAAAAABYw/m_gLK-UseYU/s1600/
clovergranny.jpg
9) See March 4 Garland Pattern
10) http://media-cache-ak0.pinimg.com/736x/10/13/8f/10138f00598ef1bfee7b8159fe605bc9.jpg
11) http://grandmotherspatternbook.com/wp-content/uploads/2012/02/3354128094_c230d758b1gold.jpg
12) https://sp.yimg.com/ib/th?id=JN.xiE%2fftdJtjyaZNtROXc56A&pid=15.1&P=0&w=300&h=300
13) See March 8 Granny Shamrock Pattern
14) http://www.cre8tioncrochet.com/wp-content/uploads/2013/01/super-easy-free-crochet-heart-pattern1.jpg
15) https://img1.etsystatic.com/000/0/5282981/il_fullxfull.210275817.jpg
16) http://s2.hubimg.com/u/9490821_f260.jpg
17) http://3.bp.blogspot.com/-TszSgSMFfVg/TxR51_TqpXI/AAAAAAAABmY/9PdUiSNoNAo/s1600/lep+4+lucky.
jpg
18) http://i1.ytimg.com/vi/j_8He623MWg/hqdefault.jpg

19) http://4.bp.blogspot.com/-ljSira3ZssM/T9Zt0z9JvWI/AAAAAAAAHa0/ZspPihwu5tI/s320/P1430342.JPG
20) http://dabblesandbabbles.com/wp-content/uploads/2013/07/Crochet_Cat_Toy_5.jpg
21) https://sp.yimg.com/ib/th?id=JN.WmwjRBNAtgtDgUsfxyH0Qw&pid=15.1&P=0&w=300&h=300 (style reference only)
22) S
23) http://4.bp.blogspot.com/_tlkclNHd8gk/S78Rhi-4jBI/AAAAAAAAFac/RiEF99OiFtQ/s1600/Vic%27s+red+shawl+and+black+jacket+002.JPG
24) http://2.bp.blogspot.com/_6BQiq4EtUXI/S1EanNtOXMI/AAAAAAAACGM/ppBgTRzv0bw/s400/CROCHET+BOOK+COVER.jpg
25) http://www.allcrafts.net/images/cropurse/184.jpg
26) http://media-cache-ak0.pinimg.com/236x/be/17/92/be17920e5b2cb11ddc5c3395997b6f80.jpg (style reference only)
27) http://www.artfire.com/uploads/product/4/624/13624/5813624/5813624/large/hand_crocheted_skirt_and_tops_for_fashion_doll_6099__cce0a0da.jpg
28) http://www.mooglyblog.com/wp-content/uploads/2012/12/Crochet-Chain-Link-Necklace.jpg (style reference only)
29) http://www.mooglyblog.com/wp-content/uploads/2012/12/Crochet-Chain-Link-Necklace.jpg
30) http://3.bp.blogspot.com/-lRxhxRIimxM/UHRpfTY8foI/AAAAAAAAC8k/u2dXqhqwV0k/s1600/SnowmanHat_Poms.jpg
31) http://www.favecrafts.com/Sewing/Cleavage-Be-Gone (style reference only)

April

1) http://3.bp.blogspot.com/-vBhsDeccWLE/TlHklfTf6RI/AAAAAAAAEo0/t2hWpvA_Jkk/s1600/blue+cushion+1.jpg
2) https://sp.yimg.com/ib/th?id=JN.bY46vrU40aCsdJ1HVZ6EjA&pid=15.1&P=0&w=300&h=300
3) http://1.bp.blogspot.com/-c9FI5R1M_XU/UQq9N907huI/AAAAAAAAEm0/wALkvSRFqQk/s1600/BunnyHat.jpg
4) http://1.bp.blogspot.com/-7LCFSe8Lbc8/UdiFSK-LtvI/AAAAAAAAQfk/FbuGBCykgEY/s1600/Barbie+crochet+cocktail+dress+004.JPG (style reference only)
5) http://www.crochethooksyou.com/wp-content/uploads/2010/12/Easy-Crochet-Bookmark.jpg
6) http://media-cache-ak0.pinimg.com/736x/eb/02/b2/eb02b2b95be32757f871e113ffb889a5.jpg
7) https://sp.yimg.com/ib/th?id=JN.Y3pFV2icAJGHW%2fvAWylgig&pid=15.1&P=0&w=300&h=300 (style reference only)
8) http://4.bp.blogspot.com/-RNvumaYM9fI/T2Ys3HWdJFI/AAAAAAAAAoU/K1PbCKS09bQ/s1600/Egg+Coaster+Set+re.jpg
9) http://2.bp.blogspot.com/-RDCEzkiOeb8/UXmqsYWpS5I/AAAAAAAAAks/5Fg5cpxRIsY/s1600/bunnyloveypattern.jpg
10) http://www.crochetmemories.com/patterns/i/lacycross1.jpg
11) S
12) S
13) http://cherishedbliss.com/wp-content/uploads/2013/03/Mini-Crochet-Easter-Egg-Baskets3.jpg
14) https://sp.yimg.com/ib/th?id=JN.m40Urydx8qY8nnA%2fLDDw%2bw&pid=15.1&P=0&w=300&h=300 (style reference only)
15) http://cf2.primecp.com/master_images/AllFreeCrochet/Checkboard-rug.jpg
16) http://4.bp.blogspot.com/-rBdktibqj14/UYKCkM7DSyI/AAAAAAAAFTo/s3L_RjfGsQY/s1600/NewbornBabyBooties2.jpg
17) http://i2.wp.com/www.jjcrochet.com/blog/wp-content/uploads/2012/11/Crochet-Baby-Bear-Hat-s.jpg
18) https://sp.yimg.com/ib/th?id=JN.4yOjIlx5vv4SQC1uUVGX7w&pid=15.1&P=0&w=300&h=300
19) https://img0.etsystatic.com/043/2/6700357/il_340x270.647131876_fs22.jpg (reference only)
20) http://img1.etsystatic.com/037/0/8963944/il_570xN.544872817_mmcp.jpg
21) S
22) http://cf2.primecp.com/master_images/Crochet/gingham-dishcloth.jpg
23) http://fc07.deviantart.net/fs71/i/2012/257/5/9/amigurumi_baby_octopus_keychain_by_erysne-d5ekir1.jpg
24) http://3.bp.blogspot.com/-Yp_6vq2qtUM/T1IpVHaR6GI/AAAAAAAABQg/qB4O69ZAwZc/s1600/maracas_amigurumi_baby_rattle_tutorial_pattern_easy_cotton_wool.JPG

25) http://4.bp.blogspot.com/-7mTyEgOsSI4/UkmjORummjI/AAAAAAAAC_w/NOVsEzu_-Rk/s1600/100_8385.JPG
26) http://in1.ccio.co/oD/c5/64/il570xN417592365m20a.jpg
27) S
28) https://sp.yimg.com/ib/th?id=JN.puKNl0i2LAYJ%2bGm2SaPWuA&pid=15.1&P=0&w=300&h=300
29) http://media-cache-ak0.pinimg.com/736x/bb/57/72/bb57724ae8ad4e913a53e8e235f6c3bd.jpg
30) http://creativejewishmom.typepad.com/.a/6a011570601a80970b019b0171894c970b-800wi

May

1) http://images.coplusk.net/project_images/51367/image/full_3570936022_4d27731c2a_b_1272548717.jpg
2) https://sp.yimg.com/ib/th?id=JN.oO%2bf745VUKWDzfVHqFvc3A&pid=15.1&P=0&w=300&h=300 (stuff instead of making case)
3) S
4) http://d1nr5wevwcuzuv.cloudfront.net/product_photos/202784/Solid_lavendar_original.JPG (style reference only)
5) http://grandmotherspatternbook.com/wp-content/uploads/2013/06/7391588584_b3cbcd191b.jpg
6) http://i.ytimg.com/vi/dHB6SdGUmf8/maxresdefault.jpg
7) https://lh4.googleusercontent.com/-tsyrSOaaxng/TX0ShG6GtQI/AAAAAAAAAd8/TxNwKVbCem8/s1600/FV_Red.jpg
8) http://3.bp.blogspot.com/-PfEvb3D6ziM/TntSXgOnKQI/AAAAAAAAAHo/heOPbvw1DoQ/s1600/Crochet+brooch.jpg
9) https://sp.yimg.com/ib/th?id=JN.6NVEdpGwmd%2bp1NQ21T96cw&pid=15.1&P=0&w=300&h=300
10) https://sp.yimg.com/ib/th?id=JN.IC2mGzA2miEj4p%2b7YcHt3w&pid=15.1&P=0&w=300&h=300
11) http://1.bp.blogspot.com/-QKreZhzDDac/TaBEc-QLo6I/AAAAAAAAAXI/IJ_n2i0MLB0/s320/pink+pillow.jpg (no ruffle)
12) http://simplycollectiblecrochet.com/wp-content/uploads/2014/06/Baby-Rattle-Blocks-Free-Pattern-by-SimplyCollectibleCrochet-2c.jpg
13) http://3.bp.blogspot.com/_Jcn6FisT5qM/Sbl3zS4G5bI/AAAAAAAA_E/W4XKe3WZgYU/s320/bottle+covers.jpg
14) http://media-cache-ak0.pinimg.com/736x/23/0b/31/230b317704d993f640187438da90009d.jpg
15) http://img0.etsystatic.com/000/0/6404355/il_570xN.330195758.jpg
16) http://www.crochetspot.com/wp-content/uploads/2011/01/crochet-belts.jpg (reference only)
17) http://i.ytimg.com/vi/E0Tvx4FX0_k/maxresdefault.jpg
18) http://cf2.primecp.com/master_images/Crochet/Crochet-Newsboy-Cap.jpg
19) http://cache.lionbrand.com/stores/lionbrand/pictures/80063ada.jpg
20) S
21) https://sp.yimg.com/ib/th?id=JN.fjbIALm2immMLUX0KbzsPQ&pid=15.1&P=0&w=300&h=300 (chain, not ruffle edging)
22) http://www.hookedonneedles.com/uploaded_images/Janes-blanket3-789606.JPG
23) http://www.petalstopicots.com/wp-content/uploads/2013/08/crochet-flower-paper-clips-1-of-2.jpg
24) http://stitch11.com/wp-content/uploads/2012/10/0081-768x1024.jpg
25) https://farm9.staticflickr.com/8080/8297363198_6da46b1ed7_z.jpg
26) http://jp5.r0tt.com/l_eba6cc20-e2f9-11e1-aa56-59d257700005.jpg (tassels instead of flower)
27) https://img0.etsystatic.com/004/0/5574618/il_570xN.374371382_l2gv.jpg
28) http://www.crochetnmore.com/dogbandanapix.jpg
29) S
30) https://img1.etsystatic.com/037/1/7123806/il_570xN.607386345_4urz.jpg
31) https://sp.yimg.com/ib/th?id=JN.aZ1b3rcDYfC9pBd40IWp4w&pid=15.1&P=0&w=300&h=300
32) http://img1.etsystatic.com/000/0/6727646/il_570xN.324132431.jpg

June

1) http://annemarieshaakblog.blogspot.nl/2012/10/apple-paperclip-tutorial.html
2) http://cre8tioncrochet.com/2013/04/bridal-garter-free-crochet-pattern/
3) http://www.desi88.com/wp-content/uploads/2014/05/ring-bearer-pillow-knit-pattern.jpg

4) http://media-cache-ec0.pinimg.com/236x/89/e0/34/89e03431a0da1eff4a25df0ca5562ccf.jpg
5) https://sp.yimg.com/ib/th?id=JN.ypNMgFNk3fkqEla7MR6HJg&pid=15.1&P=0&w=300&h=300
6) http://4.bp.blogspot.com/-398HRLvnP6o/TdvKm4N4MlI/AAAAAAAAALU/NUWd3ukFyy0/s1600/IMG_1170b.jpg
7) http://3.bp.blogspot.com/-vYOJmK02DGY/UaQYGfbMRGI/AAAAAAAAH3c/WIRVenVZpG0/s1600/IMG_8885.JPG
8) http://media-cache-ec0.pinimg.com/736x/45/66/67/4566670fbb63c1b443b90688e73c958b.jpg
9) http://media-cache-ak0.pinimg.com/736x/75/c0/9a/75c09a7fb98f510996ae2b160165bbf6.jpg
10) http://www.tinytimtams.com/wp-content/uploads/2012/02/DSC0245.jpg
11) http://www.learn-how-to-crochet.com/wedding-bell.html
12) http://3.bp.blogspot.com/-d6FxvNPsero/TZj--U3z_6I/AAAAAAAAADE/Hi9m5ZFSlvg/s1600/crochet%2Bmesh%2Bshopper%2Bbag%2Bw%2Bflower.jpg
13) http://www.allfreecrochet.com/Wedding-Crochet/Wedding-Favor-Bags
14) https://tubachingching.wordpress.com/2008/05/06/easy-peasy-catnip-mouse/
15) http://2.bp.blogspot.com/-1sApiRM2Xig/Uai92VCotEI/AAAAAAAAArc/6jM_fKNnf1o/s1600/2013-05-31+15.11.00.jpg
16) http://media-cache-ak0.pinimg.com/736x/e9/44/53/e9445319c268f6f4c4d021b3de14605d.jpg
17) http://www.crochetnmore.com/bridalhankie.htm
18) http://3.bp.blogspot.com/-KNMEJZvNIZw/T_TgKKBqwpI/AAAAAAAAAk0/eiF2aQymFYw/s1600/Sprite+Bangles+03.jpg
19) http://www.jennyandteddy.com/wp-content/uploads/2013/10/9-crochet-bow-hair-clip-450x300.jpg
20) http://www.mooglyblog.com/wp-content/uploads/2012/06/wool-striped-wallet-interior.jpg
21) http://www.ehow.com/how_12093820_make-baby-crochet-tutu-dress.html
22) http://cdnpix.com/show/imgs/c366cb92f6f24db5c27d09e379651535.jpg
23) S
24) https://sp.yimg.com/ib/th?id=JN.zcPzkNNu6qHDHNfE3Qn3fg&pid=15.1&P=0&w=300&h=300
25) http://artthreads.blogspot.ca/2012/05/monday-project-something-blue-bridal.html
26) S
27) https://sp.yimg.com/ib/th?id=JN.%2fYINnzRFLNcU5z8xk%2bD3gg&pid=15.1&P=0&w=300&h=300
28) http://www.lionbrand.com/patterns/80305AD.html
29) S
30) http://www.learn-how-to-crochet.com/basket.html

July

1) http://media-cache-ak0.pinimg.com/736x/fd/ec/15/fdec153a0a69128ff65d20141deaf3d9.jpg
2) http://media-cache-ec0.pinimg.com/736x/cc/43/21/cc432197f0476fa7a219db9352024dc0.jpg (style reference only)
3) https://sp.yimg.com/ib/th?id=JN.NKmmz6eIsnBu7EwC2%2bOrdg&pid=15.1&P=0&w=300&h=300
4) http://crochet4you1.tripod.com/photos/POT.JPG
5) https://s-media-cache-ak0.pinimg.com/236x/2d/89/c0/2d89c0e98b6c662ebc100e2196de2f55.jpg
6) http://djiqd110ru30i.cloudfront.net/upload/759075/pattern/18187/full_9207_18187_LilCuteCrochetFlower_1.jpg
7) S
8) http://img1.etsystatic.com/000/0/5622199/il_570xN.158578117.jpg
9) http://img1.etsystatic.com/000/0/5622199/il_570xN.158578117.jpg
10) http://media-cache-ak0.pinimg.com/736x/de/a0/cc/dea0ccdd377436757458eb983ec28906.jpg
11) http://images4.ravelrycache.com/uploads/elizabeth-ray/96091537/rug3_medium2.jpg (style reference only)
12) http://blog.expressionfiberarts.com/2012/07/25/bohemian-barefoot-sandals-free-crochet-pattern/
13) S
14) http://beacrafter.com/crochet-pink-striped-tank-top/
15) http://media-cache-ec0.pinimg.com/736x/48/66/65/48666519ae658c1bb863c80f1e09f4fe.jpg (style reference only)
16) http://mcdn.zulilyinc.com/images/cache/product/350x1000/1284/youngcolors_A137-R.jpg (style reference only)
17) https://img0.etsystatic.com/047/0/9318108/il_570xN.693660452_f1xe.jpg (style reference only)

18) http://katiescrochetgoodies.com/2014/07/free-usa-cozie-pattern.html

19) http://2.bp.blogspot.com/-2l_nSd1f6yQ/T-Ygg-zZQ0I/AAAAAAAABUk/TLjhF1Vrib8/s1600/
baby+hat+and+bootee+set-cree+crochet+patterns+%25282%2529.JPG

20) http://2.bp.blogspot.com/-2l_nSd1f6yQ/T-Ygg-zZQ0I/AAAAAAAABUk/TLjhF1Vrib8/s1600/
baby+hat+and+bootee+set-cree+crochet+patterns+%25282%2529.JPG

21) http://crochetncrafts.com/crochet-sandals/

22) http://www.favecrafts.com/Crochet-Bags/Crochet-Summer-Tote

23) http://donnascrochetdesigns.com/printerfriendlyone/red-white-blue-chair-pad-free-crochet-pattern.html

24) https://sp.yimg.com/ib/th?id=JN.GXH14hk8%2fEAyfPZcmC9R5Q&pid=15.1&P=0&w=300&h=300

25) S

26) http://www.allfreecrochet.com/4th-of-July-Crochet/All-American-Apron-from-Lion-Brand

27) S

28) http://www.favecrafts.com/Pet-Crochet-Patterns/Crochet-Dog-Doo-Doo-Bag-Holder

29) http://media-cache-ec0.pinimg.com/736x/56/ca/90/56ca909debe03b6d5bcd3cd93913dd76.jpg

30) http://1.bp.blogspot.com/_FU3TM3a9Urc/TEeYMin9rBI/AAAAAAAAAdY/GYo5MMcQIIo/s1600/
EGCrochetTubeHolder4.jpg

August

1) http://www.crochetnmore.com/9x13casseroletotepix2.jpg (style reference only)

2) http://media-cache-ak0.pinimg.com/736x/53/f5/47/53f5476be4c4a26afea87bd84d5a3120.jpg

3) http://deltiondotorg1.files.wordpress.com/2013/07/il_570xn-463707261_1tcr.jpg?w=470&h=352

4) http://2.bp.blogspot.com/-IEKJjvI3AOI/Td3PQ3axRLI/AAAAAAAAH0w/WVHBhhKtDqk/s1600/Crochet_
Ribbed+Dishcloths_Tutorial_DSC_6105.jpg

5) http://media-cache-ak0.pinimg.com/736x/53/f5/47/53f5476be4c4a26afea87bd84d5a3120.jpg

6) http://2.bp.blogspot.com/-XJHKl7vQ2HI/UsA5aSutQjI/AAAAAAAAACQ/udpz4q-_Y1E/s1600/
infinity+scarf+crochet+pattern.jpg (style reference only)

7) https://farm4.staticflickr.com/3557/3348446684_dd9fed4899.jpg

8) http://calleighsclips.blogspot.ca/2012/07/free-pattern-superhero-capes-and-masks.html

9) http://calleighsclips.blogspot.ca/2012/07/free-pattern-superhero-capes-and-masks.html

10) http://www.craftown.com/images/32/2/1888/sb%205%20v2.jpg

11) S

12) http://www.lionbrand.com/origpics/l10271a.jpg

13) https://whomadethat.files.wordpress.com/2013/03/crochet-bolster-issue-49.jpg?w=261&h=261&crop=1

14) http://www.crochet-world.com/images/contents/walker_caddy_300.jpg (style reference only)

15) S

16) http://www.artfire.com/uploads/product/8/168/70168/2870168/2870168/large/hot_pink_beaded_crocheted_
sash_or_belt_small_teen_or_ladies_b21b51d8.jpg (style reference only)

17) https://s-media-cache-ak0.pinimg.com/236x/d5/c4/c1/d5c4c1e9eb627f411c0859066d03ef96.jpg

18) http://allcraftsblogs.com/dolls/crochet_striped_shift_doll_pattern/crochet_striped_shift_doll_pattern.html

19) http://allicrafts.blogspot.ca/2010/10/free-pattern-jingle-ring-toy.html

20) https://sp.yimg.com/ib/th?id=JN.OiJIbdUDM9AUY2cN7AaEYg&pid=15.1&P=0&w=300&h=300 (style
reference only)

21) S

22) S

23) https://sp.yimg.com/ib/th?id=JN.%2br6u3FxHP1xR%2bqAloHfw4Q&pid=15.1&P=0&w=300&h=300

24) http://cdn.instructables.com/FEN/QJD7/H994T4V9/FENQJD7H994T4V9.MEDIUM.jpg

25) S

26) http://www.artfire.com/uploads/product/5/945/23945/4423945/4423945/large/pink_and_blue_bingo_
bag_0ce74ceb.jpg

27) http://lh4.ggpht.com/-vpgwILPDGUg/TaDQaQPi58I/AAAAAAAAADU/QZNuKr3_Ntc/DSCF0233a.jpg

28) http://www.crochetnmore.com/emmasbabyrattle.htm

29) http://3.bp.blogspot.com/-hs1dni9leF4/Ty0L1tT13BI/AAAAAAAADc4/5XJUQTUboyg/s1600/
crochet,+feb+3+009.jpg

30) http://www.artfire.com/uploads/product/8/978/14978/314978/10314978/large/fuschia_sparkle_crochet_hat_
and_scarf_set_made_for_american_girl_dolls_5ef69ad5.jpg

31) S

September

1) http://media-cache-ak0.pinimg.com/736x/a5/45/f0/a545f007827df814dcfb10f33f9fa399.jpg (style reference only)
2) S
3) http://4.bp.blogspot.com/-XLMQWByZZwU/To_3B6qG9JI/AAAAAAAAANw/3mCRRTgRJPY/s1600/Crocheted+Beanbag1.jpg
4) http://cache.lionbrand.com/stores/eyarn/upload/20110708/couponholder1.jpg (style reference only)
5) https://sp.yimg.com/ib/th?id=JN.vMYUzuHBvxXkzp1loV%2fPSg&pid=15.1&P=0&w=300&h=300
6) http://img1.etsystatic.com/000/0/5141789/il_570xN.264814563.jpg
7) https://sp.yimg.com/ib/th?id=JN.3J191tK5RG1YKN%2be0KwE1w&pid=15.1&P=0&w=300&h=300
8) S
9) http://jp5.r0tt.com/l_50a2d270-d1a6-11e1-ae87-e7af1cf00005.jpg
10) http://suzies-yarnie-stuff.blogspot.ca/2009/03/doggie-kong-c.html
11) https://sp.yimg.com/ib/th?id=JN.vmIlkcnwjN65UcDnxl4QNw&pid=15.1&P=0&w=300&h=300 (style reference only)
12) http://i.ytimg.com/vi/H2KAS6utzT4/hqdefault.jpg (style reference only)
13) http://bonanzleimages.s3.amazonaws.com/afu/images/3170/6297/IMG_0001.jpg
14) S
15) http://4.bp.blogspot.com/-p402Yc6IpWc/TgEETJ-AgnI/AAAAAAAACo8/FfeK_0cUNH0/s1600/teachersgifts5.jpg (style reference only)
16) http://media-cache-ec0.pinimg.com/736x/75/8e/56/758e56460844a47653a3860a93a65017.jpg
17) http://media.tumblr.com/tumblr_lm5kxrZdMq1qj1dkj.jpg
18) http://jp7.r0tt.com/l_8188c1c0-23b1-11e2-b000-01162e100007.jpg
19) S
20) http://media-cache-ak0.pinimg.com/736x/e5/04/77/e50477348b264ff284636d214f3e48ab.jpg
21) http://media-cache-ec0.pinimg.com/736x/0f/14/0b/0f140bf6993b4f65e1695e53a05a0571.jpg
22) http://2.bp.blogspot.com/_tPvRo0xaLUI/TCI9ArgjyDI/AAAAAAAAA1Y/8R7lY_0DN5E/s400/JoAnnes+finger+puppets.jpg (style reference only)
23) http://i25.photobucket.com/albums/c66/Wibit/Eyemask.jpg
24) S
25) S
26) https://sp.yimg.com/ib/th?id=JN.jeFNGGEMAVJvUX8gAN4m%2bg&pid=15.1&P=0&w=300&h=300
27) http://sarainakko.blogspot.ca/2011/02/earmuff-headband-crochet-pattern.html
28) https://opgrat.files.wordpress.com/2012/06/crochet-hat.jpg
29) http://d2droglu4qf8st.cloudfront.net/1005/30/169347/Simple-Triangle-Shawl_Medium_ID-583384.jpg?v=583384
30) http://media-cache-ak0.pinimg.com/736x/a8/3d/b9/a83db9c4492c938285d156b7c4e5671d.jpg (style reference only)

October

1) http://www.allfreecrochet.com/Hats/Crochet-Chemo-Cap
2) http://pumpkinsbythepieratharborvillage.blogspot.ca/2012/09/how-to-crochet-halloween-treat-bags.html
3) http://diyods.blogspot.ca/2008/10/sad-news-but-hey-you-get-free-pattern.html
4) http://web.archive.org/web/20121019052659/http:/naidascrochet.tripod.com/patterns/eyeballs.html
5) http://www.favecrafts.com/Halloween-Crafts/Spider-Web-Crochet-Pin
6) http://www.favecrafts.com/Halloween-Crafts/Spider-Web-Crochet-Pin
7) http://goodknits.com/blog/2012/09/25/crochet-simple-mask/
8) http://stitch11.com/wicked-wizard-witches-hat/
9) http://www.bustingstitches.com/2012/08/fluffy-princess-tutu.html
10) http://r.search.yahoo.com/_ylt=AwrBTv4nM.tVjfsABPrrFAx.;_ylu=X3oDMTE0czEyOWhlBGNvbG8DYmYxBHBvcwMxBHZ0aWQDVklQQ0ExMV8xBHNlYwNzYw--/RV=2/RE=1441506216/RO=10/RU=http%3a%2f%2fwww.crochetconcupiscence.

com%2f2013%2f04%2fchain-link-crochet-necklaces%2f/RK=0/RS=WaYXK2Zg8INRVjYXurinUWY1Yy8-

11) http://www.nyanpon.com/2012/10/kitten-ears.html

12) http://www.ravelry.com/patterns/library/kitty-cat-hat-and-tail

13) http://r.search.yahoo.com/_ylt=AwrBTvruM.tVcwgA8w7rFAx.;_
ylu=X3oDMTE0czEyOWhlBGNvbG8DYmYxBHBvcwMxBHZ0aWQDVklQQ0ExMV8xBHNlYwNzYw--/
RV=2/RE=1441506415/RO=10/RU=http%3a%2f%2fwww.allfreecrochetafghanpatterns.com%2fIndividual-
Squares%2fBreast-Cancer-Square/RK=0/RS=_lL6aUUd9vIjz6VhyiTGW9tT8PQ-

14) http://donnascrochetdesignstheblog.blogspot.ca/2007/09/free-crochet-pattern-devils-horns-hair.html

15) http://r.search.yahoo.com/_ylt=A0LEV2MSNOtVYyIAwSfrFAx.;_
ylu=X3oDMTE0czEyOWhlBGNvbG8DYmYxBHBvcwMxBHZ0aWQDVklQQ0ExMV8xBHNlYwNzYw--/
RV=2/RE=1441506451/RO=10/RU=https%3a%2f%2fwww.pinterest.com%2fexplore%2fpirate-eye-
patches%2f/RK=0/RS=Jss88CJuCc79FcM8fZ7ihZvnJgo-

16) http://www.allfreecrochet.com/Halloween-Crochet/Crochet-Hippie-Costume-Red-Heart-Yarns

17) http://www.petalstopicots.com/2013/10/cauldron-halloween-crochet-pattern/

18) http://r.search.yahoo.com/_ylt=AwrBTvlHNOtV1_IADRTrFAx.;_
ylu=X3oDMTE0czEyOWhlBGNvbG8DYmYxBHBvcwMxBHZ0aWQDVklQQ0ExMV8xBHNlYwNzYw--/
RV=2/RE=1441506503/RO=10/RU=http%3a%2f%2fpinterest.com%2fpin%2f394276142349520156%2f/
RK=0/RS=KuUSGfVB7ZteWgGMcI6Fl16q_78-

19) http://vickiehowell.com/2011/09/from-the-archive-boo-treelicious-ornaments/

20) http://www.favecrafts.com/Crochet-Baby-Hats/Baby-Pumpkin-Crochet-Beanie

21) http://www.lionbrand.com/patterns/L0257AD.html?keywords=noImages;ss=&r=1

22) http://www.lionbrand.com/patterns/L0255AD.html?keywords=noImages;ss=&r=1

23) http://www.lionbrand.com/patterns/L0624.html?keywords=noImages;ss=&r=1

24) http://www.lionbrand.com/patterns/L0259AD.html?keywords=noImages;ss=&r=1

25) http://www.allfreecrochet.com/Halloween-Crochet/Raggedy-Doll-Wig-Red-Heart-Yarns

26) http://r.search.yahoo.com/_ylt=A0LEV2RmNOtVCRwAd.HrFAx.;_
ylu=X3oDMTE0czEyOWhlBGNvbG8DYmYxBHBvcwMxBHZ0aWQDVklQQ0ExMV8xBHNlYwNzYw--/
RV=2/RE=1441506534/RO=10/RU=http%3a%2f%2fwww.etsy.com%2flisting%2f176225923%2fbreast-
cancer-awareness-pink-ribbon/RK=0/RS=tPxBg0haf3IFsxWqyJ4a37Xw7PQ-

27) http://www.bfranklincrafts.com/CraftIdeas/CraftIdea-HalloweenBasket.html

28) http://r.search.yahoo.com/_ylt=AwrBTvmMNOtV4o4AIdTrFAx.;_
ylu=X3oDMTE0czEyOWhlBGNvbG8DYmYxBHBvcwMxBHZ0aWQDVklQQ0ExMV8xBHNlYwNzYw--/
RV=2/RE=1441506573/RO=10/RU=https%3a%2f%2fwww.etsy.com%2flisting%2f88056347%2fcrochet-
orangepumpkin-coasters/RK=0/RS=3PXv2UKahsMcqbRaBxHAbdnv1zU-

29) http://r.search.yahoo.com/_ylt=AwrBTvmMNOtV4o4AIdTrFAx.;_
ylu=X3oDMTE0czEyOWhlBGNvbG8DYmYxBHBvcwMxBHZ0aWQDVklQQ0ExMV8xBHNlYwNzYw--/
RV=2/RE=1441506573/RO=10/RU=https%3a%2f%2fwww.etsy.com%2flisting%2f88056347%2fcrochet-
orangepumpkin-coasters/RK=0/RS=3PXv2UKahsMcqbRaBxHAbdnv1zU-

30) http://r.search.yahoo.com/_ylt=A2KLj9LINetVSVkABGD2FAx.;_ylu=X3oDMTBxNG1oMmE2BHNlYwNmcC
1hdHRyaWIEc2xrA3J1cmwEaXQD/RV=2/RE=1441506888/RO=11/RU=http%3a%2f%2fthestitchinmommy.
com%2f2014%2f05%2fcrochet-striped-dishcloths.html/RK=0/RS=9.SMrVQBcrN_bzY2WwkFi5eYmmo-

31) http://r.search.yahoo.com/_ylt=A0LEV2r1NetVyGYA8b7rFAx.;_
ylu=X3oDMTE0czEyOWhlBGNvbG8DYmYxBHBvcwMxBHZ0aWQDVklQQ0ExMV8xBHNlYwNzYw--/
RV=2/RE=1441506934/RO=10/RU=http%3a%2f%2fcrochetingclubforadults.blogspot.com%2fp%2fcrochet-
sweaters-and-wraps.html/RK=0/RS=4yG_iOqVoHtZp21q1tQJh97hgII-

November

1) http://crochetpatternbonanza.com/wp-content/uploads/2014/10/crochet-hat-hdc.jpg

2) https://farm2.staticflickr.com/1196/5142972206_050bce0543.jpg

3) http://static.artfire.com/uploads/product/3/643/11643/1111643/1111643/large/crocheted_pumpkin_pot_
holder_53637ee4.jpg

4) http://www.crochetspot.com/wp-content/uploads/2010/12/022.jpg

5) S

6) http://www.planetjune.com/blog/images/pumpkin2.jpg

7) https://img1.etsystatic.com/065/0/10938274/il_570xN.752619289_mb4q.jpg

8) https://sp.yimg.com/ib/th?id=JN.hUHIjyU6R1PbKcDJcfG0IA&pid=15.1&P=0&w=300&h=300
9) http://media-cache-ak0.pinimg.com/236x/ee/26/8d/ee268d18a69c48b38623ddf78b3d8c37.jpg
10) S
11) http://d1nr5wevwcuzuv.cloudfront.net/product_photos/2867464/101_0055_20(2)_original.JPG
12) http://lamaisonbisoux.files.wordpress.com/2012/05/crocheted-reusable-grocery-bag-by-cassie-edwards.jpg
13) http://www.favecrafts.com/Crochet-Socks-and-Slippers/Felted-Crochet-Slippers-from-Bernat
14) http://www.mooglyblog.com/wp-content/uploads/2012/10/crocheted-fall-wreath.jpg
15) http://images.coplusk.net/project_images/174503/image/102489_2F2014-06-11-170719-Acorn.jpg
16) http://media-cache-ak0.pinimg.com/736x/23/38/c2/2338c2ba51e0a29e3814b8856b4b11d9.jpg
17) http://restyledjunk.com/wp-content/uploads/2012/08/new-crochet-pumpkin-applique.jpg
18) http://crafterchick.com/wp-content/uploads/2013/03/Little-Red-Riding-Hood-Crochet-Pattern-picture.jpg
19) S
20) http://media-cache-ec0.pinimg.com/736x/42/1b/bd/421bbd3b9c57b3b0587c6bfe2d5a8c15.jpg
21) http://i.ytimg.com/vi/8iiTVo3exj8/hqdefault.jpg
22) http://1.bp.blogspot.com/-Tnf8IPV8HUE/VGbPF34CKNI/AAAAAAAAMJ8/9n6Q7_FBxXk/s1600/CrochetPie1.jpg
23) http://1.bp.blogspot.com/-U4bHxhY9g6Q/VGbPF7eobGI/AAAAAAAAMJ4/LJucnu5-ITE/s1600/CrochetPie11.jpg
24) https://sp.yimg.com/ib/th?id=JN.kO9PZayTtxJiuYapdyJuyA&pid=15.1&P=0&w=300&h=300
25) http://img0.etsystatic.com/000/0/5891042/il_570xN.322780188.jpg
26) http://media-cache-ec0.pinimg.com/736x/e4/3a/4c/e43a4ccc5b65ea18f9adbb308024f7f9.jpg
27) http://goddesscrochet.com/2015/02/27/ponytail-hat-neckwarmer-free-crochet-pattern/
28) http://www.beginner-crochet-patterns.com/images/RuffledBlanket1904.jpg
29) http://media-cache-ec0.pinimg.com/736x/2e/60/a3/2e60a320f5707705474999a687ffd27d.jpg
30) http://www.wikihow.com/images/thumb/4/46/Crochet-a-Blanket-Step-8.jpg/670px-Crochet-a-Blanket-Step-8.jpg

December

1) http://www.craftown.com/cropat35.htm
2) http://www.favecrafts.com/Crochet-for-Christmas/Crocheted-Christmas-Trees-from-Lily-Sugar-N-Cream
3) http://www.favecrafts.com/Crochet-for-Christmas/Pinwheel-Garland-from-Red-Heart-Yarn
4) http://www.favecrafts.com/Christmas-Crafts/Crochet-Snowman-Family-from-Bernat
5) http://www.favecrafts.com/Ornaments/CrochetOrnaments
6) http://www.favecrafts.com/Crochet-for-Christmas/Christmas-Pinwheel-Placemat-and-Coasters-from-Red-Heart-Yarn
7) http://www.favecrafts.com/Crochet-for-Christmas/Christmas-Pinwheel-Placemat-and-Coasters-from-Red-Heart-Yarn
8) http://www.favecrafts.com/Crochet-for-Christmas/Simp
9) http://whiskersandwool.blogspot.com.au/2011/11/christmas-wreath-ring-christmas.html
10) http://mariannaslazydaisydays.blogspot.co.uk/2013/09/easy-snowflake-christmas-decoration.html
11) http://www.ravelry.com/patterns/library/christmas-time---bell
12) http://www.allfreecrochet.com/Crochet-Bag-Patterns/Half-Skein-Purse
13) http://greedyforcolour.blogspot.ca/2011/12/christmas-bauble-tutorial.html
14) http://danettesangels.tripod.com/patterns/santa_hat.html
15) http://www.favecrafts.com/Crochet-for-Christmas/Elf-Size-Stocking-Ornament
16) http://crochetparfait.blogspot.ca/2012/12/new-years-eve-fascinator-hat.html
17) http://mousenotebook.blogspot.ca/2011/10/little-crochet-moment.html
18) http://www.crochetnmore.com/christmascandle.htm
19) http://web.archive.org/web/20010817123807/http:/www.cei.net/~vchisam/groovy/7021hat.html
20) http://3.bp.blogspot.com/-_MooooWLzZ0/TlRCMfgX_tI/AAAAAAAADHw/G-4Sovjo3cc/s320/Crochet+Clutch+Bag.jpg
21) http://www.favecrafts.com/Pet-Crochet-Patterns/Holiday-Cat-Collar-from-Red-Heart-Yarns
22) S
23) http://media-cache-ec0.pinimg.com/736x/8c/09/73/8c09736675c13b0efcf8f5fec961fd0c.jpg
24) http://www.allfreecrochet.com/Scarves/Party-Scarf-Red-Heart

25) http://www.favecrafts.com/Crochet-Sweaters/Crochet-Shawl-for-Summer-from-Caron
26) S
27) http://media-cache-ak0.pinimg.com/236x/2d/d8/af/2dd8af2046df29c802ca225120d6678e.jpg
28) http://2.bp.blogspot.com/_7_JlgVZWAwY/TEOLeuzqi8I/AAAAAAAAABY/KLjiT2VX_Lw/s1600/Candy%2BCane.JPG
29) http://attic24.typepad.com/.a/6a00e551101c548834017d3ed95008970c-500wi
30) http://www.favecrafts.com/Crochet-for-Christmas/Elf-Size-Stocking-Ornament
31) https://sp.yimg.com/ib/th?id=JN.izcmsVxYEFAJzrP1EcBhcg&pid=15.1&P=0&w=300&h=300

Mini E-Book Pattern Pictures (For Reference Only)

1) http://web.archive.org/web/19991008235940/members.aol.com/undcvrsis/music.html
2) http://www.repeatcrafterme.com/2014/10/c-is-for-cat-crochet-cat-applique.html
3) http://www.crochetnmore.com/rowcountwreathcoaster.htm
4) http://www.crochetnmore.com/heartshairtie.htm
5) http://www.crochetnmore.com/lunchmoneypurse.htm
6) http://www.crochetnmore.com/roundcasserolecarrier.htm
7) http://www.crochetnmore.com/handlepotholder.htm
8) http://www.crochetnmore.com/wheelbookmark.htm
9) http://www.crochetnmore.com/fiestacdcoaster.htm
10) http://www.favecrafts.com/Kitchen-Crochet/Border-Pot-Holder-and-Dishcloth-Crochet-Pattern
11) http://www.lionbrand.com/patterns/L50047.html?noImages=
12) http://www.lionbrand.com/patterns/90513AD.html?noImages=
13) http://www.lionbrand.com/patterns/yp-bathMat.html?noImages=
14) http://www.lionbrand.com/patterns/BK4K-0605009.html?noImages=
15) http://www.lionbrand.com/patterns/70461AD.html?noImages=
16) http://www.lionbrand.com/patterns/L10635.html?noImages=
17) http://www.lionbrand.com/patterns/70585AD.html?noImages=
18) http://blog.a-common-thread.com/post/41608196936/pattern-mesh-crochet-necklace#.VW6PJUmNS00
19) http://theshtickido.blogspot.ca/2013/01/heart-to-heart-bookmark-with-pattern.html
20) http://www.bevscountrycottage.com/preemieround.html
21) http://www.bevscountrycottage.com/thumb-booties.html
22) http://www.moonarts.com/blog/free_patterns/pages/chunky-crochet-print.htm
23) http://thecraftytortoise.blogspot.ca/2010/08/key-fob-pattern.html?m=1
24) http://web.archive.org/web/20050307100154/www.crochetpartners.org/Patterns/CPpat165.html
25) http://www.freecraftunlimited.com/crochet-christmas-bells.html
26) Checkerboard scarf - http://www.artfire.com/uploads/product/3/733/65733/2065733/2065733/large/pdf_-_checkerboard_scarf_knitting_board_pattern_9c94cb03.jpg
27) Beginner's bib - http://media-cache-ak0.pinimg.com/736x/6d/01/82/6d01824dfaff38da734f94131ad15832.jpg
28) Ear bud covers - http://media-cache-ec0.pinimg.com/236x/29/28/28/2928285d5a5282faa6ef25d62cff551b.jpg
29) Baby afghan - http://cf2.primecp.com/master_images/Crochet/pretty-pink-afghan-and-pillow-set(1) .jpg
30) Baby pillow - http://cf2.primecp.com/master_images/Crochet/pretty-pink-afghan-and-pillow-set(1) .jpg
31) Dish soap bottle apron - http://www.crochetspot.com/wp-content/uploads/2015/06/Dish-Soap-Apron-300x300.jpg

Thank you for reading "365 Days of Crochet – 365 Patterns for 365 Days"

If you have enjoyed it, please leave a review on the Amazon website.

You can find more of my work at amazon.com/author/whitelemon

58804473R00142

Made in the USA
Lexington, KY
17 December 2016